Charles Woodruff Shields

**Philosophia Ultima**

Vol. III

Charles Woodruff Shields

**Philosophia Ultima**
*Vol. III*

ISBN/EAN: 9783337236724

Printed in Europe, USA, Canada, Australia, Japan

Cover: Foto ©Thomas Meinert / pixelio.de

More available books at **www.hansebooks.com**

Photographed by Adrian Pockliz

Sincerely Yours,
Charles W Shields

# PHILOSOPHIA ULTIMA

OR

## SCIENCE OF THE SCIENCES

VOL. III.

THE SCIENTIFIC PROBLEMS OF RELIGION
AND
THE CHRISTIAN EVIDENCES
OF THE
PHYSICAL AND PSYCHICAL SCIENCES.

BY THE LATE
CHARLES WOODRUFF SHIELDS, D.D., LL.D.,
PROFESSOR IN PRINCETON UNIVERSITY.

WITH A BIOGRAPHICAL SKETCH
BY
WILLIAM MILLIGAN SLOANE

NEW YORK:
CHARLES SCRIBNER'S SONS.
1905.

# CHARLES WOODRUFF SHIELDS.

## A BIOGRAPHICAL SKETCH

### BY

### WILLIAM MILLIGAN SLOANE.

# CHARLES WOODRUFF SHIELDS.

I.

The ideals of youth are seldom realized, and yet some men see the fruit of their labors, being so blessed that after a long and laborious life, they die as young in feeling and in enterprise as they were in early youth. In his eightieth year Charles Woodruff Shields was as much himself, as fully in possession of all his fine powers and qualities as he had been in the prime of his years. It was therefore with a sense of fulfilment that he left in the hands of a friend certain manuscripts for posthumous publication as the completion of his life work. His choice fell upon one who is a layman to both lines of the study which so engrossed the author, a fact interpreted as meaning that the editor was to confine himself strictly to the task of verbal correction, and to avoid all effort at revision or rearrangement of the matter. This is the more evident as most of the philosophical and apologetic material had already been printed in one form or another, and had had the careful revision of the author. What follows as the last division of the "Final Philosophy" is therefore given exactly at it was intended to stand, and in connection with the two preceding volumes needs no introduction.

II.

The author of these chapters was fully aware of the position he had taken and of all the responsibilities incident to the selection of a title which was almost a challenge: though personally one of the most modest of men, he was fearless to a fault in the exposition and defence of the truth as he saw it. He was convinced that all the sciences could be united into one Christian philosophy, and that all denominations of Christian believers could be united into one visible church of Christ. In no sense did he conceive that the "final" word in philosophy was to be spoken by him, but he did believe and was not ashamed to declare that these exalted ideals would never approach realization unless the plan were outlined and fruitful suggestions were made towards its accomplishment. This he essayed to do and in the effort he deployed extraordinary powers of research and of assimilation. This was not all, for as it stands the "Final Philosophy" is far more than a suggestion, it is a system more or less complete of Cosmic philosophy, based on a synthesis of all the empirical sciences in their natural order of an ascent which culminates in theology, or rather in a theistic ontology derived from Revelation as a valid source of data.

In the same way the author of the "United Church of the United States" (1896) suggested with the strength of a firm conviction and the force of a historical expert that practical Church unity was within reach if only a beginning were discussed and made. For him the most striking phenomenon of contemporary history was the elasticity of the federal system in politics, a system which in his own country comprehended in a roomy edifice men of every land and tongue, of every tradition and practice, provided only they were devoted to the essential idea of liberty under law. He could see no good reason why in some similar way men of a common faith should not, under an elastic constitution, mass their forces against the forces of infidelity and worldliness. The question of church unity was for him an eminently practical one, to be solved in a churchmanlike and politic way. Assiduous in his study of the historic forces which had rent the reformed churches into denominations, he proposed a method of reintegration which was based on the most sacred convictions of believers and on the lessons of the past.

## III.

The personality of Dr. Shields was as engaging as his mind. He was elegant and urbane, sensitive and fascinating, a man of refinement and culture, with all the charm of manner which springs from self-respect and consideration for others. His company was eagerly sought by the best society and his conversation was stimulating and refreshing. He loved the atmosphere of quiet studies, but he was happy in the world and sensitive to its charms. No man could be more ardent and industrious in the pursuit of knowledge, nor more contemplative in its interpretation; yet he had abundant leisure for friendship and the duties of his home. His love for his university was a passion, and he served her with a devotion which ennobled her life and his own. In his veins ran the blood of old colonial stock, north and south, his view of his country was correspondingly catholic and patriotic.

The endearing qualities of the man were as marked as the wide range of his learning. Constructive scholarship is not always gentle, far from it, and it is interesting to trace the origin and evolution of the man who is both a gentle man and a learned man. This combination was the preëminent characteristic of Dr. Shields: it was due partly to heredity and partly to a broad and varied training.

Mere pride of birth is vanity. The world is full of men and women whose personal insignificance is only heightened by the achievements of the ancestors from whom they claim descent. But on the other hand, there are many who are stimulated to great energy by the knowledge that there courses in their veins the blood of men who have lived on a high plane and who have achieved something for God and fatherland. Among the notes of Dr. Shields, written late in life and evidently as a pastime, are some remarks on the subject which are of much interest in explaining the character of the man. I like, he said, to discern the honorable ancestry of a friend in his character and in his countenance.

For myself, however, I must be content with a modest pedigree which is good enough as far as it has been traced. If it can boast of no crowns or coronets among its crests, yet it shows no blot or bar sinister upon its shields. The name itself may hint of the knightly esquire of heraldry (scutum, écuyer); and in fact both the Scottish and the English branches of the family have borne, with differences, the device of three shields upon their escutcheon. The surname has even been traced far back among northern myths to Scyld or Schild, father of the demigod Odin, the founder of both the Norman and the Saxon dynasties of southern Europe. As these two lineages became blended after the Conquest, it would be easier to claim them both than to choose between them.

In later times, he continues, the family was lowland Scotch or northern English by turns, as the border line shifted during the wars of the two kingdoms. The place name is still found on both sides of the Tweed, as borne by hall or hamlet at Shieldfield and Galashields near Melrose Abbey and by the two seaport towns, North Shields and South Shields, on the site of old Norman and Roman ruins on both sides of the Tyne. To myself I seem to have lived mentally in borderland, and if subconscious effects of ancestry may assert themselves in one's tastes, I like to look back for a historical beginning to that romantic region so celebrated in the Border Minstrelsy and so hallowed in the more heroic annals of the Border Covenanters. The ballad of Chevy Chase is attributed by antiquarians to "one Rychard Sheale, minstrel"; and in another old ballad the name appears among the Scots with whom the Englishman was at feud—

"And Anton Shiel, he loves not me."

When the feuds became religious as many as eighteen of the name were ranked with the Presbyterian martyrs. Chief among them was James Shields, a bonnet laird of Haugh Head, in Lauderdale, whose two sons, Michael Shields and Alexander, wielded their pens vigorously enough for Christ's

Crown and Covenant. Michael was clerk of the Societies, as the outlawed Covenanters were called, with Sir Robert Hamilton for their chief, and afterwards published their proceedings in a volume with the quaint title "Faithful Contendings Displayed," from which the philosopher Sir William Hamilton has since derived proof of his claim to the baronetcy. The other son, Reverend Alexander Shields, had a most eventful career. Graduating from Edinburgh University in 1675, he pursued his studies in Holland, returned to England, was ordained by the Presbytery of London and became amanuensis to the great non-conformist divine John Owen. During the persecutions of James II he was taken to Edinburgh, subjected to torture at the Tolbooth and cast into the dismal prison of the Bass Rock, from which he escaped in woman's clothing. He then succeeded the martyred Renwick as preacher to the hunted bands of worshippers on the moors and mountains, and issued for them their "Informatory Vindication," published in Holland; at the same time publishing his own chief treatise: "Naphtali, The Hind Let Loose, or An Historical Representation of the Church of Scotland for the Interest of Christ." On the coming of William of Orange he espoused the "revolution settlement," and was made chaplain of the famous Cameronian regiment, exhorting them to the desperate battle at Dunkeld, which ended in a psalm of victory. After serving for ten years as minister at St. Andrew's he was appointed by the General Assembly senior minister to the ill-fated Darien expedition, and after severe hardships and disappointments died on the homeward voyage in the island of Jamaica. "It is not easy to conceive," says Macaulay, "that fanaticism could be heated to a higher temperature than that which is indicated by the writings of Shields. Yet there was then in Scotland an enthusiasm compared with which the enthusiasm of even this man was lukewarm. The extreme Covenanters protested against his defection as vehemently as he had protested against the Black Indulgence and the oath of supremacy." It should be added, however, that he afterward showed the same moderated enthusiasm as a zealous advocate of church unity in his final work entitled "An Inquiry into Church Communion."

The writer of these notes firmly believed that genealogy was an important part of history. It is very interesting to see how much the inspiration of what men of his name and his blood had done affected his own life work. The borderland and marches of science, literature, and philosophy were the scenes of his labors as those of conterminous kingdoms had been the scenes in which his forbears had fought and suffered and died for the same lofty ideals which were the mainspring of his own life: ideals expressed in the nineteenth century by the unity of all learning and the unity of the whole visible Christian church.

The remaining portions of these genealogical notes are scarcely less interesting, although they are historical as well as personal and genealogical. They are given without comment or revision because they need neither.

IV.

In the colony of Virginia since the close of the seventeenth century, there have been three distinct settlements of the Shields family. They were successfully planted in eastern Virginia, in the valley of Virginia, and in midland Virginia, and may be located by the unquestioned authority of Henning in the counties of York, Augusta, and Halifax. The name also appears on the map of Virginia as a place name in each of these districts.

The first settlement was made probably by direct migration from England to the banks of the James River. This branch of the family is mentioned occasionally by Bishop Meade and its genealogy has been sketched by President Lyon G. Tyler. It has intermarried with the families of Marot, Bray, Minge. Page, Armistead, Bryan, and Tyler and it became distinguished in the Reverend Samuel Shields of the colonial church, in Colonel James Shields of the

Colonial Army, in Captain John Shields of the Revolutionary Army, and more recently in Dr. William J. Shields of Williamsburg and Dr. Charles H. Shields of Richmond.

The second settlement was made by emigration from Scotland and north Ireland through Pennsylvania into the Shenandoah Valley, where, by the liberal policy of Governor Gooch, the Scotch-Irish were then finding a refuge from religious persecution. I have been able to glean but little information in regard to this settlement. As early as 1749 Thomas Shields purchased a portion of the Beverly tract, two hundred acres in extent, for six shillings, agreeing to pay one ear of Indian corn on Lady Day next to secure possession. There is also on record an inventory made in 1750 of the estate of James Shields, full of interesting details as to the domestic life of the time and place. The will of John Shields, freeholder, is recorded in 1772, naming his wife Margaret and children John, Thomas Robert, Mary, William. It is probable that some members of this family did military duty in the Colonial and Revolutionary Wars, as the name occurs in the muster-rolls of Colonel Lewis, of Colonel Hite and of the Muhlenburg Regiment when it was engaged in the battles of Brandywine and Germantown and encamped at Valley Forge. Beyond these fragmentary items, no fuller information has been obtained in regard to the Augusta County family.

Distinct from these two settlements, with no traceable connection to either of them, a third Shields settlement was made by migration into Virginia from the colonies of Delaware and Maryland, where, as appears by the public records of those States, a number of persons of the name had been settled for one or two generations. As early as 1654 the Maryland Archives mention Robert Sheels, and in 1689 Thomas Shields, and in 1694 John Shields. There are also recorded wills in Queen Anne County of Catherine Shields, 1717; and of Susanna Shields, 1735; in Talbot County of James Shields, 1759; in Somerset County of Elizabeth Shields, 1766; in Frederick County of Elizabeth

Shields, 1769, and in Newcastle County, Delaware, of Robert Shields, 1796. The Maryland muster-rolls of the Revolutionary Army contain the names of Lieutenant Archibald Shields, Lieutenant Caleb Shields, Captain John Shields, Commissary Edward Shields and Privates James, John, Patrick, and William Shields.

These persons were probably of Scottish or Irish origin and naturally Episcopalian; in connection with the established church of the colony. Of some of them but little has as yet been ascertained, but it is positively known that about the middle of the eighteenth century two brothers, Archibald and Thomas Shields, of Delaware, married two sisters, Rebecca and Anne Bayard, daughters of Samuel Bayard of Bohemia Manor, Maryland, from whom are also derived the distinguished Bayards of Delaware and New Jersey. The descendants of Archibald Shields have been widely scattered throughout the Southern States: among them is the Honorable William Bayard Shields of the United States Court, New Orleans, La., who married Victoire Benoist, daughter of a French Catholic refugee. The grandsons were Thomas Rodney Shields, William Bayard Shields, the Honorable Joseph Dunbar Shields of Natchez, Miss., and Gabriel Benoist Shields. The great-grandsons are the Reverend VanWinder Shields, D. D., Rector of St. John's Church, Jacksonville, Fla., and Dr. W. B. Shields of St. Francis, Arkansas.

The other brother, Thomas Shields, who married Anne Bayard, afterwards settled in Virginia. Among his descendants are Colonel John Shields of Poplar Vale, Va., who married Anna Jane Moncure, daughter of a certain Mr. Robinson; also Lieutenant Wilmer Shields, U. S. N., who was son of Purser Thomas Shields, and married Julia Devereux Scott. Also, Wilmer Shields, who married Eliza Runkle, daughter of Captain Thomas Conway of Pittsylvania County, Va. To these should be added James Shields, son of the first Thomas, who was born near Sassafras River in Delaware, married Elizabeth Graham of Christiana, and migrated to Halifax, now Pittsylvania Co., Va., where his family was seated until the Revolutionary War.

At this point it will be interesting to notice the influence of environment as well as heredity, upon family character. During the latter part of the eighteenth century the community dwelling between tide-water and the mountains on the east side of the Blue Ridge was as intermediate in its characteristics as in its situation. Therein were blended the social and religious elements of the eastern and western colonists. It should be remembered that in contrast with the Puritan of New England, both the Covenanter and the Cavalier of Virginia had been Royalists, devoted to the house of Stuart, and also zealous Churchmen, the one attached to Presbytery and the other to Episcopacy. When united under William of Orange, they had settled their ecclesiastical feud by establishing the Presbyterian Church in Scotland and the Episcopal Church in England. And not long afterwards in the New World they found themselves again neighbors with only the Blue Ridge between them; but with new common interests taking the place of the old border warfare. The tolerance granted to the Presbyterian Churchmen of midland Virginia was altogether creditable to the colonial governors: it had already ample legal precedent in the mother country as well as in Virginia law, and there was really nothing now to prevent the free intercourse and fusion of the two races and creeds. The product was a type of Virginian, distinguishable alike from the luxurious planter of the lowlands and from the hardy freeholder of the uplands, yet retaining much that was best in both of these stocks without their defects and vices.

This commingling of the two strains showed itself not only in the inherited traits of individuals and families, but also in certain affinities and interchanges which have long since been forgotten or but seldom noticed. It is a remarkable fact that some great political leaders like Madison, Light-horse Harry Lee and even Randolph of Roanoke were not educated at William and Mary, but at Nassau Hall in the school of statesmanship founded by the patriotic Witherspoon. It is a no less remarkable fact that Princeton College instead of looking to New England for Presidents such as Dickinson, Burr, and Edwards, now summoned from Virginia the eloquent Davies, who was Patrick Henry's model, the accomplished Stanhope Smith, who was President of Hampden-Sydney, and Dr. Archibald Alexander, also President of Hampden-Sydney, and founder of the Princeton School of Divinity. Thus it was that the seeds of old civilizations as transplanted to a new soil, flowered into a new form of culture as strong as it was graceful.

Besides this difference between eastern and western Virginia, there was a still further difference of social atmosphere between the northern and southern sections of midland Virginia.

It may not be easily explained, but it appeared in the impassioned genius of Patrick Henry and John Randolph as compared with the trained statesmanship of Jefferson and Madison. It appeared still more strongly in the Presbyterian College in Prince Edward as contrasted with the liberal University afterwards founded at Charlottesville. And it also appeared in the gradual decline of the Cavalier and Episcopal elements in the southern counties. It would seem that these counties, after having been devastated by two civil wars and drained of their best blood by emigration to the Western States, now retain but little of their former prestige. Bishop Meade in his day lamented the extinction of the Church throughout this region and remarked that the names of such churchmen as Madison, Henry, Read, Carington, Watkins, Venable are no longer to be found in the vestry-records of parishes though enrolled among the trustees of Hampden-Sydney College. John Randolph bitterly deplored the decay of the gentry in the county of Charlotte where he lived, attributing its degeneracy to the attacks of Jefferson upon the church establishment and the law of primogeniture. The old régime, however, still lingered some time after the Revolution. Dr. James W. Alexander depicted it as it existed in his father's time. There is no portion of the State or country where the bright side of the planter's life is more agreeably exhibited. The district has always been remarkable for its adaptation to the culture of a particular variety of tobacco which usually commands high prices, and it has therefore abounded in slaves, although the estates are less extensive than in the cotton districts of the remote South. The proprietors enjoy the comforts and luxuries of life in a high degree, and almost every family has some man of liberal education within its bosom. Hospitality and genial warmth may be said to be universal. Nowhere in the South has the Presbyterian Church had greater strength among the wealthy and cultivated classes. Dr. William Henry Foote skilfully traces the same society to its sources and elements: " Coming from different divisions of the European stock, mingling in society on the frontiers, amalgamating by marriage, moulded by the religious teachings of Robinson and Davies, they formed a state of society and morals in which the excellencies of the original constituent parts have all been preserved. The courtly manners of Williamsburg, the cheerfulness and ease of the Huguenots, the honest frankness and stern independence of the English country gentleman, the activity and shrewdness of the merchant, the simplicity of republican life—all have been preserved."

Into this frontier region in 1757 came certain members of the Shields family of Delaware through Maryland down the Chesapeake Bay. The first of the name on record was Patrick Shields, of the County of Halifax and Colony of Virginia, planter, who for two hundred and twenty-five pounds purchased twelve hundred and sixty acres of rich tobacco-growing land on Sandy River, next to Colonel Byrd's tract, the " Land of Eden," and not far from Leatherwood, the purchase of Patrick Henry. During his lifetime he deeded portions of this land to his children Samuel, James, John, and Elizabeth Read, and by his will, September 22nd, 1770, he bequeathed his own plantation to his wife Jeane and son Joseph, together with a negro servant Phyllis and a roan mare and colt; also 50 pounds to his son Robert, and 10 pounds to his " grandson Patrick and son of Samuel." The will is conventional in form, beginning with a confession of his Christian faith in the doctrine of the resurrection.

The next interesting record nine years afterwards is another will so much briefer that I will cite the whole of it:

In the name of God, Amen. I, James Shields, of Pittsylvania County, Virginia, being in perfect health, mind, and memory, do constitute, make and ordain this my last will and testament in manner and form following:

And first of all my lawful debts to be paid. And to my beloved wife Elizabeth I give and bequeath her third of my estate, and to my son Patrick I give and bequeath the other third of my real and personal estate, and to Molly my daughter the other part. I also will and desire that my son Patrick over and above his share have so much to be paid from my estate as will pay his learning through the several degrees of the college: and I do hereby constitute my beloved wife my whole and sole executrix of this my last will and testament, and do hereby revoke, disallow and annul all former will or wills whatsoever, and do make and confirm this only to be my last will and testament. As witness my hand and seal this third day of August in the year one thousand seven hundred and seventy-nine.

And as my wife is with child if the child lives I desire that it may have its due and equal share of my estate.

James Shields (L. S.).

Teste
  John Smith,
  Samuel Shields,
  Joshua Cantrill.

This document, brought to light after a lapse of one hundred and twenty-five years, is a remarkable confirmation of family tradition in every particular. It was evidently written somewhat hurriedly, in view of the fate which might befall a soldier of the Revolution. One may fancy him tenderly leaving the paper with his wife, as he rode away never to return. The disastrous siege of Savannah followed on October 10th, and the will was probated December 21st, 1779. The executrix and "beloved wife Elizabeth" was the above-named Elizabeth Graham of Christiana.

In reference to the family of Elizabeth Graham some traditions may here be interesting. Her father, a Covenanter as well as a Graham, had narrowly escaped the sword thrust of another Graham before he fled to the Colonies. The story runs in the family that the dragoons of bloody Claverhouse thrust their swords into the very thicket in which he was concealed, but without discovering him. He crossed the sea in the same ship with the family into which his daughter afterwards married. The two families before their emigration, it is said, lived on opposite sides of the Irish Channel where it was so narrow that they could tell when it was washing day on the other shore by descrying the clothes hung to dry. It is also said that Graham on settling in Delaware built his house in part of bricks brought with him in the vessel and marked with his initials, and as late as 1821 Senator Tipton, a friend of the family, reported that he had seen the house and noticed the initials. Beyond such home-like traditions there are no European annals of Elizabeth's family. Her little, worn Bible which she bequeathed to the oldest son of the oldest son, because of its register showing title to Scottish properties, has come to her great-grandson, water-stained, tattered, and alas, without the register. It was accidentally dropped into a stream which was being forded by another ancestor on one of his preaching excursions. The lost pedigree might have helped to decide whether she came from the Grahams of Menteith, or of the Grahams of Montrose, who boasted of the handsome and gallant Dundee, as much praised by the Cavaliers as he was hated by the Covenanters.

But to return to the will. The unborn child proved to be another daughter. Left alone with three young children and in charge of a plantation, Elizabeth Graham Shields married a neighboring planter, General Burnett, whose name was gratefully given to one of her grandsons, Henry Burnett Shields. Her two daughters married husbands who rose to wealth and public office in Tennessee. Her son Patrick, so thoughtfully provided for in the will, became Judge Shields of Corydon, Indiana. He was born in Pittsylvania, May 17th, 1773. His boyhood was passed in the Virginia plantation mode of life with the church and school at home and in a neighborhood then exceptionally good. Dr. Archibald Alexander thus notices it in his Journal: " Tuesday, August 7th, 1792, I preached at Sandy River. The house was very full of people who seemed desirous to hear. I don't remember that any to whom I have preached since I was on my tour were apparently more affected than these." One of these listeners may have been young Patrick, then nineteen years old. In accordance with his father's will he was educated for the law in Hampden-Sydney Academy and William and Mary College.

To his uncle's name Patrick his parents had added the name Henry in compliment to their intimate friend the patriot orator, but in after life he preferred to write his name simply " P. Shields." I have, however, official documents signed " P. Henry Shields." The boy was educated carefully, according to his father's directions. At one time William Henry Harrison, the future President, was his classmate and thus became his lifelong friend. On the sixth of December, 1798, he was married to Mary, daughter of Rev. Clement Nance, by his cousin Rev. James Read. The Nances were an old Virginia family, first seated as early as 1641 in Henrico County, from thence migrating into other counties and intermarrying through successive generations with Isham, Vaughn, Lanier, Giles, Palmer, and Pleasant. After the Revolution Clement Nance removed with his family to the Northwest Territory. It was not long before his son-in-law decided to follow him, drawn into the general westward movement.

His father's estate, which was valued at seventeen thousand pounds, having become depreciated through the failure of the Continental currency, he surrendered the home plantation to his mother and sisters and accepted as his portion two thousand six hundred and sixty acres of wild land in the Blue Grass region of Kentucky, which was then still the County or District of Virginia. About the year 1803, with his wife, two young children, and a negro servant, Sam, and doubtless other emigrating families, he made the long and difficult journey over the mountains into Kentucky. On arriving at Lexington he found that owing to the dishonesty of a business agent, made easy enough by the chaotic state of land titles at that time, he was unable to secure possession of his land and must simply begin the world anew. For a time he remained with some of his Graham connections in Mercer County, but at length he decided to join his wife's relatives beyond the Ohio River, where land was more easily obtained.

With his family, household goods, and cattle in a flatboat, he floated down the Kentucky and Ohio rivers to a point below the Falls where his relatives, having seen the boat approaching, were waiting to welcome him after the long separation with hysterical tears of joy. In the unbroken wilderness he entered a section of land; this time with no flaw upon the title. Upon my study wall now hangs the parchment deed to this tract signed by President Monroe as recorded in the general land office at Washington. Here with the aid of his servant was cleared the first patch of ground in the wilderness and the first crop of grain was raised only to be destroyed by severe frost in autumn. A local chronicler describes the cabin which he erected as much better than those of that time: " It was built almost entirely of blue ash logs and nearly full two stories in height. Shields in a short time gathered around him a settlement of some size and wielded considerable influence among the settlers." His spacious cabin being the most commodious in the neighborhood became almost a public resort, the place where political and religious meetings were held. It was also for a time the seat of the Territorial authorities until the government was established in the neighboring village of Corydon. The building was in due time replaced by a more commodious brick building, styled by the ruder settlers—the folly of "stuck-up" Virginians.

There is no doubt that Shields was the pioneer of all that band of Virginians, a score or more of families that subsequently followed his lead and became citizens of this township. He was soon, on December 8th, 1808, commissioned by his old classmate Governor William Henry Harrison as judge of the Court of Common Pleas, the first appointment of this kind for the territory, which then included the region since divided into the States of Indiana, Michigan, and Illinois. In 1811 he went to the defence of the border with General Harrison as a mounted rifleman and volunteer aide. In the battle of Tippecanoe his horse received a bullet in the head, but was not killed and was safely brought back home with him again. When Indiana became a separate territory under Governor Posey, January 7th, 1814, he was commissioned judge of the Circuit Court of Harrison County, the first president judge in that territory; and in the year 1816 he was appointed a member of the Constitutional Convention which met at Corydon for the organization of the Territory into a State.

### V.

These pages were written by Dr. Shields in his seventy-ninth year and amply suffice to show that his force was not in the least abated. Their interest is far from being either personal or local, for they are a contribution to American history as showing the sources of the strength and culture characteristic of many small but vigorous communities through the central and further West. Though life was very primitive in Corydon, Indiana, the people had as their leaders men of the first importance from the viewpoint of education, family, and energy. As the years went on and material prosperity blessed the efforts of the pioneers, they gave the same attention to their intellectual and spiritual necessities as they gave to their bodies and their estates. Churches and schools were established on firm foundations, their sons and daughters were trained in piety and patriotism. When James Read Shields, son of Patrick Henry, came to man's estate he sought and found a wife among the best and most refined families of the East. Being president of the bank of New Albany in the State of his birth, and a ruling elder in the Presbyterian church of the same town, he married Hannah Woodruff of Elizabethtown, New Jersey.

This was the fact which determined the career of the only child of the marriage, who was born on April fourth of the following year at his father's home in New Albany. The ancestors of Hannah Woodruff for four generations on both sides lie buried in the graveyard of the First Presbyterian Church of Elizabeth. They were descendants of a well-known Yorkshire family, which emigrated to Massachusetts in 1638, went thence to Southampton, Long Island, and with a number of others removed thence to the Carteret district of New Jersey. They were a line of devout Presbyterian church folk. Mrs. Shields was trained in the "nurture and admonition of the Lord" as her parents understood it, and her well-worn books of devotion were a cherished possession of her son. She is well remembered by the present distinguished Chancellor of the State, William J. Magie, who recalls that she was a famous Bible scholar. Her pastor, the Rev. John McDowell, D. D., a Princeton graduate of 1801, and a founder of the Princeton Seminary, received into the church the grandmother of Dr. Shields and, by both baptism and confession, his mother: he likewise delivered the charge at the installation of her son as a minister, and baptized his oldest daughter.

Samuel Woodruff, one of the same family, had long since identified the family with the interests of Princeton College, an institution founded to represent the religious culture which, by a larger catholicity, had outgrown the conservative type from which it had sprung. He was a trustee from its founding in 1749 to his death in 1768, and is the first to have remembered that institution by a bequest. He was a prosperous merchant and a pillar of the church. In the founding of the college he was, of course, intimately associated with all the leading spirits of the time and place, in particular with Boudinot, Stockton, and Belcher the governor of the province, he himself being a member of the Council. The society from which the founders of Princeton stood forth had a marked character, being both aristocratic in feeling and ecclesiastical in its standards. Dr. Shields wrote of it in this connection, as follows: " Between the extremes of Northern and Southern culture, it laid stress upon forms, and titles, and costumes, while insisting on the claims of virtue and piety. There was in it a touch of English gentility over the harshness of the Puritan, the strictness of the Covenanter, the staidness of the Hollander, the primness of the Quaker, the grace of the Huguenot, and the gayety of the Cavalier. At one time, indeed, all these elements seemed to have been fused together under the eloquence of that Presbyterian clergyman of the Church of England, George Whitefield, who was then traversing the colonies, like another Apostle to the Gentiles. The Reverend Mr. Chandler, Missionary to the little flock of St. John, wrote home to the London Society in disgust, that schism was becoming a mere " ecclesiastical scarecrow," churchmen and dissenters being so mixed up together that they would not discriminate between " Episcopal and ye leathern mitted ordination " which his neighbor, the Reverend Jonathan Dickinson, had been defending in sundry learned essays. The preceding rector, good old Mr. Vaugn, had died on the same day with Dickinson, exclaiming, when told that his friend was also dying, " Oh, that I had hold of the skirts of brother Jonathan!" This passage has been quoted because, in its literal truth, the writer was holding up the mirror for himself as a sitter for his own portrait.

Dr. Shields was in a marked degree what inheritance made him, a man of exactly this social and ecclesiastical mould.

In response to a request for a few intimate details concerning the mother whose influence was almost paramount in her father's life, Mrs. Stockton, of Morven, writes:

My grandmother's marriage was looked upon by her large family connection, then living in Elizabethtown and New York, as cutting her off entirely from her family and almost from civilization, and so it was natural that my father should have been sent to her sister, Phebe (Woodruff) Rankin, in Newark, to be educated.

New Albany, where my father lived in 1837, was a very primitive place at that time; the first Presbyterian church, and the different clergymen who supplied its pulpit, were the only social interests of the town. My grandmother, although of English descent, was much more the type of a Scotch Presbyterian, and my father has often told me of the breakfasts his mother used to give to the visiting clergymen, a custom still quite common in Scotland.

She also held "parlor meetings," or ladies' prayer-meetings, at her house on Main Street, which had a beautiful garden running down to the Ohio River, "planted with borders and shrubberies," of which my grandmother took personal care.

My grandfather has left this description of her, which he wrote for his eldest granddaughter:

"She was a little below the ordinary size of women, well favored and straight in her person. Her forehead high, her features good, complexion fair, with a well-shaped nose resting between her gray or hazel eyes—her countenance on the whole was that of serenity and sense, attractive to all, being entirely destitute of that doll-faced beauty that is so prominent in the features of many women; one look at her invited a second and then a third; she was rather retiring and modest in her deportment; she rose early, delighted much in flowers, and employed her leisure moments in reading. The Bible was her first book, then the religious books and papers of the day. She was mild and amiable in disposition, and very kind to those who came within reach of her acquaintance; very conscientious in the discharge of her duties to God and her fellow beings, benevolent to the poor and the church; cheerful, but not given to levity.

"For upwards of thirty years we lived together in peace, sharing in each other's joys and sorrows until the evening of August 21st, 1856, when she ceased to be with me."

After her death it was found that she had treasured every letter her only child had ever written her, and even those from her own people in which his name was mentioned.

In contrast to the austere life led by my grandmother in the West, I quote from a letter written at Elizabethtown in the first year of her marriage. "We have had a visit from Lafayette, and a most splendid bower was erected for his reception; I blistered my hands tying greens for it, but it paid with the honor of shaking hands with the general. Hannah! he looks very much like Mr. Nelson, on the hill, so you can fancy you have seen him; our bower, it is said, stands next to Castle Garden (the port on the battery); I was in it one evening, previous to his arrival, and it really appeared like enchantment; it is, Hannah, indescribable; I have just finished his memoirs, which have been published since his arrival here. They are very interesting."

My father was baptized by the Reverend M. R. Welles, pastor of the Presbyterian Church. His early childhood was very lonely; his mother was his only companion as well as teacher. When he was three years old, he read the first chapter of St. John's Gospel at her knee. He had many salutary lessons from her. As he has somewhere written he began during this time to write a journal of resolutions and penitential confessions, such as he had read in the memoirs of some precocious young saint of the day. But his wise mother, pointing out its marks of conceit and vanity, promptly suppressed the effusion. These lonely days playing by her side in the sunny garden readily account for his shyness and reserve. He had no playmates until he went to school in Newark in 1837.

In 1839 he and two of his schoolmates owned a small printing press, and for a few months "The Aurora," a monthly paper, Printed, Published and Edited by Shields, Butler & Co., was the fruit of their leisure hours. This child's paper was largely subscribed for by "The Aunts" living in the East, and its poetical effusions were contributed by the *young ladies* of the neighborhood.

My father's maternal grandmother, Mary (Mulford) Woodruff, daughter of Lewis Mulford III and wife of Parsons Woodruff, was much interested in his spiritual welfare; in 1838 she writes: "Give Charles my love and tell him that I was much gratified to see that he was attending to so many studies, and especially the Bible class. I hope he will be thankful that his parents can give him so good an education, which is the best of gifts." When she was told that he had joined the Presbyterian Church in 1841, and was to be sent to college, she writes: "I think there is a blessing that attended you that your child should be brought out of natural darkness. I hope he will press forward to the prize of the high calling. I feel gratified to have one of my grandchildren a professional character."

She lived until she was eighty-five, and kept constantly in touch with her grandson. He was expected to pay his respects to her on coming and going to college. In 1843 she writes again: "Professor McLean called here during the vacation. I told him I thought Charles would be home-sick, as he never had been away from home. He said if he was he would send him on to spend a few days with us, but as he did not come we concluded he is very well contented."

While my father was in the seminary she writes: "You wish to know what we think of Charles; we are all very much pleased with his visit. He has improved greatly in regard to his diffidence; you will no doubt be pleased to hear that he asked a blessing at the table with perfect confidence, while Mr. Wood and Mr. Millpaugh were both present."

My father's letters gave detailed accounts of his holidays spent with his aunt, Mrs. Rankin, his uncle, Archibald Woodruff, at whose "establishment in Newark" his grandmother lived after her husband's death, and in New York, at 20 Spring Street, with his aunt, Charity Wood, of whom he was very fond.

VI.

Having been a diligent student at the New Albany high school, the boy of twelve was quite ready for better training than New Albany could afford. Accordingly his education was not interrupted by his entrance on the work of the Newark Academy, already a famous school. Four years sufficed to prepare him for Princeton, as a sophomore at least, and possibly a junior. The summer of 1842 he spent at home, and on October 31 he started for the college, already so dear to him, in company with two friends. From this time onward, for some years, his letters to his mother and other relatives contained many things of general interest. He traveled by boat to Wheeling, thence by stage to Harper's Ferry, Washington, and Baltimore, and thence by train to Philadelphia, and Princeton, which he reached on November 9. The cost of this journey was thirty-three dollars and six cents. The careful accounting is characteristic.

Presenting himself as a candidate for the junior class, he was examined by Vice-President McLean and Professor Topping. They found him, for so high a standing, deficient in the languages, and advised him to enter the sophomore class; but as they did not forbid him trying to join the higher one he concluded so to do, and easily made good all deficiencies. His college bill was a hundred and six dollars and eight cents; this he paid immediately and further bought furniture costing fourteen dollars. He then established himself with his friend, Walter Mann, at No. 20 East College, and was ready for the work and play of college life.

As might be expected from one of his birth and training his first impressions of Princeton relate to its religious character. More than a third of the students, he wrote, are professors of religion, and many others are seriously disposed. The religious restraint cast around them is very great. Beside daily prayers in the chapel there are also nightly prayer-meetings, conducted by some of the faculty and pious students, lectures on Monday evenings, Bible lessons, etc., etc. Within less than three weeks he had himself joined the Philadelphian Society, and had signed a constitution drawn up in the handwriting of James B. Taylor, who, in his own words, was the founder and chief member of the society—a society, it may be remarked in passing, which was the forerunner and almost the parent of all the numerous religious associations of students in American colleges. Further, the students were not permitted to leave the grounds on a Sunday, except by special dispensation.

The routine of his life is graphically described: A little after six in the morning we have what is called a "rouser," a term most significant of its use. It consists of a most melodious concert of bells and horns (one of the latter is blown in each entry of the different colleges) together with the howling of neighboring dogs by way of a symphony. This should effectually rouse most of the students, it would seem; I have slept through it once, notwithstanding. After a half an hour for dressing the college bell rings for prayers. At prayer-hall the roll is called, delinquents marked, a chapter read, and a prayer made by one of the tutors. At eight we go to breakfast. Study hours are nine to eleven. recitation till twelve, and so on for the remainder of the day. The students generally walk after evening prayers till supper, and we have some beautiful walks. Professor McLean's prayer-meeting (comes) immediately after supper, Thursday evenings a lecture at Dr. Rice's church from either himself, Professor McLean or Alexander alternately(?) in the sophomore recitation room, which we of course attend. After prayer-meeting Walter and I trim our study lamp and seat ourselves by a good grate fire to study. The sermons we have in prayer-hall are of a strange order. It is a difficult thing to please the students, and some of the professors seem to bend their efforts to obviate this difficulty. What would you think of a grave metaphysical discourse (Dr. Hodge of the Seminary) on the "existence of the Deity"? A sermon (Professor Dod) on the best method of study?

Throughout these and all his letters there is constant and tender mention of home affairs, with never ending expressions of affection. His first examination closed on January 28th, 1843. He felt some uneasiness as to gaining distinction in mathematics, and he did not. There is mention of his regular reading of the "Observer" and the "Presbyterian": also of careful study in "Alexander's Evidences" and "Locke's Essay." His time, he found, was almost engrossed by his studies, and by the constant, faithful performance of his religious duties.

A letter of September 2nd, 1843, is very interesting: I have become attached to study, he writes. What in the first place necessity imposed, habit has consented to, and fastened upon me. The natural offspring of this is a thirst after truth. We juniors are now beginning to come in possession of the seniors' peculiar privileges. We have a lecture in the morning (of which we are obliged to take notes, and which we are obliged to transcribe neatly in a large blank-book, together with drawings and illustrations, to be subjected to the supervision of the professor) and in the afternoon a recitation upon it. The last week we had Professor Dod on architecture. He is a splendid lecturer and has, besides his class, an audience of the ladies and gentlemen from out in the town. I have been delighted with the subject, and especially with the method in which he presents it. I do not believe that, in aptness and facility of utterance, there is his equal in the United States. He completely carries you away and makes you feel like another being, even on such a plaything as architecture. Oh, two sermons which I have heard from him this session, I can never forget!

They have sunk into my heart. He is the greatest man that ever came under my personal observation. He has his mind completely under control—can do with it what he pleases, and it is remarkable that he never fails of making his sentences intelligible, is never confused and indistinct in his words, has neither too many nor too few, even when most hurried and dealing with most abstract subjects. He has preciseness of ideas—preciseness of utterance; and complete mastery over his mind to a degree as near to perfection as I can imagine. The wonder is that such a man would be content to be cooped up in the little village of Princeton.

In another letter he thus characterizes Dr. John McLean: " He is all benevolence. He has a soul large enough to take in the whole world; although most severe in his administration of college discipline he has not an enemy among the students. They all go to him as an adviser and friend. He always gives them his private reproof and warning before he proceeds to more rigorous measures. He is a complete exemplification of the Christian, and labors more assiduously and conscientiously than any other member of the faculty for the spiritual good of those who are under his instructions. As to his success in his professorship I cannot speak so favorably, I am really afraid my knowledge of Greek is not very much brightened by my college course."

The industry of the man, and the opportunities for education which he enjoyed in Princeton at that time, are well illustrated by his enumeration of the studies he pursued in and out of college: his class-room work in mathematics included mechanics, analytical geometry, differential and integral calculus, and the contents of Olmsted's text-book of astronomy; in the classics he read the Captivi of Plautus, Juvenal and the Œdipus Tyrannus; and with these he had instruction in the Evidences, and in Locke's Essay, together with lectures on architecture. He had also private lessons in elocution and French. The spring holiday he spent in Newark, where his mother was visiting with her family, and in September he returned to New Albany to pass the autumn holiday at home. His expenses for the year were three hundred and fifty-three dollars and twelve cents.

The senior year was begun by the purchase of a syllabus of Professor Henry's lectures, Brande's Encyclopedia, Hedge's Logic, and Blair's Rhetoric. The holidays were spent in New York and Newark respectively; he graduated on July 27th, 1844, and returned home by way of Niagara. His expenses for the year were three hundred and eighty-one dollars and fifty-four cents.

The letters he wrote during this period glow with a warm affection for Princeton, and express a high appreciation of the advantages he there enjoyed. They likewise exhibit the heart-searchings of a generous mind and of a manhood devoted to duty, and scanning the future to find its leadings. On the subject of his opportunities in different lines he wrote at various times with keen discrimination. Toward the close of the year he declared: " I can truly say that no portion of my life has been to me so pleasant as that which I have spent at college. The friendships formed there are like no others—they are between equals, all have the same object in view, and the same end to strive after; and, therefore, they are purer and freer from those temptations which an intercourse with the world is likely to produce. In fact, I have never known before what it was to have a real friend and to separate from him. I mean, of course, such a companion as similar tastes and a common interest endear to us. I have really become attached to Princeton. As the days of my sojourn draw to a close, and I recount the pleasant friendships which I have formed, I feel confident I shall leave with regret."

During this year young Shields was managing editor of the Nassau Literary Magazine, and took the Alpha medal for an essay in connection with other literary work in Whig Hall. Chapel exercises were at five in the morning during summer, and he allowed himself but six hours of sleep, such was his untiring zeal in the performance of the many tasks which gave him such a full and fruitful life. In one of his letters he thus describes his room: " Imagine, then, after having deposited carefully the dirt upon a respectable mat at the door, and having received in response to your knock a couple of simultaneous 'holloas' from within, you step upon a neat carpeted floor—please sit down—I must apologize for the dilapidated appearance of that chair—it lost its rockers and one of its arms one rainy morning in a desperate exigency of kindling-wood—be cautious how you trust yourself in that other one—its limbs are relaxing with the feebleness of old age—however, there is that other remaining one which I can recommend to you as trustworthy. Having given you the necessary precautions for your safety, you may now proceed in your examination with nothing to molest you. You see that double cylinder stove before you. It is a very convenient, economical affair, with its set of dampers to regulate the temperature, only addicted to a curious habit of letting the fire go out once or twice daily. This will lead you readily to account for that hill of short wood you see behind it. In the southeast corner you observe a collection of old umbrellas, bandysticks, old shoes, broom, etc., etc."; and so he runs on for a page or two with his enumeration of collected rubbish.

There were sixty-seven members in the class, and among them were many destined to be famous in after life: James C. Welling, president of Columbian, now George Washington, University in the national capital; the Hon. H. S. Little, of Trenton; Col. Edward A. Wright, of Newark, N. J.; Governor A. H. Colquit, of Georgia; the Rev. Noah H. Schenck, of Brooklyn, and in the seminary Bishop Littlejohn, of Long Island. Charles Godfrey Leland, though in the class of 1845, was his warm friend. From the entire number of his classmates about one-third were destined for the Christian ministry, and it was not extraordinary that Shields, with his pious zeal and profound religious nature, should have begun to consider its claim upon him. As early as December, 1844, he became a regular attendant at the exercises of trial preaching in the seminary. The faculty of Princeton

College was composed of men who were not only great, to mention only Henry, founder of the Smithsonian Institute, and James Waddell Alexander, almost the foremost Presbyterian divine of his day, but they were one and all, lay or clerical, men of devout minds. Their influence on young Shields had been, as we have noted, very profound, and but a short distance away in the seminary of the Presbyterian Church were men, Alexanders and Hodges, spiritually akin to the college professors and equally fascinating by their intellectual attainments. Shields expressed in his letters many doubts as to his spiritual strength, earnestly entreating his mother to pray that he might have more holy thoughts, more heavenward aspirations. He had many fits of despondency, and wrote often of disappointments, of temptations, of his unfitness and unworthiness for the high and sacred calling of the ministry. At last, however, his decision was taken and announced. One seems to read between the lines that Dr. McLean influenced him in this, unconsciously to the student; be that as it may, the earlier boyish judgment of the doctor's scholarship was entirely revised, and, though the appearance and manner of the saintly man seemed unfortunate to the youth, he spoke in the highest terms of his professor's learning in a tone utterly different from the first; and this at the time when his judgment was ripe and he was in the midst of choosing his profession for life. His parents were content that their boy should be a clergyman, but they were firm that it must be in the church of his birth, a Presbyterian minister; and that he should pursue his theological studies at home. Although there is evidence that Mr. Shields already considered taking orders in the Protestant Episcopal Church, as some of his closest associates at Princeton actually did, yet on that point he did not make a firm stand, so earnest were the representations of his mother; but his arguments for remaining in Princeton during his theological training were so eloquent and convincing that in that respect his parents yielded.

## VII.

It was at the end of his senior year that a new college calendar, substantially the one still in use, was adopted and inaugurated. Accordingly, the holiday, after the momentous decision was taken, scarcely afforded more than a breathing space, and it was with some sense of exhaustion that the laborious student entered on what proved to be the most important phase of his education. His routine work proved in itself a very serious task, and for a time he was much depressed over his inability to take it with the cheerful heart which alone goes "all the way" in a responsible and solemn profession; in fact, his health was actually jeopardized and he was compelled to seek recreation and recuperation in a visit to his parents of some length, before the close of the first year. He returned, however, at the opening of the second year in vigorous health, with his mind clear, his faculties alert, and all doubts dispelled. Thereafter there was no interruption in a long course of congenial study; he pursued with ardor, not alone the regular course of study, but the avocation of philosophical research which was destined to become a life work.

Of the distinguished men who taught him he formed the highest opinion; as was indeed inevitable for one endowed as he was with a friendly and appreciative mind. Dr. Alexander's simple talks, he wrote, talks in which he utters great truths with such familiarity and plainness, or Dr. Hodge in one of his convincing doctrinal discourses; there is no such thing as resisting either. Dr. Alexander is plain, simple and precise, having just the qualities and manner necessary to give lucid, common sense views on vexed metaphysical points, and detect the folly of fine-spun theories. Dr. Hodge is logical and comprehensive, just what he ought to be in his branch, to give rigid and correct interpretations of Scripture. Professor Addison (Alexander) I would not attempt to describe; he completely stupefies me every time I hear his talk, such a stream of words, and so much meaning. He is my model of a Christian scholar.

Upon one of the manuscripts of the young theologian is this remark by the Old Doctor (Alexander) as he was reverendly called: Mr. Shields has a very pleasing, plaintive manner of speaking. In these days when energy and force seem to be so much courted, it is very pleasing to meet with that more winning and soothing style.

In the case of Dr. Shields it is true that the child is the father of the man. He had not fairly entered college before he began to ponder the Wie, Wo, und Wann? of the German poet. But for him the oracle was not entirely dumb; though he heard only in part and in whispers, yet he seemed to catch words and thoughts, alike of weight and import. These he carefully noted and pondered; almost from day to day, certainly from month to month. By the time he was in the Seminary and had secured his full measure of health and vigor, the desire for system took possession of his very soul. Fortunately, the instinct and love for history were well developed in him; the air of the universities was then heavy with what the jargon of the hour styled German "neologism," supposed to be lethal to all Christian faith; and for many weak heads the draught was too strong, so strong that rationalistic intoxication was a common phenomenon. But Shields, with a little knot of friends, had cool heads and an abundance of hard common sense. They thoroughly knew much of what men had already thought, and of how they had behaved in consequence. They determined to know more, and to give all the pressing problems a thorough investigation in the light of human experience. The group consisted of W. A. Lord, W. A. Dod, A. N. Littlejohn, J. C. Welling, and C. W. Shields; they were all notable men, nearly every one became distinguished in after life. Three of these choice spirits the present writer has been privileged to know; their learning and refinement were so noteworthy that they would have been marked men in any land and in any circle.

In connection with these men, therefore, Shields began a thorough and exhaustive examination of the philosophies both of the past and of their own day. The philosophic synthesis of systems which he had formed early in his intellectual life appears to have served him well as a point of departure even in his more exhaustive studies. But he preserved from first to last an open mind; the debates of the little club were continuous during the seminary course, each contributed his share, and the conclusions of each were either consciously or unconsciously modified by the results of the general discussion. Two profound convictions remained in Shields's mind: the unity and continuity of human thought, the unity and continuity of the divine purpose as exhibited in the historic church. These matters he fully explained to his mother, and between the lines of his letters she seemed to read his leaning toward the Episcopal Church. At all events she considered the probability so great as to be, from her point of view, an imminent danger, and with all her weapons, ecclesiastical and personal, she combated the idea in her letters. She was so far successful that her son proposed to spend a year in Germany before entering on the work of the ministry. This course was equally distasteful to his good mother, who seems, from one rather doubtful reference, to have dedicated her son to mission work in the West. In a letter from one of his friends mention is likewise made of another missionary scheme; namely, work in the foreign field. This probably has no further significance than that the conscientious young minister had casually, at least, considered every possibility in the dedication of his life.

The result of all these deliberations was the conviction that he was still too young to enter on the work of the Presbyterian ministry, and that he could spend another year at Princeton with excellent results, both in ripening his mind and in strengthening the foundations of his scholarship. In this decision he had determined the course of his life. No longer attached to the membership of a class or even of a group, his mind had free course for independent development, and his habits of omnivorous reading were confirmed, were settled into their groove without the support of comradeship. His own feeling throughout later life was that the quiet, detached, reposeful, intellectual life of this year had been fertile almost beyond that of any other. Before it was over he had found his line; and from it he never deviated to the very end. Determined on the practice of his profession, at least for a time, many of the sermons he prepared were of a marked philosophical cast.

During the holiday after leaving Princeton, which he spent at New Albany, he made the acquaintance of Miss Charlotte Elizabeth Bain, of Galway, New York. Later, when he went to spend some time with an aunt in the city of New York, while preaching in various pulpits, the acquaintance was continued and ripened into love. On November 22nd, 1848, they were married in Stamford, Connecticut, by the Reverend John McElroy. The happy life together began in Brooklyn, where, with his wife and her sister, he established himself during the time of his probation, as a supply in various pulpits.

He was an accomplished preacher from the first. Licensed as a candidate on February 2nd, 1847, he chose as his text: "And Enoch walked with God and was not, for God took him." One of his hearers wrote: "The introduction was most beautiful, and the whole sermon was one of exceeding excellence, chaining the attention of the audience throughout." The first pulpit which he supplied was in Philadelphia. The proof of his great power as a preacher came in the form of three calls, almost simultaneously, in 1849. One was from Salem, Massachusetts; one from Hempstead, Long Island, and the third was from the Pearl Street Church of New York. He was in much doubt as to which of the three he should accept. After mature deliberation, in which the question of his wife's health had to be carefully considered, he finally decided for Hempstead. Referring jocularly to his decision, he had decided, he said, on the old negro's advice: "Go where there is the most devil and the least pay."

He was ordained in November and entered at once on his work at a salary of five hundred dollars a year. His task had been made clear in advance. Writing on the subject, he said: "They wish a minister who will give himself up to a great deal of social visiting. The country portion of the congregation, which forms the greater part, are especially solicitous on this point. They seem to feel that they have hitherto been much neglected, and have signified their desire to the session that it should be stipulated with their new pastor that he should bestow more attention upon them —should go out occasionally and spend the day, etc., etc. They are not a reading people," he wrote in another letter; "there are three men here who own fortunes who can scarcely write their names, and there is not one family or person in the village (as far as I have become acquainted) who is of a congenial taste. I feel this deficiency very much, as I am afraid if I remain here long I shall lapse into neglectful habits of study, preaching, and so forth." It was apparently as a matter of secular education for his people that early in 1850 he delivered a course of public lectures on architecture, modelled on those of Professor Dod, which he had so greatly admired. There is in one of his letters of the time an interesting reminiscence of older customs. The clergymen in attendance at a funeral were provided with certain mourning insignia, among them an ample scarf of linen to be worn over the shoulder. Of these Mr. Shields had so many that they served as a sufficient provision for all the shirts he could wear.

During the summer of 1850 there came a call from the Second Presbyterian Church of Philadelphia. This he naturally accepted, and in November he was installed, the charge being delivered by Dr. John McDowell, and the sermon being preached by Dr. H. A. Boardman. This was a very important church, and the young pastor took hold with a will. During the year ending October 1st, 1851, there were held ninety-four public services, at seventy-three of which the pastor preached. He likewise delivered thirty-six lectures, and during the year twenty pews were rented. To the end of his pastorate his zeal never abated, and he left the active work of preacher and pastor in the full tide of success. Among his leading men were such influential citizens as Charles McAllister, Charles E. Morgan, Judge Joel Jones, and Judge John K. Kane. His friends were men of mark in the community, such clergymen as George and Walter Stewart, Richardson, Brown, Van Rensselaer, Chester, Mann, Cuyler, and Engles, editor of the " Presbyterian." Two of his intimate personal friends were the Hon. Furman Sheppard, and Elisha Kent Kane, then in the height of his renown as an Arctic explorer. Over the remains of the latter, five years later, he preached a funeral sermon of such power as to attract attention from the entire community.

In short, Mr. Shields took his place at once as a great force in the city. This was the more remarkable in view of the conditions then prevailing. As Bishop Henry C. Potter said in his memorial address, delivered after the death of his friend: "I was a boy in Philadelphia at that time, and I can remember how swift we of different communions were to fasten upon one another's failings, and how little love was lost—or found—between us! What was most prized then was a master of polemics—there is little doubt that the orthodox believer, when he looked at his heterodox neighbor, complacently thanked God that he was not as other men were! Does anybody wonder that the sensitive and devout scholar turned from the ministry, in which it was often demanded that the preacher should meet such expectations or be lectured by his deacons—turned, I say, from such a conception of the office of the pulpit to the professor's chair?" For fifteen years the pastor of the Second Presbyterian Church was a faithful servant of his people and of his community, warning, admonishing, edifying, and cheering all who sought his kindly offices.

The life of these years was stimulating in all directions. He found time to indulge himself in extensive reading, and occasionally to write verses of a fugitive sort, which relieved his own emotional nature and gave great pleasure to many discriminating readers. But the serious side of his private study was dedicated throughout the entire period to a continued and careful consideration of the great problems which had absorbed him in earlier years. As early as 1855 he published a thoughtful article on "Presbyterian Polity," and a volume entitled "A Book of Remembrance." The latter is a beautiful allegory of the inner life; it had a wide circulation through the Presbyterian publication board, and ran through several editions. So important were his contributions to philosophy and theology that in 1860 he delivered the annual address at the Princeton Commencement and received the degree of Doctor of Divinity. In an address delivered long afterward, at the centennial celebration of the American Philosophical Society, he said that he remembered Philadelphia as a city in which his early labors found generous appreciation, to which he became attached by the strongest ties of his life, and which he had ever remembered, as the exiled Greek remembered his *dulcis Argos,* the sweet home of art and letters and refinement.

This sentiment was doubtless awakened as much by recollections of his private as of his public life in that city. During the early years he had lived through the heats of summer in the suburb of Torresdale. There, on August 9th, 1853, his wife died, leaving him a widower with three children still in infancy. For eight years he devoted himself to nourishing and cherishing them with double affection and devotion. During the summer of 1856 he was in Newport, Rhode Island, filling the pulpit of the Congregational church, of which the well-known Dr. Thayer was pastor. He remembered all the simplicity of Newport living as he then saw it; no cottage life, no Ocean Drive, no Bellevue Avenue; just the old town, three large hotels, and many boarding houses. The morning hours were spent in the quiet of the modest residence, dinner was at three, and the gayety was a drive after that to Fort Adams, or to the " Beaches," and then to the " Glen " for tea. There he first met Miss Elizabeth Kane, of Philadelphia, who was visiting her cousin, General John van Rensselaer. Their acquaintance was destined in time to become a romance, and it was to this meeting that he always attributed his enduring affection for Newport. He did not return until 1877, but the place had still, even heightened charms for him; and it was in the study of a house he built for himself, on a site overlooking Ochre Point, that he wrote many chapters of his Philosophia Ultima.

This friendship led also to the forming of many intimacies in Philadelphia. These are worth enumerating because they greatly influenced the later life of Dr. Shields, affording him the pleasure and stimulus of social and intellectual companionship, which everywhere made him one of the initiated. Fernrock, the country seat of Judge Kane, was the centre of a group, many members of which were destined to eminence in later years. Among them were Miss Lilly Macalister, who, as Mrs. Lawton, held a unique position in Washington society from the days of Buchanan to the second administration of Cleveland; there were the daughters of Fanny Kemble, Sarah and Fanny Butler, the former married to the late Owen J. Wistar, and the latter to the Hon. James Lee, now Dean of Hereford, England; there was Miss Charlotte Wood, wife of the late Vicar of Wakefield, the Reverend Edward Bell; there were also Thomas Hicks, and three medical students, J. Da Costa, S. Weir Mitchell, and John K. Kane, a son of the house; of course, too, there was Dr. Elisha Kent Kane, of the Navy, who returned thither to recuperate from his voyages in the Arctic. It is easy to understand the attractions of such congenial friends to a hard-working pastor, glad to seek relief for a season from the cares of a large city church.

## VIII.

In 1861 Dr. Shields published a pamphlet entitled "Philosophia Ultima." It contained a digest of his philosophical studies up to that date. It was an essay, partly historical, partly critical, claiming that eventually there would issue from a complete system of knowledge, which reason and revelation are combining to produce, a final philosophy; in other words, that sooner or later there would be a conclusive harmony of science and religion. This paper was almost a defiance of the orthodox thought of America as it then was, for it had no apologetic motive whatever, though it claimed that the relation of apologetics to philosophy demanded the most careful study from the philosophical point of view. In the view of the Presbyterian Church it was erroneous to make philosophy the arbiter between science and religion; to emphasize the opposition of science and religion was unduly to enlarge the area of apologetics, to introduce an unphilosophic element into philosophy, which at most is but the handmaid of theology. The essence of Dr. Shields's position was that between true religion and true science there could be no conflict, but that between the "crude, unproved hypotheses put forth in the name of science, and the human, fallible dogmas claiming to express the Bible" there was already joined a bitter conflict, and that it was a proper task of philosophy to sit in judgment on the claims of both, but to purge the evidence and establish the facts beneath the claims. On the one hand, the importance and value of certain so-called scientific hypotheses, on the other, the importance and value of certain so-called religious dogmas; from a determination of these would finally issue a harmony of secular and religious thought. Such was the revolutionary position of the manifesto. Of set purpose the proud title was a challenge.

## IX.

In order to gain a hearing the challenger must enter the lists; these were already marked and enclosed for the appellant, partly in the existing conditions of thought, partly in the position which Dr. Shields had established in the Philadelphia community, and especially in the esteem which he enjoyed at Princeton. His claim to a professor's chair was manifest. Accordingly the idea engaged the attention of many influential people, and the agitation took form almost immediately. In due time it became evident that his chair must be in philosophy, as far removed from the field of Christian apologetics as was necessary to secure and keep a clear perspective. The ideal situation was manifestly in Princeton College, as his *alma mater* was then popularly styled. When the Presbyterian Church located its chief and oldest seminary at the doors of Princeton College, it did so with the clear intention that the interaction between the two institutions should redound to the advantage of both. Their relations have ever been close and harmonious; yet their chairs have been held by men of the most divergent views, and their policies are for the most part avowedly distinct. It would be no breach in custom for a graduate of both to maintain in the undenominational college what the Calvinistic theology of the seminary might not admit, the more so as Dr. Shields was a convinced and consistent Calvinist himself. By 1865 the matter was arranged, and in that year he was made professor of the harmony of science and revealed religion. This was the first chair of the kind to be established in any American college. Princeton contributed from its meagre funds six hundred dollars, the rest of the salary was provided by subscriptions of friends to the project most of whom were in Philadelphia: later, when the professor inherited a modest fortune, these sums were all scrupulously repaid.

On August 25th, 1861, Dr. Shields had taken to wife his dear friend Miss Elizabeth Kane, whom he had so long admired and who had been the inspiration for much of his best work. They lived on Rittenhouse Square, and what with the duties of a growing family, increased by social activities incident to a new sphere, life was so full and exacting as to make very difficult, if not impossible, the pursuit of philosophical studies. The endless cares of the pastor weighed heavily upon him, feeling as he did that his period of ministerial work had been faithfully absolved. It was with delight that he hailed his Princeton call, and the vista which it opened of congenial work and study. The last years of his Philadelphia pastorate were, however, not so far absorbed by public duties but that he found time to publish a Presbyterian prayer-book, thus inaugurating in the church of his birth the liturgical movement which has reached the stage set forth by the action of the General Assembly in 1904, approving the report of their committee on the order of common worship. Dr. Shields's book contains a historical statement of the work of the Savoy Conference, in which the language of the English prayer-book was modified to satisfy the scruples of Presbyterians with a view to the unity of an Anglican Catholic church. The body of the book contains all existing historical material for such a manual. While the volume has never attracted general attention, yet several editions have been sold, and it has been a constant reminder of the possibility in the contemporary age of what was contemplated at the outset of modern history. Further, the introduction gave evidence of thoroughness in historical research, and displays a mastery of material in style and form which did not pass unnoticed by historians. He was later to be honored with the burden of historical teaching; which he did not seek and which was far from being congenial to his tastes.

Dr. Shields established himself with his family in a comfortable and conveniently situated cottage, where he dispensed a generous hospitality, spiritual, intellectual, and material, for many years. For some time his income was small; but, such as it was, the gracious presence of his wife and his own genial personality made his hearthstone a centre of influence from the beginning. There radiated from it a spirit of refinement and culture which made it a power among his colleagues and his students. The first period of his Princeton life was one, however, of some disappointment and much sorrow. As his family grew in numbers and in age, the demands upon his slender resources increased steadily. Much of his work was that for which he was prepared: the writing and delivery of lectures, the chapel preaching, and the general routine of the professor's life, but there was alarming and fatal sickness in his family, and increased expense had to be met by exertions which though remunerative did not advance the cause to which he had devoted himself. As the crown of sorrow, Mrs. Shields died in 1869. Again he found himself in widowed solitude, charged with all the care which little children demand from both their parents.

Always sensitive and retiring, it now seemed as if he must remain a sad and discouraged recluse. For a little time it was such a life that he led. But the well-spring of a higher life was copious and strong within him; as in many similar instances his mind and his books provided balm for his wounded spirit and in renewed study he found a measure of consolation. At last he felt the impulse to original composition, and in the summer of 1870, working day after day, far into the night, he began to set down the ideas he hoped to embody in his first book. Among the younger men who had enjoyed the privilege of some intimacy with Dr. Shields was one who was destined to reach great distinction as a biblical scholar and who is now (1905) a professor in the University of Leipsic, Caspar René Gregory. After months of solitary labor, his older friend called the young scholar to his service; their intimacy grew apace and after the autumn of the year they were much together in the evenings, frequently, too, in the afternoons; and sometimes in the mornings as well. At last Dr. Gregory came to pass long periods of time, weeks together, under his friend's roof.

His account of the author's labors and methods gives a clear insight into the genesis of the volumes, as they grew on Dr. Shields's hands.

With reference to his sources, says Dr. Gregory, I was for some time librarian of the Seminary Library, and I used to search out all kinds of things at first hand for him. An old copy of Petrus Lombardus, the Master of Sentences, sticks in my memory; and philosophers of all kinds, and scientific men in general. So far as I can remember, the longest hunt I had, referred to Galileo; and I scarcely venture now to say what the last point was, save that the aim was to get authentic testimony about his trial; testimony that was not in books. It is quite possible that some note of mine about it is still among Dr. Shields's papers. I went to a then very old and very world-forsaken, I think French, monastery in Baltimore; it seems to me that the priest or the monk whom I there saw was very suspicious, and that I got nothing out of him. I was more successful at Philadelphia, at the Bishop's house near the Cathedral. There I met a priest who, I think, had been the Secretary of the Bishop at the Vatican Council; his name escapes me at this moment; I think of Hauptmann, Hausmann, or Hoffman, but the chances are that it was something very different; he is probably, if still living, a dignitary of the Church, for he was learned, facile, and in favor. He at once entered into the spirit of the thing and, after we had rummaged around for a while, he said that he thought he had seen an account of the trial or some quotations from proceedings at the trial in, I think, an Italian Review. This he found, and a footnote gave just what we were looking for. Dr. Shields was greatly pleased when I got back to Princeton with the notes. That is enough about the sources. Dr. Shields, I always found willing and desirous to get back to and down to the original sources.

Taking then the accessible sources, often, of course, a volume or two of the given author, Dr. Shields wrote with the greatest care an abstract of the opinions of the author, often several pages long. Such longer summaries he then again reduced to shorter ones, tearing the old ones up. Finally, I objected to his destruction of the preliminary work and he laid these papers away; whether they still exist or not I do not know. From these abstracts he proceeded to the writing of the given chapter in his book. How long he wrote and rewrote and tore up I cannot tell. I kept remonstrating with him and insisting upon it that he must begin to settle the manuscript for the press. I should say that I read everything as he wrote it, or he read it to me. I worked at my own work, then largely philosophy and history, at the window side of his table, a large table, doubtless still at Morven or Newport, while he worked at the room-side of the table, so that we were hours together there. And then we would go to chairs at each side of the little wood fire, where he would read Tennyson or Matthew Arnold, or something else nice, to me, or we discussed heaven and earth, and the rest of creation or non-creation. To go on: at last I said, "This must stop. You must give me the beginning of Volume I, and I shall copy it off and lay it away, and that will be as if it were printed, and you must let it alone and go on with the rest. And so for II, and III." And we did that. How far the process actually went on before I left for Leipsic, on May 9 (sailing May 10), 1873, I cannot now remember. I take it for granted that the most of I, much of II, and a little of III (do not ask me how far I, II, III reach) was done, and of course he was working away on the piles of abstracts for the rest of it. I put the copied-off, quasi-printed, parts into one of the drawers on my side of the table.

As to persons, it should be mentioned that Dr. Welling, when he first came to Princeton, lived at Dr. Shields's and was thus for some time closely with him, talking over and, I think, hearing everything, although I cannot now say just how much he read or heard of the book. Dr. Shields did not have much to do with people in general, although he was, of course, ever friendly to all. Once or twice we called on

John Miller, after he came back to Princeton, for he amused and interested us. He was full of thought, and totally reckless in what he said. Once he appalled us by saying, I think in the presence of his lovely wife, in the midst of a theological argument: " Now, if I should murder my wife——" We knew there was no danger of it, but it was an uncanny way of pointing a position.

These pleasant memories of Professor Gregory suggest the character of his friend, as it was then formed and as it remained substantially to the last. His scholarship was marked by three qualities; it was based on the rock of original research, it was special within limits carefully related to the whole field, it had the clearness which Descartes says is the test of truth. In his friendships he was careful to select those of the strongest individuality, so that the interchange of relations might increase the vital forces of all concerned. Then, as now, Princeton abounded in men of strong purpose and of fearless personality, utterly indifferent to the levelling forces so active in the outer world. The intercourse of such persons with each other results in the sharpening of minds and wits, in the challenge and retort, the feint and guard, which are conducive to chivalric liberty, reciprocity of sympathy, and vigorous execution of tasks. Busy scholars guard their privacy as a sacred thing, and carefully maintain the conventions of life; the hours of leisure are correspondingly free and joyous. The atmosphere thus created was a congenial one for the training of Dr. Shields's natural powers, and he throve in it despite his sorrows and his cares.

Moreover, he was in hearty sympathy with the policy of the university to which he belonged, a policy based on tradition and on the conditions of its means and geographical site. Established in protest against ultra conservatism, it was committed to hearing the other side on all disputed questions; its constitution was founded in the liberal arts and sciences, and to the cultivation of these it was irrevocably committed. Whatever the future had in store, the present path was clearly defined; in the words of a famous son of Princeton, her scholars were not to be citizens of some petty principality, but freemen in the commonwealth of knowledge. The place itself has been, from the first, a haunt for men of all sections in our federal union; it bred the rebels of 1776 under Witherspoon, it saw Washington's greatest strategic achievement, it saw the recognition of American independence, its vane pointed first South and then North in the Civil War, it had first introduced science into the curriculum of American colleges, in short, both theoretically and historically it stood for liberty without license.

With such aspirations and such a past, the task of development along its chosen course would have been easy for the college, had its resources been adequate to its aspirations; but unfortunately such was not the case, and no member of her faculty could escape the performance of work for which he was known to be capable. The most conspicuous gap in her course of study was the absence of all instruction in secular history, except as it was given incidentally to the instruction in other departments. Dr. McCosh succeeded to the President's chair at the opening of the college year in 1868. He at once inspired all the friends of the university with confidence in his guidance, and delighted them with his shrewd insight into the character of his task. Enthusiasm increased as his projects were realized one after another, and his colleagues were ready for almost any sacrifice. In 1870, therefore, Dr. Shields assumed the work of teaching modern history, the college assuming the whole of his salary. For thirteen years he lectured on European and American civilization, on English constitutional law, on philosophical history, and on social science. So brilliant and thorough was his work, in spite of the energy which it took from his chosen field of labor, that the compulsion to continue for so long was really of his own making. He obtained relief at the last only by sheer will-power, in the determination to sacrifice a portion of his salary that he might devote himself solely to his specialty. For no part of his activities is he held in more grateful remembrance by his pupils than for the inspiration they received from his large and forcible views of history, and for the enduring impulse he gave to the development of historical studies in Princeton University.

His intellectual discouragements, therefore, were in the main due to his own qualities and abilities. He nevertheless felt them keenly, and was often impatient as time flew by and the field he had surveyed remained untilled. A born and fearless pioneer, it seemed hard that he should not enter on the task of occupying and improving his preëmptions. What was more, he was for long an academic preacher, second to none in eloquence and edification. He held his student audiences spellbound in the college chapel, and visiting strangers thronged to hear him. A number of his most famous and best remembered sermons were printed by request. They remind one of the "Old Doctor's" criticism, when the professor was yet a student. Their tone is distinctively that of the plaintive scholar, who has noted the conditions into which he was born, and holds himself responsible for those in which he lives. They abound in felicitous phrase, in happy illustrations, and in philosophic insight. They console while they instruct, they encourage while they warn, they combine the fire of conviction with the charm of melancholy. To the preparations of these sermons their author gave lavishly of his time and his force, so much, indeed, that in them he cultivated his literary gifts to a higher perfection than in either his lectures or his books. It was his sufficient reward that his hearers were appreciative and grateful. When, after many years of such service, he felt compelled to devote his life to what he regarded as higher duty, it was not without regret that he relinquished the stimulating pleasure of regular ministerial service.

Considering the natural sensitiveness of Dr. Shields, and the circumstances under which he had entered upon his duties in Princeton, it was not strange that he desired to know how he stood in the opinion of his public. On this point he consulted one of his intimate friends, William Baker, the well-known author of several striking books, among them the novel which not long since absorbed a host of critical readers, " His Majesty Myself." In a letter dated November 11th, 1866, Mr. Baker wrote: " I have only two small statements to make. Whether or not you will think them worth the paper and the time spent in reading this, you must decide. Imprimis, Dr. Duffield accompanied me to this city. In an incidental way he told me that you gave the utmost satisfaction in your chair to all. He was even enthusiastic about your present and future in Princeton. Since coming here I have heard that Dr. Hodge, of Princeton, has been speaking of your course in a manner most flattering to yourself. This I have direct. Moral: Do not be so sensitive. You are too self-conscious, too introspective. Forget your own existence. Be so absorbed in, say, the culture of—even turnips, if nothing else—the youth about you, as to have only a traditional memory of yourself. I believe if one could know and care as little for one's self as a tulip does, or a nightingale, one would be that much the more fragrant and melodious for it. What a sage I am, am I not?" The recipient of this letter profited much from it; for it looks at present as if he might have kept it by him for a time. At all events, he eventually acquired, as was just, the well earned self-confidence without which men are after all broken reeds.

The high esteem and affection which was expressed to Mr. Baker by Dr. Duffield, of the college, and Dr. Hodge, of the seminary, in their utterances of consideration for Dr. Shields were universal with all his colleagues in both institutions. He easily attained to respect and popularity, and his eminence was never disputed. Possibly the degree of confidence which his associates placed in him was most clearly expressed in the fact that throughout his long connection with Princeton, they regarded him as the one man best fitted for the most difficult of tasks, the preparation of the record to be spread on their minutes concerning the character and services of those who by death or resignation were taken from the service of the college. In him they recognized the typical Princetonian, steeped in the college history and feeling, endowed with a splendid gift of expression and able to gauge the proportionate value of services rendered, as no other could. Besides, his human sympathy, tempered by disciplined emotions, would, as it did, surely result in a fine literary cast to such a record. The many such estimates from his pen are alike adequate and beautiful. Were the old fashion of elaborate epitaphs still in vogue, these polished and terse characterizations would well commemorate virtue and gladden the hearts of posterity. It is a misfortune that they must ever remain inaccessible to all but the antiquary.

## X.

With the revolving years the home of Dr. Shields became a centre of social importance, which afforded the highest and purest pleasure to his neighbors and to strangers alike. In his oldest daughter, as she grew to woman's estate, he had a helper and companion abundantly fit to preside at his hospitable table and welcome his guests to a well-ordered house. The students and other young visitors made life cheerful and gay. Into their amusements the head of the family threw himself with zest; for one of their most important enterprises he made a dramatic version of Tennyson's "Princess," carefully studied with reference to the exigencies of the amateur stage. It was duly acted by his children and their friends under his careful management, and with such success that he was persuaded to publish it in a little volume which has been of use to many similar companies of young folk. These, and like recreations of an elevating character, gave a distinguished quality to the household. Miss Shields deserves more than a passing mention. She was her father's support, and a mother to his children; a woman of most uncommon parts, of brilliant attainments and trenchant wit; her company was eagerly sought by her equals in age and by her elders; children were her adoring friends. After her marriage she presided over her husband's home as she had over that of her father, and "Springdale" was a centre of influence quite as important as her father's house; after her grandfather's death, Dr. Shields came into his comfortable inheritance, and made his home with her until her untimely death. Her memory is still green with those who were young in Princeton during her mature life; and men now verging over the term of middle life pay hearty tribute to the power for good which she exercised over those who were favored with her friendship.

When her younger sister became Mrs. Stockton, it was possible for Dr. Shields to purchase "Morven," the ancient seat of her husband's family, and there in the companionship of his children and grandchildren, he spent the remaining years of his life. In this acquisition Dr. Shields took the most intense delight. He wrote of it that it had been the joy of Richard Stockton, scholar and statesman, who had been a student at Elizabeth, where he met Annis Boudinot, daughter of Elias, president of the first congress. As Mrs. Stockton she came to the ancestral home in Princeton, and fixed upon it the poetic name of "Morven," taken from the scene of Ossian's poems. As a manorial estate it originated in a grant from William Penn to an earlier Richard Stockton, in 1701, of a tract of five thousand five hundred acres, embracing the present grounds of the university and the village of Princeton. Nor was it a matter of little interest to him and to many others, that by a coincidence, after a lapse of a hundred and thirty years, branches of the Stockton and Woodruff families, so closely associated in colonial times, should so long after be connected by marriage, and come into possession of the Morven mansion at a juncture when otherwise that family seat would have passed out of a succession in which it had been maintained for two centuries. Within its walls on the due month and day occurred a notable celebration of the two-hundredth anniversary of the grant. There were gathered for the festival many descendants of both stocks, and the present holders of lands whose title rests in the grant. The ceremonial was that of the far-off olden time, as were the costumes; the arrangements, carefully studied by Dr. Shields in anticipation of the event, and with reference to the background of his historic house, were admirably carried out in all particulars, and impressed those present with the dignity of their heritage, and with its accompanying responsibilities, exactly as he had desired. The place is as famous by its later associations as by its origin, and its owner looked upon its possession as a public trust. To all visitors on the high festivals of town and gown alike, its doors were open for inspection; and very often in lavish hospitality.

Reference has already been made to the tender associations which endeared Newport to Dr. Shields; among his first cares after his succession to his inheritance was the purchase of a field on the then sparsely settled Ochre Point. There he built a cottage after his own ideas, and he furnished it in the exercise of his chastened and exquisite taste. From 1877 onward Newport was his summer home, except for a single year, the holidays of which were spent in a European tour, which gave him the greatest possible pleasure. His visitors at Newport found him one of a select circle of literary and other friends, no member of which was more sought after than himself. In the companionship of eminent men and women he found refreshment and strength; as has been said, in the quiet of his study on Ochre Point much of his profoundest thinking and best writing was done. One of his activities was his connection with the "Town and Country Club"; of it Mrs. Julia Ward Howe was the president and he was the vice-president. Its membership is in all respects remarkable, comprising the keen minds of many sections of the country, and its proceedings afforded to Dr. Shields a valuable stimulus; the honor it paid him is sufficient evidence of what he did for it. These and his Princeton associations in winter were the sources from which he renewed his perennial youth. He was in the full enjoyment of all the activities which rendered his life so rich and varied, when death overtook him at Newport during his eightieth year, on August 26th, 1904. He literally "fell on sleep"; in a moment, without pain or warning, he was unconscious, and in that state he departed this life.

### XI.

Dr. Shields died in the communion and orders of the Episcopal Church. The circumstances under which he changed his denominational connection were as characteristic as any other events of his life. Not far from Morven stands the Princeton Inn, a hostelry founded and managed by graduates of the college in order that students and their friends, graduates and their families, may enjoy the amenities of life in quiet comfort. This purpose appealed to the master of Morven in every way, as elevating the social life of the undergraduates, inviting the friends of both the institutions to lengthened sojourn, and bringing strangers to visit with leisure the historic sights of the town and surrounding country. Devoted to the cause of true temperance, he did not hesitate to sign the application for license required of hotels by the law of the State, and followed the example in so doing of other neighbors, men of the first position in the country and the community. For some years this fact, as was to be expected, attracted no attention whatever. But when one of the surges of intemperate agitation against temperance, in favor of total abstinence, which arise from time to time, lifted its crest in all the Eastern college towns, it broke also over Princeton. The crusaders attacked Dr. Shields as a Presbyterian minister, and sought to accumulate capital at his expense. Their influence reached far, and appeared in the sessions of the Presbytery to which he belonged. It finally became clear that a very delicate and embarrassing issue was to be joined. His first and natural impulse was to meet it without compromise and stand on the ground of personal liberty, which has always been that of his church and of his own. He was little disturbed by the abuse and vilification of fanaticism, and was quite ready to try conclusions with his opponents. In time, however, he had a change of conviction. It appeared that the General Assembly of the Presbyterian Church had advised against the endorsement of a license as a reprehensible complicity with the liquor traffic; just as it had characterized card-playing, theatre-going, and dancing as " unscriptural, immoral, and improper "; and while the modifying circumstances of the Princeton Inn might well have given him a firm standing for the defence of private judgment, yet it was possible that a long and protracted struggle might ensue. From this he shrank, partly because of sensitiveness, partly because he did not wish to involve his friends in troublesome litigations in the church courts, while above all he desired to avoid the scandal of Christian brethren infringing the apostolic injunction against the judgment of another man's servant. He determined, therefore, to withdraw from the ministry of his ancestral church, and avoid the embarrassment it might cause to its many members who did not see eye to eye with him.

But whither should he go? He felt bound to examine himself thoroughly, and weigh the claims of all the reformed churches; this he did earnestly and deliberately. The decision which he reached might have been foreseen; as indeed it was, by many of his intimate friends. Among the many elements within the fold of the Presbyterian Church in America there has always been one, which was essentially Scotch in its attitude toward Presbyterian ordination, holding their own orders to be as apostolic as any others. They have also stood firmly on the historic ground of reform as opposed to protest and schism. These are they who, when separated from the ministrations of their own church, naturally gravitate toward the one other communion of Protestants which maintains a similar position. A divine-right Presbyterian stands closer to the Episcopal Church than to any other branch of the Teutonic church. These matters were always, as we have seen, close to the heart of Dr. Shields; and further, his belief in liturgical worship had now brought him to the conviction that all eclecticism in that regard was vain, that the reunion of Protestant Christendom could better be accomplished on the basis of the Book of Common Prayer than on any other. It was certain, therefore, that his decision would fall as it did. Moreover, among the clergy of the Episcopal Church he had many, many personal friends, and there, as he felt, was held the orthodox view of temperance; the scriptural view, antagonistic to that which criticised the conduct of the Son of Man and which "was invading His church, and defacing His sacrament." On December 14th, 1898, he received the first orders of the Episcopal Church from Bishop Scarborough, of New Jersey, in the chapel of the Good Shepherd, in the city of New York. On May 28th, 1899, he was further ordained to the full ministry of that communion in Garden City Cathedral by Bishop Littlejohn, of the Diocese of Long Island, his lifelong friend and comrade. Not long afterward he was elected a trustee of the General Theological Seminary in New York. Before that institution he delivered the Bishop Paddock lectures on the "Evidences of Christianity," which form a part of the following volume. His services as a preacher were in frequent requisition in the pulpit of Trinity Church, Princeton, and elsewhere. From Trinity Church, in Princeton, he was buried, and from its pulpit Bishop Potter, of New York, preached an eloquent discourse in memory of one whose highest ideals were unity of the faith and unity of the church of God upon earth.

May we suppose, said the Bishop, that it cost Dr. Shields no pang to sunder ties and end companionships which, in their origin, reached back for generations, and were as truly a part of his mental and emotional identity as anything can be? There were men whom he met every day, who loved and honored him—as who that really knew him could help doing?—and who had no smallest doubt as to the honesty of his motives, or the integrity of his action, in any step that separated him from his earlier associates; but who could never forget that a certain action had been determined upon by him, and that a certain step had been taken. When these men met him, with whatever continuance of the old warmth and cordiality, they knew and he knew, that there was one group of subjects that were to be avoided, and one realm of discussion even the outer portals of which were never any more to be opened! And yet, continued the Bishop, with what gentle dignity and gracious self-restraint, through it all, he bore himself! Yes, and with what true nobility of largeness and charity did this ancient University bear herself toward him! One can easily imagine, on the part of associates and authorities from whom he separated, something of resentment, because of action on Dr. Shields's part, which some of them thought inconsistent, if not positively disloyal. But if they ever thought so, they never said so; or if they said so, they said it with such cautious reserve that it never came to outside ears. And I must confess, for myself, that there has always seemed something especially dear and beautiful in the fact that, with Princeton, its social and its intellectual life; and best of all, with that great University in which so long he was a professor—that with all these he remained identified to the last! Long may his memory survive here as that of a true scholar, a pure and most lovable man, who brought to great opportunities great gifts, and who used them, with unwearied fidelity, for God and man!

These appreciative words are strictly and literally true. The attitude of the university continued in the end what it had been in the beginning, what it has ever been in like instances, sympathetic to every man who sincerely seeks the truth of faith and conduct in the light given to him. For example, Dr. Patton, President during fourteen years of Dr. Shields's professorship, was the most outspoken critic of his colleague's work in philosophy, the fearless champion of the orthodoxy as held in the Princeton Seminary. His was the only criticism which ever moved Dr. Shields from the even tenor of his studies, and induced him to defend his positions. Yet in the minute which he prepared for the faculty on the resignation of Dr. Patton, he did not miss a single one of the great milestones which had characterized the passing administration; its growth in material and intellectual equipment, the maturity which it had reached in academic development, the new spirit of research, and the educational method by which it had been marked. To his rare logical skill, acumen, and familiarity with living issues, there is also a sincere tribute. In turn Dr. Patton has put on record the esteem in which he held Dr. Shields, and the position he had taken. I have no reason to believe, he said in the "Princeton Bulletin," that when he (Dr. Shields) took orders in the Episcopal Church his views respecting the validity of his own Presbyterian ordination had undergone a change; and I am confident that his Calvinistic theology underwent no revision, either before or after he left the Presbyterian ministry. To those who knew the circumstances it was not strange that Dr. Shields, so late in life, entered the ministry of another church; and to those of us who knew, and loved, and trusted him, his change of denominational relations made no difference in our sense of fellowship with him. He was to us the same genial, gentle, lovable, refined, and scholarly Dr. Shields that he had always been; and we were only sorry that the roll of ministers of the Protestant Episcopal Church had been enriched through our loss of a name that had long adorned our own. These words of one who is now the president of the Princeton Theological Seminary, are a fitting pendant to those of Bishop Potter.

John Calvin was indeed one of Dr. Shields's heroes. The aspersions cast upon the great reformer, he regarded with contempt and disgust; in 1893 he published a monograph, recondite in its learning and fiercely polemic in its argument, which spurns the accusation that Calvin burned Servetus. No one has yet risen to refute it. So strongly had the theme taken hold of the writer's imagination that he saw the dramatic qualities of it in a clear light, and as an avocation he composed a drama entitled, "The Reformer of Geneva," which was published and widely read. Charles Dudley Warner, Laurence Hutton, Weir Mitchell, Henry M. Baird, and other experts like them wrote of it in unstinted praise; newspapers like the Philadelphia *Press*, the *Christian World*, of London, and the New York *Evening Post*, reviewed it sympathetically. Perhaps the highest tribute came from Professor Dowden, the famous British critic. He wrote: It seems as if a few hours were too short a time to allow of real acquaintance with so large an output of mind. But I have read it all with eager interest, and with close attention—breaking off last night and resuming my reading at five this morning. It is a piece of history lifted into drama with, I am sure, remarkable fidelity, and certainly with remarkable vividness. All the characters live, and the action does not flag or falter. There is rare strength and dignity, with a touch of hidden tenderness and pathos, in Calvin; and I can well believe your Servetus to be the real Servetus. The love of La Fontaine and your creation, Idelette—a nest in the storm and rocking trees—is a strenuous love, and it is duly subordinated to the tragic interests. I seem to understand the life of Geneva better than I ever did before, and I thank you for a possession of enduring value.

## XII.

This, with the other appreciations of Dr. Shields's work in preaching, in teaching, and in literature, have been given, lest the reader might think of him as a mere dilettante in all these lines of work, so versatile was his genius and so varied his avocations. The evidence adduced, to which much might be added, is quite sufficient to prove the contrary. Nevertheless, in this age of high specialization, the wide scope of Dr. Shields's interests and activities had something to do with the interest taken in that which was his life work. Too many concluded, on insufficient grounds, that no man could do the basic and thorough work which he aimed to do, when his energies were so engaged elsewhere. The day of the polymath had gone, and finite powers must be content with knowing little about many things if they were to grasp much about anything. Such a view, widely prevalent, is the worst heresy of our times, and is the force which has debased our intellectual standards to a level on which charlatanism thrives. No high standard of either knowledge, judgment, or expression is possible unless set by men of extensive learning, and intensive study within a broad field. Moreover, professional and technical investigation, the results of the highest specializations, are themselves legitimate subjects of examination. No scholar is in greater danger than he who confines himself exclusively to work within narrow bounds; and just such men suddenly, in the natural and overmastering desire for generalization, are they who proceed to establish great principles on insufficient data. The best antidote for such rashness is in exactly the line of work which Dr. Shields essayed to do, and in just the equipment which he sought to provide for the comparative method as applied to determining the order and value of the sciences, human and natural. To judge him the court must be at least as well trained in the principles of a transcendental and metaphysical philosophy as he was. So far is this true that it would be almost impossible to draw a jury of such sufficient intelligence as to fit it for trying the case. In his field of inquiry Dr. Shields found that, often, if not always, it had been necessary to exchange the advocate for the judge. Men like Locke, Descartes, Leibnitz, Berkeley, and above all, Butler, were quite as much philosophers as apologetes if not more so; and did not hesitate to sit in judgment on the case which they themselves presented. If Dr. Shields found himself compelled at times to a similar course, his capacity for umpirage was due to the broad sympathies, the extensive learning, and the inclusive experience of life, the phases of which have been indicated if not described.

The passion for systematized knowledge is as old as civilization, and the effort to unify science began with Plato. From his day to this the list of writers who have attempted a classification of the sciences is unbroken. The pamphlet entitled "The Order of the Sciences," which Dr. Shields published in 1882, was the first essay made in America to deal with the question. Had the author but lived a year longer he would have had the gratification of reading in Professor Robert Flint's history of the subject an appreciative tribute to the work. Dr. Flint had evidently not seen the later modifications of the "Order," and the changes made in the theory of their development, which was published in various journals, and are now given in the author's final revision, partly in this volume and chiefly in the preceding one. Nevertheless, in Dr. Flint's exhaustive treatise Dr. Shields is first among the American names; and to his somewhat embryonic outline the most respectful consideration is given, accompanied by high praise. What is even more striking is the fact that the definition of philosophy as "scientia scientiarum," a definition much disputed by Dr. Shields's American critics, is adopted by the learned Scotchman as a matter of course, a definition requiring no defence.

In Flint's judgment, the treatise, small and merely introductory as it is, ranks among the best; and he declares that while its exhibition of the scheme of scientific distribution is clear and skilful, its criticism of other classifications is also discriminating and incisive. In the order of time and the estimate of capable critics, as well as by the further elaboration of his subject, Dr. Shields appears to be the Nestor and founder of this department of philosophy in our country. Of course, Flint and Shields, alike in accepting "scientia scientiarum" as a definition of philosophy, are also alike in confining that definition to theoretical philosophy, "as a scheme of the sciences, as an inquiry into the nature and limits of knowledge, and as a doctrine of being and becoming —or, in other words, philosophy as positive, critical, and metaphysical." Both were well aware that this, while the most of philosophy, is not the whole of it; that "practical applicability is a necessary consequence of theoretical accuracy." The quotations are from the former of the two authors, but the latter has in his second volume, and in conversation, repeatedly said the same thing. Indeed, had Dr. Flint ever seen Dr. Shields's second volume, he would have recognized a close kinship of mind with the earlier writer. Neither would surrender an inch of the territory won by sound theory to the pragmatic meddlers who, in their assumptions, discard not merely the relations of the sciences, but even the conditions of knowledge and the very nature of both existence and causation, as immaterial to the concept of a universe and its order. Difficulties must needs arise, and they can never be composed either by observation or by analysis; there must be a synthesis, and it can never be reached by apathy and neglect.

The great task which the author set for himself early in life was completed in his old age when he had prepared the following pages for the press. It had not occurred to him to preface their publication by any apology for the book; his work was no longer tentative, and had received the encomiums of so many able critics on the continent of Europe, in Great Britain, and at home, that he might justly feel his place to be assured. Moreover, he was a man of apostolic temper, clear as to his theme and its bearing, faithful in the performance of a plain duty which had been revealed to him in the most searching self-examination. Not given to polemics, he was nevertheless a master in attack and argument, fond of the fray, and the last to leave the field. To the three volumes of the "Final Philosophy" he gave the best of his life, and by their contents he wished to be judged. It is not likely that posthumous opinion, any more than that of his contemporaries, will go to the extreme of honeyed panegyric. His subject is too abstruse and recondite for any general agreement thereon to be easily reached; but that he will be gratefully regarded as an able surveyor in the field, and that he will be felt to have established many important principles of procedure, seems certain to the present writer. His claim to remembrance in the United States as a pioneer is undoubted; and furthermore, even those who cannot accept his main thesis are sure to appreciate the incidental value of an erudition marked by sympathy, richness, and a cosmic scope.

This memoir is not the place in which to detail either the praise or the blame, the assent or dissent, with which his most important work has been received. In fact, until now the work has been incomplete, and with this volume it is for the first time before the public in its entirety. There may, in consequence, be some revision of opinion; if so the object of this brief memoir will have been secured, provided the chosen few, who alone can appreciate and judge the life work of Dr. Shields, derive from it any information likely to elucidate the spirit in which he began and finished his task.

# BIBLIOGRAPHY

COMPILED UNDER THE DIRECTION OF E. C. RICHARDSON

## BOOKS AND PAMPHLETS

Address at the funeral of John K. Kane. Feb. 24th, 1858. n. p. [1858]. 15 p., 8vo.

Biographical sketch. (See Welling, J. C. Addresses, lectures, and other papers. 1904. Pref., 9-19.)

Book of remembrance; a New Year's gift. 1867. 18mo. Pres. Bd.

Church unity; five lectures delivered in Union Theological Seminary, N. Y., 1896. N. Y., Chas. Scribner's Sons, 1896. 12mo.

Commemorative sermon on Henry Steele Clarke. Jan. 24th, 1864. Phila., Leisenring, 1864. 21 p., 8vo.

Course in the harmony of science and religion, first part, Themes and questions from Butler's Analogy. Princeton, Stelle & Smith [1868]. 103 p., 22.4 cm. [8vo]. 28mo.

Directory for public worship, and the book of common prayer considered with reference to the question of a Presbyterian liturgy. Phil., W. S. & A. Martien, 1863. 48 p., 8vo.

Discourse in memory of William Darrach, M. D., May 21, 1865. 1865. 8vo., 23 p.

Discourse on Christian politics, delivered on Thanksgiving day, 1851, in Philadelphia. Phil., Deacon & Peterson, 1851. 31 p., 23.5 cm. [8vo].

Essays on Christian unity. 1892.

Final philosophy. N. Y., 1877. 8vo.

Final philosophy; 2d. ed. N. Y., 1879. 8vo.

Funeral discourse on Joel Jones. Philadelphia, Feb. 6, 1860. Phil., Deacon & Peterson, 1860. 16 p., 16.9 cm. [16mo].

Funeral eulogy at the obsequies of E. K. Kane. Phil., Parry & McMillan, 1857. 34 p., 16mo.

Harmony of science and the Bible. Princeton, Robinson & Co. 13 p., 22.2 cm. [8vo].

Historic episcopate; essay on the four articles of church unity proposed by the American House of Bishops and the Lambeth Conference. N. Y., Chas. Scribner's Sons, 1894. 12mo.

Introductory lecture on the relations of science and religion. Phil., 1866. 8vo.

Liturgia expurgata; or, The Prayer-book amended according to the Presbyterian revision of 1661, and historically reviewed. Phil., W. S. & A. Martien, 1864. 188 p., 17.2 cm. [16mo].

Logic applicable to religion. n. p. 103 p., 22 cm. [8vo].

Manual for worship, 1862. 180 p.

Order of the sciences; an essay on the philosophical classification and organization of human knowledge. N. Y., Scribner's Sons, 1882. 103 p., 19.2 cm. [12mo].

Philosophia ultima. Phil., Lippincott, 1861. 96 p., 22.5 cm. [8vo].

Philosophia ultima; or, Science of the sciences. 3d ed., rev. N. Y., Scribner, 1888-89. 2 v., 23.2 cm. [8vo].

Preces ecclesiasticæ; the forms of public devotion instituted by Calvin, John Knox, Martin Bucer, Micronius, and used in the Presbyterian Church, newly collected and collated. N. Y., Scribner, 1856. iii, [1] p. 23.9 cm. [8vo].

Purely instrumental character of ministerial labor; a discourse. October 18, 1850. Phil., Moore, 1851. 24 p., 22.7 cm. [8vo].

Reformer of Geneva; an historical drama. [Princeton, privately printed, 1897.] 108 p., 25.8 cm. [4to].

Religion and science in their relation to philosophy; an essay on the present state of the sciences. N. Y., Scribner, Armstrong, & Co., 1875. 69 p., 19.2 cm. [12mo].

Scientific evidences of revealed religion. N. Y., 1900. 8vo. Paddock lectures. 1900.

Sketch of the life of Elisha Kent Kane, from a new ed. of "Arctic explorations." Newark, Bliss & Co. p. 749-766, 8vo., por.

Syllabus of the problems of natural religion as solved by analogy. n. p. 103 p., 8vo.

Themes and questions from Butler's Analogy. n. p. 38 p., 8vo.

United Church of the U. S. N. Y., Scribner's Sons, 1895. xi., 285 p., 8vo.

What is truth? A discourse preached in the College chapel, Princeton, N. J., Sept. 30, 1886. Princeton, Robinson, 1866. 20 p., 8vo.

## EDITORIAL WORK

Bacon, Francis. Philosophical works; ed. by C. W. Shields. 1870.

Presbyterian Church. Book of common prayer, ed. by C. W. Shields. Phil., W. S. & A. Martien, 1864. xxiv, 637 p., 16mo.

Presbyterian Church. Book of common prayer, ed. by C. W. Shields. N. Y., Randolph & Co. xxiv, 637 p., 16mo.

Tennyson, Alfred, 1st baron. Princess; a drama adapted from the poem of Alfred Tennyson, [by C. W. Shields for the Princeton Dramatic Association.] Princeton, Press pr. establishment, 1878. 28 p., 8vo.

## MAGAZINE ARTICLES

Arctic monument named for Tennyson by Dr. Kane. 10 p. Cent. mag., 1898. v. 56, p. 483-492.

Doctrine of Calvin concerning infant salvation. Pres. and reformed review, 1890. v. i., p. 634-651.

Does the Bible contain scientific errors? 9 p. Century mag. 1893, v. 23, p. 126. Abstract of this paper in Princeton Univ. Bulletin, 1893, v. 5, p. 13-14.

Ecclesiastical situation. Churchman, 1894, June 23. Abstract in Princeton Univ. Bulletin, 1894, v. 6, p. 101-102.

The Hon. Furman Sheppard, late attorney of Philadelphia, class of 1845. Princeton Univ. Bulletin, 1895, v. 7, p. 92-94.

The Hon. Samuel Woodruff, trustee of Princeton College. Princeton Univ. Bulletin, 1892, v. 4, p. 2-9.

Hypothesis and dogma in the sciences. Presbyterian and reformed review, 1891, v. 2, p. 294-606. Princeton Univ. Bulletin, 1890, v. 2, p. 58-59. (Abstract.)

Lambeth articles of church unity. Princeton Univ. Bulletin, 1894, v. 6, p. 6-7. (Abstract.)
Philosophy and apologetics. Princeton review, 1879, v. for Jul.-Dec., p. 198-207.
Professor Dod's lectures on architecture. Princeton Univ. Bulletin, 1897, v. 9, p. 63-64.
Reason and revelation in the sciences. N. Y., Presbyterian Review Association [1885]. 21 p., 24 cm. [8vo]. From the Apr. (1885) no. of the Presbyterian review.
Religious lessons of the deluge. Theological and literary journal, 1853.
Review of Comte's positive philosophy. Princeton review, 1858.
Social problem of church unity. Century mag., v. 40, 1890, p. 687-697.
Trial of Servetus. Presbyterian and reformed review, 1893, v. 4. 353-389. Abstract in Princeton Univ. Bulletin, 1894, v. 6, p. 15-16.
Two current fallacies in the higher criticism. Princeton Univ. Bulletin, 1897, v. 9, p. 4-5. Summary of a paper read in N. Y., Feb. 17, 1897.
United churches in the U. S. 22 p. Cent. mag., 1886, v. 34, p. 74 ; 1888, v. 35, p. 254.

# PREFACE.

The aim of this treatise is both philosophical and apologetical. It is designed at once as a contribution to the philosophical scheme of knowledge, and as a vindication of the Christian religion.

In its philosophical character it forms part of a logical structure of the sciences which is set forth in the two preceding volumes, outlined for the convenience of the reader in the Summary, which follows this Preface.

In its apologetical character it comprises, in the first part, those religious problems which have emerged in the various sciences, as first discerned by Bishop Butler, but now more scientifically restated, together with some additional questions which have arisen since his day, such as the Problem of Theism, The Miraculous Evidence, and The Historical Evidence, so far as they are affected by modern speculation and research. In the second part, are comprised those Christian evidences, peculiar to our own age, which are accumulating in the physical sciences, astronomy, geology, and anthropology, and in the psychical sciences, psychology, sociology, and comparative religion, and which, in the philosophical sciences, it may be, are destined to yield a full demonstration of the truths of revealed religion.

It should be stated that this volume, in connection with its new material, contains substantially the "Bishop Paddock Lectures on the Scientific Evidences," which here reappear in their proper and final setting in the scheme of the Ultimate Philosophy.

In pursuing these philosophical studies, on the apologetical side of the work I have come in contact with a modern phase of Biblical study, known as the Higher Criticism, so far as it bears upon the Scientific Evidence. The peculiarity of this criticism is, that, while apparently occupied with the mere literary form of the Holy Scriptures, it has been steadily involving their revealed content and reconstructing their essential purport. It will be found that I have favored the utmost conceivable freedom of scholarship within the legitimate bounds of Biblical Criticism, but without adopting conclusions which are based upon mere hypothesis and assertion; and it will also be found that even to such critical hypotheses I have given a fair hearing, though often seeing in them little more than an antiquarian interest.

## EDITOR'S NOTE.

The author had already put through the press, though in another form, most of what is contained in this volume of the Philosophia Ultima. Accordingly, in the text which follows, the style, verbiage, and diction are entirely those of the author, even his device of capitalization, quotation marks, and punctuation, has been carefully retained as far as possible. Where there were manifest inadvertences, they have, as far as the editor knows, been rectified. The arrangement of the text is altogether that of the author himself. There is but a single passage, that at the close of the chapter on Theism, which has been supplied by the editor, and for this reason it is enclosed in brackets.

# CONTENTS.

## INTRODUCTION.

SUMMARY OF THE PHILOSOPHIA ULTIMA, . . . . PAGE 3–6

## PART I.

### SCIENTIFIC PROBLEMS OF RELIGION.

#### CHAPTER I.

##### THE PROBLEMS AS STATED BY BISHOP BUTLER.

SECTION I. THE PERSONALITY OF BUTLER, . . . . . 11–13
SECTION II. THE EPOCH OF BUTLER, . . . . . . 13–17
SECTION III. LITERARY DEFICIENCIES, . . . . . 17–21
SECTION IV. LOGICAL DEFICIENCIES, . . . . . . 21–25
SECTION V. METAPHYSICAL DEFICIENCIES, . . . . 25–27
SECTION VI. RELIGIOUS DEFICIENCIES, . . . . . 27–31
SECTION VII. THE VALUE OF CHRISTIAN EVIDENCE, . . 31–32
SECTION VIII. THE LOGIC OF CHRISTIAN EVIDENCE, . . 32–39
SECTION IX. THE PROBLEMS OF CHRISTIAN EVIDENCE, . 39–40
SECTION X. THE NEW SCIENTIFIC EVIDENCE, . . . 40–44

#### CHAPTER II.

PROBLEM OF THEISM, . . . . . . . . 45–64

#### CHAPTER III.

##### THE MIRACULOUS EVIDENCE. THE MYTHICAL THEORY OF REVEALED RELIGION.

SECTION I. SUBTLE DANGERS OF THE MYTHICAL THEORY, . 66–67
SECTION II. ORIGIN OF THE MYTHICAL THEORY, . . . 67–69
SECTION III. DEFINITION OF THE MYTH, . . . . . 69–70
SECTION IV. NEGATIVE CHARACTERS OF THE MYTH, . . 70–71
SECTION V. POSITIVE CHARACTERS OF THE MYTH, . . 71–72
SECTION VI. AN EXAMPLE OF A SUPPOSED CHRISTIAN MYTH, 72–74
SECTION VII. MYTHICAL EXPLANATION OF JUDAISM, . . 74–75
SECTION VIII. MYTHICAL EXPLANATION OF CHRISTIANITY, . 75–76
SECTION IX. MYTHICAL EXPLANATION OF BIBLICAL MORALITY, 76–77
SECTION X. THE THEORY SOPHISTICATING, . . . . 77–78
SECTION XI. PAGAN MYTHOLOGIES MERE COUNTERFEITS, . 78–79
SECTION XII. CHRISTIANITY SELF-VINDICATORY, . . . 79–80
SECTION XIII. SUMMARY OF REFUTATION, . . . . . 80–81

## CHAPTER IV.

### THE HISTORICAL EVIDENCE OF REVEALED RELIGION.

|  |  | PAGE |
|---|---|---|
| SECTION I. | THE FOUR GREAT HISTORICAL FACTS, | 82–84 |
| SECTION II. | THE BIBLICAL SCHEME OF HUMAN REDEMPTION, | 84–86 |
| SECTION III. | THE PRE-CHRISTIAN DISPERSION OF NATIONS, | 87 |
| SECTION IV. | THE PRE-CHRISTIAN CIVILIZATIONS, | 87–88 |
| SECTION V. | THE PRE-CHRISTIAN RELIGIONS, | 88–90 |
| SECTION VI. | UNCONSCIOUS PROPHECIES OF PAGANISM, | 90–91 |
| SECTION VII. | THE EPOCH OF THE INCARNATION, | 91 |
| SECTION VIII. | EXTERNAL HISTORY OF CHRISTIANITY, | 92–93 |
| SECTION IX. | HISTORY OF AMERICAN CHRISTIANITY, | 93–94 |
| SECTION X. | THE INTERNAL HISTORY OF CHRISTIANITY, | 94–95 |
| SECTION XI. | THE PROSPECTS OF CHRISTIAN CIVILIZATION, | 95–96 |
| SECTION XII. | THE PREDICTED TRIUMPH OF CHRISTIANITY, | 96 |

---

# PART II.

*SCIENTIFIC EVIDENCES OF RELIGION.*

## CHAPTER I.

### THE LOGICAL NATURE OF THE SCIENTIFIC EVIDENCE.

| SECTION I. | PRESENT SCIENTIFIC CRISIS, | 99–100 |
|---|---|---|
| SECTION II. | DUTY OF UNITED DEFENCE, | 100–101 |
| SECTION III. | THE NEW SCIENTIFIC EVIDENCE, | 101–103 |
| SECTION IV. | ITS LOGICAL PREMISES, | 103–104 |
| SECTION V. | POPULAR FALLACIES, | 104–105 |
| SECTION VI. | THE BIBLE AS PREJUDGED, | 105–106 |
| SECTION VII. | THE BIBLE AS MUTILATED, | 106–107 |
| SECTION VIII. | THE BIBLE AS IGNORED, | 107–108 |
| SECTION IX. | THE TRUE SCOPE OF REVELATION, | 108–109 |
| SECTION X. | ALLEGED SCIENTIFIC ERRORS, | 109 |
| SECTION XI. | A QUESTIONABLE THEORY, | 109–110 |
| SECTION XII. | THE FALLACY PROVES TOO LITTLE, | 110 |
| SECTION XIII. | THE CATHOLIC DOCTRINE, | 111 |
| SECTION XIV. | THE FALLACY MAY PROVE TOO MUCH, | 111–112 |
| SECTION XV. | APPROXIMATE TRUTHS, | 112–113 |
| SECTION XVI. | A DANGEROUS FALLACY, | 113–114 |
| SECTION XVII. | THE KEY-NOTE, | 114 |

## CHAPTER II.

### THE LOGICAL VALUE OF THE SCIENTIFIC EVIDENCE.

| SECTION I. | THE BIBLE MORE THAN MERE LITERATURE, | 116–117 |
|---|---|---|
| SECTION II. | THE BIBLE NO MERE ANCIENT CLASSIC, | 117 |
| SECTION III. | THE BIBLE FREE FROM PAGAN SCIENCE, | 117–118 |
| SECTION IV. | PERSONAL ERRANCY OF INSPIRED WRITERS, | 118 |
| SECTION V. | PERSONAL FREEDOM OF INSPIRED WRITERS, | 118–119 |

|  |  | PAGE |
|---|---|---|
| Section VI. | Divine Unity of the Scriptures, | 119–120 |
| Section VII. | Logical Pre-Requisites of Biblical Study, | 120–121 |
| Section VIII. | Misapplied Classical Criticism, | 121–122 |
| Section IX. | Abuse of the Higher Criticism, | 122–123 |
| Section X. | Scientific Pre-Requisites, | 123–124 |
| Section XI. | Unscientific Higher Criticism, | 124–125 |
| Section XII. | Spiritual Pre-Requisites, | 125–126 |
| Section XIII. | Rationalistic Criticism, | 126–127 |
| Section XIV. | Conservative Higher Criticism, | 127–128 |
| Section XV. | Higher Qualities of the Scientific Evidence, | 128–130 |
| Section XVI. | The Evidence of Scientific Authorities, | 130 |
| Section XVII. | The Evidence of Scientific Facts, | 130–131 |
| Section XVIII. | The Evidence of Scientific Theories, | 131–132 |
| Section XIX. | The Evidence of Scientific Marvels, | 132–133 |
| Section XX. | Valuation of the Scientific Evidence, | 133–134 |
| Section XXI. | Timeliness of the Scientific Evidence, | 134–135 |

## CHAPTER III.

### THE ALLEGED SCIENTIFIC ERRORS OF THE BIBLE.

| Section I. | Are There Errors in the Bible? | 136–143 |
|---|---|---|
| Section II. | The Physical Teaching of the Bible, | 143–144 |
| Section III. | No Teaching of Scripture Erroneous, | 144–145 |
| Section IV. | The Physical Teaching Implicated with the Spiritual, | 145–146 |
| Section V. | The Physical and Spiritual Teaching alike Non-Scientific, | 146–147 |
| Section VI. | The Physical and Spiritual Teaching alike Sincere, | 148–149 |
| Section VII. | Both alike Permanent, | 149–151 |
| Section VIII. | Both alike Suitable, | 151–152 |
| Section IX. | The Physical Teaching also Important, | 152–153 |
| Section X. | Evidential Importance of the Physical Teaching, | 153–154 |
| Section XI. | Metaphysical Importance of the Physical Teaching, | 154–155 |
| Section XII. | Philosophical Importance of the Physical Teaching, | 155–157 |

## CHAPTER IV.

### THE EVIDENCE FROM ASTRONOMY.

| Section I. | Growth of the Astronomical Evidence, | 158–159 |
|---|---|---|
| Section II. | Testimony of Astronomers, | 160 |
| Section III. | Devout Astronomers, | 160–161 |
| Section IV. | Revealed Truths in Astronomy, | 161–162 |
| Section V. | Critical Questions, | 162–163 |
| Section VI. | Evidential Literature, | 163–164 |
| Section VII. | Astronomical Hypotheses, | 164–165 |

|   |   | PAGE |
|---|---|---|
| Section VIII. | A Primitive Cosmos, | 165 |
| Section IX. | A Primitive Chaos, | 166 |
| Section X. | The Doctrine of Creation, | 166-167 |
| Section XI. | Our Planet Alone Inhabited, | 167-168 |
| Section XII. | Other Planets also Habitable, | 168 |
| Section XIII. | The Doctrine of Angels, | 169 |
| Section XIV. | A Final Chaos, | 170 |
| Section XV. | A Permanent Cosmos, | 170-171 |
| Section XVI. | The Doctrine of Old and New Heavens, | 171-172 |
| Section XVII. | The Stupendous Problems of Astronomy, | 172 |
| Section XVIII. | Astronomical Marvels, | 172-173 |
| Section XIX. | Astronomical Miracles, | 173-174 |
| Section XX. | Astronomical Difficulties of Faith, | 174-175 |
| Section XXI. | Illustration of Divine Omniscience, | 175-176 |
| Section XXII. | Physical Insignificance of Our Planet, | 177 |
| Section XXIII. | Moral Importance of Man, | 177-178 |

## CHAPTER V.

### THE EVIDENCE FROM GEOLOGY.

| Section I. | Growth of Geological Evidence, | 179-180 |
|---|---|---|
| Section II. | Testimony of Geologists, | 180-181 |
| Section III. | Geological Facts and Revealed Truths, | 181-182 |
| Section IV. | Evidential Literature, | 182-184 |
| Section V. | Geological Hypotheses, | 184-185 |
| Section VI. | The Primitive Earth a Finished World, | 185 |
| Section VII. | The Primitive Earth Chaotic, | 185-186 |
| Section VIII. | The Doctrine of Creation, | 186-187 |
| Section IX. | The Catastrophists, | 187 |
| Section X. | The Uniformitarians, | 187-188 |
| Section XI. | The Six Creative Days, | 188-189 |
| Section XII. | The Creative Days as Cosmogonic Eras, | 189-190 |
| Section XIII. | The Creative Days as Logical Stages, | 190-191 |
| Section XIV. | Critical Questions, | 191-192 |
| Section XV. | Dissolution of the Earth, | 192 |
| Section XVI. | Stability of the Earth, | 192-193 |
| Section XVII. | Doctrine of the Old and New Earth, | 193-194 |
| Section XVIII. | Geological Marvels and Miracles, | 194-195 |
| Section XIX. | Value of the Geological Evidence, | 195-196 |
| Section XX. | Geological Difficulties of Faith, | 196-199 |

## CHAPTER VI.

### THE EVIDENCE FROM ANTHROPOLOGY.

| Section I. | Growth of the Anthropological Evidence, | 200-201 |
|---|---|---|
| Section II. | The Testimony of Anthropologists, | 201-202 |
| Section III. | Anthropological Facts and Truths, | 202-203 |
| Section IV. | Evidential Literature, | 203-204 |
| Section V. | The Constancy of Species, | 204-206 |

|  |  |  | PAGE |
|---|---|---|---|
| SECTION VI. | THE EVOLUTION OF SPECIES, | . . . . | 206–207 |
| SECTION VII. | THE DOCTRINE OF THE FIRST ADAM, | . . | 207–208 |
| SECTION VIII. | UNITY OF THE RACE, | . . . . | 209–211 |
| SECTION IX. | DOCTRINE OF THE FALL OF ADAM, | . . | 211–212 |
| SECTION X. | PHYSICAL UNITY OF MANKIND, | . . | 212–213 |
| SECTION XI. | THE DIVINE IMAGE IN MAN, | . . . | 213–214 |
| SECTION XII. | CRITICAL PROBLEMS, | . . . . | 214 |
| SECTION XIII. | PHYSICAL DECLINE OF MANKIND, | . . | 215 |
| SECTION XIV. | PHYSICAL IMPROVEMENT OF MANKIND, | . . | 215–216 |
| SECTION XV. | THE FIRST AND SECOND ADAM, | . . | 216–217 |
| SECTION XVI. | ANTHROPOLOGY AND ANGELOLOGY, | . | 217–218 |
| SECTION XVII. | MIRACLES OF ANTHROPOLOGY, | . . | 218–219 |
| SECTION XVIII. | DIFFICULTIES OF EVOLUTIONISM, | . . | 219–220 |
| SECTION XIX. | THE PROBLEM OF PHYSICAL EVIL, | . . . | 220–221 |
| SECTION XX. | ÆSTHETIC IMPRESSIONS OF NATURE UPON MAN, | . | 221 |
| SECTION XXI. | THE SCENE OF HUMAN LIFE, | . . . | 221–222 |
| SECTION XXII. | THE COURSE OF HUMAN LIFE, | . . . | 222–223 |
| SECTION XXIII. | THE STORY OF HUMAN LIFE, | . . . | 223 |

# SUMMARY

### OF THE

## PRINCIPLES OF THE ULTIMATE PHILOSOPHY.

# SUMMARY OF THE PRINCIPLES OF THE ULTIMATE PHILOSOPHY.

The following statements may serve to outline the philosophical scheme which has been set forth in the two preceding volumes, and also to indicate their claims to be considered as original contributions to the study of philosophy.

### I.

Philosophy has been defined as a Science of the Sciences in distinction from Epistemology (or the science of knowledge), which is but a psychological division of philosophy; in distinction from Ontology (or the science of being), which is only the metaphysical half of philosophy; and in distinction from mere speculative philosophy, which does not always include the empirical sciences or the industrial, æsthetical, and ethical arts issuing from these sciences. Since this definition was made in 1861, Professor Flint in 1881 has attempted a similar definition which is less comprehensive and wanting in some essential details.

### II.

The method of such philosophy has been pursued as an objective study of the historical and logical development of the sciences, instead of a mere subjective study of the cognitive powers of the mind, or a purely *a priori* attempt to construct the existing body of knowledge. This objective and historical method was partially pursued by Comte and Whewell in their so-called "Philosophy of Sciences," but not to its full and legitimate results, as they are presented in Vol. II.

### III.

In arranging the sciences as objects of philosophical study, theology has been placed at the summit of the ascending series of sciences as an empirical science of comparative religion in distinction from the metaphysical theology of the Schools. Thus placed, it appears as the flower and crown of the Sciences, of astronomy, geology, biology, psychology, sociology, as based respectively upon the corresponding service of mechanical, chemical, organical, mental and social phenomena. The want of such a place for Empirical Theology in the classifications of Comte and Spencer was first discussed and supplied by the author in a memoir on "The Order of the Sciences," read before the Philosophical Society of Washington, and incorporated in Vol. II., Chap. I.

### IV.

In projecting a philosophical scheme of the sciences their metaphysical sections have been placed in logical corelation with empirical sections throughout the series from astronomy to anthropology and from psychology to theology. While Comte and Spencer have ignored the whole metaphysical region, the German classifiers, from Kant to Wundt, have recognized it, but without mapping it as systematically as has been attempted in Vol. II.

### V.

Into the metaphysical region has been admitted the problem of revelation as consequent upon the problem of knowing and the problem of being; and in solution of these problems a theopneustic (divine inspiration) theory of revelation has been based upon a realistic theory of knowledge and a theistic theory of being. Avoiding at once the gnostic theories of Schelling and Swedenborg and the agnostic theories of Spencer and Huxley, a theory of perfectible science, perfectible through the combined action of reason and revelation, has been advocated in the second part of Vol. I. and in Chap. III. of Vol. II.

### VI.

In collecting materials for such a Theory of Perfectible Science, thus based upon the harmonious action of human reason and divine revelation, their past and present relations have been historically reviewed and their existing products have been critically surveyed. As complemental to the Histories of Draper and Andrew White, the alliances as well as the "conflict" and the peace as well as the "warfare" of Science and Religion have been sketched in Part First of Vol. I.; and in Part First of Vol. II. both religious dogmas and scientific hypotheses have been together exhibited as more or less logically co-existent throughout the whole series of sciences.

### VII.

As the full result, a Science of the Sciences has been projected in accordance with the true conditions of such a science as stated in Vol. II., pp. 109-122:—(1) That it should embrace all the sciences, physical and psychical; (2) that it should include all their contents, empirical and metaphysical; (3) that it should employ both factors of knowledge, reason and revelation; and (4) that its aim and goal should be the perfectibility of science with the demonstrability of religion. The supreme law of scientific development has been announced as the converse of the law of Comte. Although the series of sciences, one after another as Comte maintained, may in their earliest stages be first theological, then metaphysical, at length positive, yet after becoming positive, thenceforward, in their mature stages, they become again more truly metaphysical and at last fully theological. Compare Vol. I., Part II., Chap. II., with Vol. II., p. 101, and pp. 321-324.

### VIII.

The second division of the Ultimate Philosophy described as the art of attaining knowledge or the constructive Logic of the Sciences, has been outlined on the basis of the foregoing principles in three parts: 1st, the Empirical Logic has been referred to such masters as Comte, Whewell, and Mill; 2nd, the Metaphysical Logic, to such masters as Wolff, Berkeley, and Butler; and 3rd, the strictly Philosophical Logic, embracing both the empirical and metaphysical regions, has been treated as including rules applicable (1) to the normal relations of reason and revelation in the sciences, (2) to the provisional relations of hypothesis and dogma in the sciences, (3) to the prospective relations of theory and doctrine in the sciences. This part of the work is designed to establish the claim of the Ultimate Philosophy to be considered as a system of perfectible knowledge, based upon the growing harmony of science and religion.

## IX.

In the course of these studies some practical principles have been enunciated; first, the philosophical value of apologetics in upholding divine revelation as a source of metaphysical knowledge within each science and throughout the scale of the sciences, a principle not yet fully recognized by some of the most Christian philosophers of our day; second, The umpirage of Philosophy between religious dogmas and scientific hypotheses, a principle at first questioned but since accepted by intelligent divines as well as devout scientists; third, The right of comparative theology, or the empirical science of religions to a place in the University curriculum as distinguished from the place of orthodox theology in a Seminary or a school of divinity. All these three principles were brought under discussion by the founding of a chair of The Harmony of Science and Revealed Religion in Princeton University, the first Professorship of the kind attempted in any American institution of learning.

# PART FIRST.

## SCIENTIFIC PROBLEMS OF RELIGION.

# CHAPTER I.

*SCIENTIFIC PROBLEMS OF RELIGION. FIRST STATED BY BISHOP BUTLER IN HIS GREAT WORK, "THE ANALOGY OF RELIGION AND NATURE."*

The "Analogy" of Bishop Butler was given to the world in the year 1736. In the same year of grace was born the orator, statesman, and first governor of Virginia, Patrick Henry, who in mature life made the Analogy his serious study, published an edition of it, and bequeathed it to his countrymen as a cure for the scepticism which had been coming in with the French Alliance during the Revolution. It is probable that this was the first American issue of the work. A hundred years have passed, and another great churchman and statesman, an English kinsman of Henry, Mr. Gladstone, has also published the Analogy, and stood forth as its champion among the leading thinkers of the age. The fresh interest thus aroused in Butler's writings would seem to make this juncture a fitting time in which to renew our estimate of his contribution to the Evidences of Christianity.

Bishop Butler has strong claims upon American churchmen of all classes. In advance of modern schools of churchmanship, he illustrated much that was best in each of them. First of all, he was an evangelical churchman. Bred a Presbyterian non-conformist, he never lost that type of doctrinal belief which is common to the Confession of Faith and the Articles of Religion and expressed in portions of the Daily and Communion offices. It underlies and pervades his whole argument, especially in the chapters on the "Opinion of Necessity" and the "Appointment of a Mediator." An evangelical, yet he was also a Catholic churchman. A century before the appearance of the Oxford tracts and the Christian Year, he enunciated some of the leading principles of those epoch-making works. On both rational and historic grounds he argued that the visible Church was essential to the perpetuation of true Christianity. In his episcopal charge on the Importance of External Religion he urged the more frequent use of the daily offices and the sacraments as means of piety. By devoutly studying the lives of the saints and other books of mystical devotion, by decorating his chapel with stained glass windows imported from Italy, popularly supposed to have been presented by the Pope, and especially by erecting a white marble cross over the communion table, he incurred the most bitter persecution as a suspected revert to Romanism. A Catholic among Evangelicals and an Evangelical among Catholics, he was still a liberal churchman. While bowing to the authority of Scripture, he declared he would not vilify reason, which is our only faculty for judging of anything, even revelation itself. When invited to the throne of the Primacy of all England, so disheartened was he by the ecclesiastical abuses about him, he said it was too late for him to "try to support a falling church," and looked hopefully away to another scene where it might flourish without the fetters of an establishment and the scandal of dissent. In his plan for strengthening and extending the church of England in the American Colonies he broached some of the very principles which have been reaped as the fruits of our political Revolution, such as the equality of denominations, the rights of the laity, the independence of the Church, the extension of the episcopate. If Berkeley could foresee in poetic fancy the "westward course of empire," it was Butler who had that glowing vision of ecclesiastical advancement which is now passing before our eyes. More than any other English prelate, if I mistake not, he may be revered as the prophet and progenitor of the Protestant Episcopal Church in the United States.*

But it is not of Butler as a churchman that I am here to speak. Nor is this his only distinction. It is as a defender

---

* Life of Butler prefaced to the Analogy by Bishop Fitzgerald, pp. 59-61.

of the faith, as the greatest of Christian apologetes, that he has received the homage of English Christendom. All churches and denominations are represented in the tribute. Bishop Fitzgerald, of the Church of England, the most accomplished editor of his work, has characterized it as "so original in its design, so perfect in its method, so profound and yet so practical in its reasoning, so earnest and yet so calm in its tone, so combining decision without dogmatism and caution without timidity, as to be justly deemed the masterpiece of British theology." Dr. Chalmers, of the Church of Scotland, could acknowledge himself more indebted to the Analogy than to anything else in the whole range of our extant authorship. President Wayland, of the Baptists, has made a similar acknowledgment with reference to his own ethical writings. President Emory, of the Methodists, has compared the position of Butler in divinity to that of Bacon in philosophy. Among lay scholars, Sir James Mackintosh pronounced it "the most original and profound work extant in any language, upon the philosophy of religion." Lord Brougham declared it to be "the most argumentative and philosophical defence of Christianity ever offered to the world." And the Duke of Argyll has termed it "an argument the greatest in the whole range of Christian philosophy, in its ramifications as infinite as the appearance of variety, and as pervading as the sense of oneness, in the universe of God." It may be doubted if any modern writer has been so generally accepted as an exponent of English thinking upon religious questions, or has exerted such an influence, directly and indirectly, in moulding its tendencies and products.

### The Personality of Butler.

In order fully to appreciate Butler as a philosophical apologete, we need to begin by recalling briefly his personality, the man himself. At first sight this might appear unimportant. The principle that the character of a writer will be reflected in his writings does not seem to apply. If ever an author succeeded in hiding himself behind his subject, and leaving us occupied with the bare logical process of thought itself, it was the author of the Analogy. In the dry light of his intelligence there is not a tinge of idiosyncrasy or egotism. The first personal pronoun, when used, brings with it nothing whatever of the disturbing influence of the personal equation. Had some Raphael alighted upon our orb, as in Milton's Paradise, his high discourse would scarcely have seemed more free from the passions and infirmities of mortals. This superficial judgment, however, disappears on connecting Butler's work with his life and his character. We can see that the young student in the Presbyterian Academy at Tewkesbury, while exchanging letters with Dr. Samuel Clarke on his "Demonstration of the Being and Attributes of God," is already in training as an apologete. When at Oxford, he was not only gaining all needed learning for his future task, but was entering the way of needed preferment, through his influential friendships with Talbot, who procured for him from his uncle, the Lord Chancellor, the post of preacher at the Rolls in London; and with Secker, afterward Bishop and Archbishop, who befriended him throughout life, and defended his memory after death. In his "Sermons," which he preached before the legal audience of the Rolls Chapel, he was enunciating those principles of ethics which were to be made the foundation of his whole apologetic. Afterward, as rector of Stanhope, in the seclusion of a rural parish, with patient toil he slowly built up, like a coral reef, that argument which contains the closely packed results of twenty years' hard thinking on the problems of philosophy and religion. Meanwhile, the world had forgotten him, and when Queen Caroline asked if Butler was dead, a shrewd courtier replied, "Not dead, but buried." He was at once drawn forth from that retirement. As Clerk of the Closet to the Queen, as Dean of St. Paul's, as Bishop of Bristol, and at length as promoted to the princely See of Durham, he acquired that celebrity and influence without which his great work might have dropped back again into obscurity and oblivion.

During all this somewhat ordinary career of student, preacher, thinker, divine, and bishop, his character was unfolding those sterling traits which, in spite of his studied self-effacement, may be discerned on every page; that ardent love of truth, the research for which he said he had designed to be the chief business of his life; that candor with which he stated the whole truth as he knew and believed it, without over-statement or under-statement; that courage with which he faced the most adverse facts and arguments and accepted the most perilous inferences; that strict adherence to his own high ideals of right and reason from which he never swerved; as well as that supreme desire for the glory of God and the good of mankind which is everywhere felt without being expressed. A glance is enough to show us that such a work could only have been written by such a man.

### The Epoch of Butler.

There is also a preliminary need to estimate Butler in the light of his epoch, of the age in which he lived. A hasty reader of his book would think otherwise. For anything that appears on the surface it might have been written indifferently in the fifteenth century or in the nineteenth century. It contains no allusion to current events and discussions. With the exception of two marginal references to Locke and to Shaftesbury, not a single English author is named. The argument proceeds as abstractly as the Differential Calculus, and every objection is examined as imperturbably as if it were a meteorolite that had fallen from some remote region of space. And yet, no writer was ever in so close vital contact with his whole literary environment, and no work more alive with the spirit of the age in which it was produced. To see this we have but to place him in his true historic setting.

Look first at the religious crisis which had been reached in Butler's day. It was but fifty years since the restoration of the monarchy and the act of uniformity. The profligate Charles had been succeeded by the jesuitical James and then by the Calvinistic William of Orange. Presbytery had been re-established in Scotland alongside of prelacy in England. Puritanism had fled to the wilds of America. That Presbyterianism which had once been the pride of the Universities, a power in the London pulpit, and a stately figure in the manor-houses of Yorkshire, was now languishing into Unitarianism under the ban of dissent. The establishment, drained of spiritual life, was thronged with place-hunters and time-servers. The superficial type of Christianity which remained was correct and comfortable. A genteel Deism, which accepted so much of religion as it had in common with natural religion, was leavening the clergy as well as the aristocracy. The old faith, like an old fashion-plate, had become pompous, pedantic, and grotesque. Ridicule was made the test of truth, and the day for serious argument seemed to have gone by. It was then that Butler, somewhat like an unbidden spectre at a revel, opened his treatise in these words: "It is come, I know not how, to be taken for granted by many persons, that Christianity is not so much as a subject of inquiry; but that it is, now at length, discovered to be fictitious. And accordingly they treat it, as if, in the present age, this were an agreed point among all people of discernment; and nothing remains but to set it up as a principal subject of mirth and ridicule, as it were, by way of reprisals for having so long interrupted the pleasures of the world."

Look also at some of the principal writers who preceded and surrounded him on either side at this crisis. On the side of Deism were marshalled the opponents of revealed religion. Nearly a century before, Herbert of Cherbury, the father of English Deism, in his treatise on "Truth as distinguished from Revelation," had maintained natural religion, the Religion of the Laity and of the Gentiles, to be the one sufficient and absolute religion. Charles Blount, in his "Life of Apollonius," a wonder-worker of Tyana, had exalted Pagan feasts of magic into comparison with the Christian miracles. Woolston had delineated his so-called "Religion of Nature" as found in the writings of Greek philosophers and Roman moralists rather than in the teachings of prophets and apostles. And then came a direct assault upon revealed religion. Toland, in his "Christianity not Mysterious," argued that revealed truths are neither against reason nor above reason, but must be freed from everything contradictory and unintelligible. Tindal, in his "Christianity as Old as the Creation," held that the natural religion of mankind neither admitted nor required an external revelation, and that the pretended Jewish and Christian revelations are defective in their external evidences and in their internal teachings. Collins, the first of the self-styled free-thinkers, attacked the prophetical evidence; and Morgan, as a moral philosopher, attacked the internal evidence. At length the assault grew desperate and undisguised. The polished Shaftesbury was sneering at the humbling doctrines and lowly graces of the Christian disciple. The truculent Bolingbroke was scoffing at the failings of Old Testament saints and the ethics of the New Testament. The half-crazed Woolston was flinging profane jests at Christian miracles and mysteries. And the vulgar Chubb, over his candle-moulds, was railing at the Apostles as liars and the Gospel as a forgery.

On the side of Christianity, meanwhile, were arrayed the opponents of mere natural religion. During the early stage of the contest, Ralph Cudworth, in his " Intellectual System of the Universe," had collected with prodigious learning the evidences of revealed religion in all Pagan literature and philosophy. Theophilus Gale, in his " Court of the Gentiles," had traced back all Greek and Roman religion to a primitive revelation as mere borrowed light from that sacred fire. Henry More had dreamed of a Platonic Trinity born of the marriage of Greek Metaphysics with the divinity of St. John. But soon there was need of a vigorous defence. Leslie, in order to meet Herbert and Blount, produced his famous " Short and Easy Method with the Deist," in which he exhibited Christianity as the one true religion, and Judaism, Paganism, and Mohammedanism, all mere natural religions, as counterfeits and impostures. Toland was answered by the philosopher Locke and by Archbishop Browne. Conybeare, as the antagonist of Tindal, maintained, in his " Defence of Revealed Religion," the insufficiency of natural religion, the necessity of a revelation, and the validity of its evidences. While Chandler was defending the prophetic evidence against Collins, and Chapman was defending the internal evidence against Morgan, Leland, in his " View of the Deistical Writers," was massing together all the Christian evidences as a rampart of the faith. At last, there was a furious sally and onset upon the assailants. The pugnacious Warburton, more than a match for Bolingbroke in savage invective, charged into the very camp of the Deists with that *argumentum ad hominem*, his " Divine Legation of Moses," and routed them on their own ground. The erudite

Bentley, having caught Collins tripping in his scholarship, demolished him with blows of ponderous learning. And the lawyer-like Sherlock, with more ingenuity than reverence, in his " Trial of the Witnesses," cited the Apostles to an imaginary session of the Inn-Court, as if to convict Woolston and Chubb of libel and perjury.

It was at the close of this heated debate that Butler appeared, not as another advocate, but as the presiding judge, after the combatants had reached the extremes of controversy. Noticing them without naming them, avoiding alike the personality of praise or invective, now accepting the premises of a deist, then rejecting the reasonings of an apologist, carefully weighing every argument, he at length summed up the whole discussion in a tone so judicial that it has been mistaken for indifference or weakness. "Those who believe," he said, "will here find the scheme of Christianity cleared of objections and the evidence of it in a peculiar manner strengthened: those who do not believe will at least be shown the absurdity of all attempts to prove Christianity false, the plain undoubted credibility of it; and, I hope, a good deal more."

Such was the man and such the age which produced the "Analogy of Religion, Natural and Revealed, to the Constitution and Course of Nature." It is the mission of some books to project the issues of the future and not merely to resume those of the past. Had Butler's work been of the latter sort, it might to-day be as dusty and worm-eaten as some of the forgotten volumes which have just been mentioned. But, unlike them, it was not only free from everything personal, local, and transient, but contained truth for all time as well as for its own time. Instead of remaining as a piece of obsolete controversy, interesting only to a former generation, it has passed into the intellectual life of succeeding generations with ever-widening influence. It is true that Mr. Matthew Arnold, in his " Bishop Butler and the Zeitgeist," has argued that it is quite behind the philosophic spirit of the age; but there could be no more striking proof of its essential vitality than some recent efforts to destroy it. After the lapse of a hundred and fifty years it has been exciting fresh discussion and demanding readjustment to the highest and best thinking of our epoch.

A history of this criticism would be interesting and instructive. I can only notice some of the deficiencies which have been alleged against Butler; and then, some of his permanent contributions to apologetic science. I speak of deficiencies rather than of defects. The former are mere neglects or omissions which do not impair the quality and effect of a work: the latter are blemishes or fallacies which inhere in the reasoning and mar and vitiate it. It will be found, I think, that Butler has some deficiencies, but only a few defects.

### *Literary Deficiencies.*

The literary deficiencies which have been alleged are the first to strike the reader. His style has been much criticised. Bolingbroke had his fling at its obscurity. "She studies," he said of Queen Caroline, "with much application the Analogy of Revealed Religion to the Constitution and Course of Nature. She understands the whole argument perfectly, and concludes with the Right Reverend Author that it is not so clear a case that there is nothing in Revealed Religion. Such royal, such lucrative encouragement, must needs keep both metaphysics and the sublimest theology in credit." To all which John Wesley incisively replied, that the Analogy was too deep for the men against whom it was written.

Obscurity, however, may be due to defects of language rather than to profundity of thought, as ripples can hide the bottom of the clearest lake. It is not easy to defend Butler's style from such superficial blemishes. His English is now somewhat archaic; his diction is at times too idiomatic and harsh, and his sentences are often long, involved, confused, and perplexing. One finds that he must turn back and read them again in order to take in the full meaning. The constant effort to understand him at length becomes tiresome. Butler himself seems to have been made aware of the difficulty of his style and defends it from the charge of obscurity: "I must take leave to add, that those alone are judges whether or no and how far this is a fault, who are judges whether or no and how far it might have been avoided—those only who will be at the trouble to understand what is here said and to see how far the things here insisted upon and not other things might have been put in a plainer manner."

And it must be granted that he bears well the test to which he appeals. Let anyone try to put Butler's ideas into clearer words and he will find it no easy task. In this respect he is the despair of his editors and commentators. It should be remembered that his works were carefully revised by his friend Archbishop Secker, and it may be added that his letters, unlike his more elaborate writings, are charming in their simplicity and ingenuousness.

Writers, who admit that he is obscure, have explained the defect in various ways. Mr. Mark Pattison thinks it due to the multiplicity of details which he wrought into the complex structure of his reasoning in his effort after logical precision. Mr. Leslie Stephen would explain this paradox by referring it to the density with which he packed his ideas, as a lonely thinker using phrases and arguments unfamiliar to the ordinary reader. The best defence has been suggested by one of his most studious editors: "There is a rough likeness," says Dr. Steere, "between the style of the Analogy and that of a legal document, and it goes deeper than might have been expected; for what makes a deed obscure to the uninitiated? Chiefly the attempt on the part of the framer to exclude all ambiguity. It looks like irony, but it is true that no written thing, when examined, is clearer than a legal document, and the object, the attained object, of all those obscure phrases is to avoid the possibility of being misunderstood. . . . Thus it is that careful students of Butler's works generally come, in the end, to have a sort of relish for his peculiar style."

When we have maintained that Butler writes "good sinewy Saxon," with vigor, simplicity, accuracy, propriety, and dignity, we must still admit, I think, that there is some remaining obscurity in his style which is not in his thought or in his theme. "It is an instance," says Mackintosh, "of the importance of style. No thinker so great was ever so poor a writer. Indeed the ingenious apologies which have been lately attempted for the defect amount to no more than that his power of thought was too much for his skill in language. How general must the reception have been of truths so certain and momentous; with how much more clearness must they have appeared to his own great understanding, if he had possessed the distinctness with which Hobbes enforces odious falsehood on the charm of that transparent diction which clothed the unfruitful paradoxes of Berkeley."

Butler has also been charged with a lack of imagination in the treatment of his theme. He lends some color to the charge by characterizing the imagination as "that forward delusive faculty, ever obtruding beyond its sphere and the author of all error;" and once he dismisses a false analogy between the decay of vegetables and living creatures, with the remark that it is "sufficient to afford the poets very apt allusions to the flowers of the field." There is in fact not a single poetical quotation in his whole treatise, and only now and then a metaphor. He has none of the negligent beauties of a writer to whom ornament comes unsought as the fruit of reading and culture. His constructive skill is that of the mere intellect rather than that of the free imagination.

This absence of the play of fancy will be regarded as a defect according to the point of view. One who would like to have his Euclid done into verse, or the Thirty-nine Articles interspersed with bon-mots and epigrams, might wish that the Analogy had more rhetorical embellishment. If Butler's taste was different, it was not because he was wanting in a sense of the beautiful. In his Sermons he defines and vindicates the ideas of order, beauty, and harmony as consistent with virtue and religion and a reflection of the Divine character itself. And in one of his chapters he likens the conviction produced by the collected evidences of Christianity to "what they call the effect in architecture or other works of art." It is the only glimpse that he gives us of an extravagant fondness for elegance in building and decoration which led him to expend large portions of his princely income upon the see-houses of Bristol and Durham, somewhat to the scandal of his contemporaries. His devotion to this most imaginative of the arts would indicate no lack of the imaginative faculty. That reredos in his chapel hints of an æsthetic ritualist, who did not dislike such symbolism as may be expressive of evangelical doctrine. Mr. Bagehot, in his "Literary Studies," forgetting or not knowing of these artistic tastes of the ascetic bishop, comments severely upon the prosaic atmosphere of the Analogy: "If the world were a Durham mine or an exact square, no part of it more expressive than a gravel-pit or a chalk-quarry, the teaching of Butler would be as true as it is now." Turn away from this picture to a stately chamber wainscoted with cedar and brilliant with storied windows, where the patriarchal prelate is seated, his white hair flowing to his shoulders and a divine placidity animating his countenance, while Mr. Eems, the precentor of St. Paul's, is playing for him upon the organ. Is this a Durham coal-pit or chalk-quarry or even an exact square?

There have been some hints of a want of originality in Butler, which have only a plausible color. Mr. Gladstone has been at pains to collect them. Hallam, it seems, has detected certain portions of Bishop Cumberland's treatise on the "Laws of Nature," though greatly modified, in the chapters on the Natural and Moral Government of God. Fitzgerald finds in Foster's "Reply to Tindal" a remarkable anticipation of the chapter on the Want of Universality in Revelation; and he also quotes and explains a striking sentence from Berkeley's "Minute Philosopher" which suggests the very phraseology of Butler: "It will be sufficient if such Analogy appears between the dispensations of grace and nature (although much should be unaccountable in both) to suppose them derived from the same author, and the workmanship of one and the same hand." A Dublin professor of divinity, Dr. Bernard, had printed a paper on "The Predecessors of Butler," among whom he names Wilkins, Colliber, and Shaftesbury as writers to whom he is specially indebted. Agreeing with such critics, Mr. Mark Pattison goes so far as to declare that the merit of the Analogy lies in its lack of originality, as a mere rearrangement and summary of all the actual and possible opinions which came within the scope of the argument. There is no need to defend Butler from such charges. Anyone who will take the trouble can find scattered through his pages in abundance the ideas and phrases of preceding and contemporary writers. Butler himself says, in one of his prefaces, "A subject may be treated in a manner which all along supposes the reader acquainted with what has been said upon it both by ancient and modern writers and with what is the present state of opinion in the world concerning such subject." Like many another great author he reproduced the results of his reading unconsciously without a thought of plagiarism. Had he endeavored to connect them with marginal references and citations, his page would have been encumbered with more notes than text. He did not choose thus to leave his masterpiece standing among the chips of the workshop.

Of all the literary deficiencies alleged, it may now be said that at their worst they are superficial and unimportant. The truth is, that Butler had no literary ambition. Though tempted by the grandest of themes, he simply wrote to be understood. Though gifted with an architectonic genius, he preferred the severe Doric to the ornate Corinthian in the construction of his argument. Though the most original of thinkers, he did not disdain the thoughts of the humblest writers.

### Logical Deficiencies.

The logical deficiencies alleged against Butler, like the literary deficiencies, pertain to the form rather than the substance or purport of the Analogy. As a piece of reasoning it has often been admired. Someone likens every sentence of it to a well-considered move in chess. Apart from its high religious purpose or rather in connection with that purpose, it has long served as a mental gymnastic for the training of Christian thinkers in the English universities and American colleges, ranking in educational value with the higher logic and mathematics. Mr. Mark Pattison, though he inconsistently removed it from its place among the Oxford studies, commends " the solid structure of logical argument, in which it surpasses any other book in the English language." Nevertheless, some objections have been brought against it, which are primarily logical in their nature.

It has been accused of a fallacious use of the *ad hominem* argument. Dr. Martineau speaks quite bitterly of its irritating effect upon the believers in natural religion, and declares that it hurts and browbeats all who take any ground between theism and orthodox Christianity. It should be remembered, however, that in reasoning from the premises of the deist, Butler could have intended nothing personal to them as individuals or as a class, since he agreed with them as far as they went, and their system of natural religion was almost as generally accepted in that day as the Copernican system of astronomy in our day. In like manner, he argued upon the premises of the Necessitarian or Fatalist only in order to convince him that his premises were untenable, and to bring him, as well as the Libertarian, under the obligations of religion. So also he reasoned upon the theories of prudence and benevolence, because they might contain moral elements not inconsistent with his own theory of essential virtue. Always, indeed, his manifest aim was not so much to succeed in an argument as to arrive at the whole truth.

Butler has also been charged with the fallacy of the argument *ad ignorantiam*. It may be granted that Mr. Stephen finds an instance of it, perhaps the only instance of a flaw in Butler's reasoning, where he argues from our ignorance of the whole system of things, that animals, like infants, may survive death as undeveloped moral agents and find some unknown place and purpose in the future economy. With less pertinence Mr. Matthew Arnold complains of his frequent appeals to our ignorance as based upon assumed knowledge of an unknowable Deity; whereas he bases such appeals upon the facts of our situation, upon the incompetency of reason and the incomprehensibility of the universe. He shows that the Christian scheme, like the scheme of nature, in its immensity and complexity, transcends our utmost capacity of thought, and almost loses his patience with a caviller who fancies that he knows enough of it to criticise it. "Let reason be kept to," he exclaims, "and if any part of the Scripture account of the redemption of the world by Christ, can be shown to be really contrary to it, let the Scripture, in the name of God, be given up. But let not such poor creatures as we, go on objecting against an infinite scheme that we do not see the necessity or usefulness of all its parts, and call this reasoning."

He has been charged with fallacies of analogy. His daring

comparison of the loss of souls to the waste of seeds in Nature becomes as revolting as Mr. Goldwin Smith has depicted it, if pushed beyond the exact point of the comparison—which is that souls, like seeds, were designed, not for destruction, but for perfection. The terrible impression of the ruin of so many moral agents may be lessened when the circumstances in which the analogy fails are brought into view, viz.: that souls, unlike seeds, are free moral agents which may be saved from destruction; that souls, unlike seeds, will be saved according to their own action and opportunity; and that souls, unlike seeds, cannot be lost in the dreadful ratio of millions to one, if the immense majority of mankind, the heathen and infants, be included with believers in the number of the saved.

The fallacy of the *petitio principii* has also been charged against Butler. Mr. Arnold seems to accuse him of begging the question by assuming what he is trying to prove—the existence of a future life of which we have had no experience. It would be enough to reply, that he offers his analogical argument as supplemental to the "proper" or "natural and moral proofs of immortality." Strictly speaking, however, we can have no experience of anything future; no more of our future life in this world than of our future life in another world. But we can reason from our present experience to the probability of either, with greater or less degree of evidence. From our experience of a former state of life in the womb and in our infancy we can anticipate the state of mature age, and after death a still higher state of being as unlike the present as manhood is unlike infancy or unlike the embryo before birth. And then, on the basis of this proved immortality, we can argue from our experience of moral rewards and punishments in this world and from the observed tendencies of virtue to prevail over vice, that the divine government, though imperfect here, will be completed hereafter in another world, where existing hinderances will have disappeared. In the same manner Butler has anticipated Mr. Arnold's objection to theism as an implicit assumption wanting in the element of experience. All such objections are reducible to the absurdity of maintaining that we can prove nothing which we have not experienced.

Butler's reliance upon probable evidence as sufficient to determine belief and practice has been much questioned as tending to a *reductio ad absurdum*. Mr. Leslie Stephen accuses him of representing "doubt as a ground of action;" and the ridicule of Matthew Arnold becomes so merry as to become contagious: "If I am going to take a walk out of Edinburgh, and thought of choosing the Portobello road, and a travelling Menagerie is taking the same road, it is certainly possible that a tiger may escape from the Menagerie and devour me if I take that road; but the evidence that he will is certainly, also, much lower than what is commonly called probable. Well, I do not, on that low degree of evidence, avoid the Portobello road and take another." Had the ingenious critic only read the first paragraph of the work before him, the tiger of his logic would have appeared there rampant: "We cannot indeed say a thing is probably true upon one very slight presumption, because, as there may be probabilities on both sides of a question, there may be some against it, and though there be not, yet a slight presumption does not beget that degree of conviction which is implied in saying a thing is probably true."

Butler's critics have also depreciated his general conclusions as meagre and unsatisfactory. They dwell upon a supposed "breakdown" of his argument, its "puny insignificant outcome," and his own judgment of its inconclusive character, and draw pathetic pictures of him at the close of his treatise as seated in mournful dejection or staggering like a blind giant out of Doubting Castle. It is simply astonishing that critics of such intelligence should so mistake faith for doubt, candor for concession, and courage for weakness. If Butler proved anything, he proved all that he meant to prove. From his first page to his last page he is ever insisting that a demonstrative proof of Christianity is in the nature of the subject unattainable; that imperfect beings must be guided by probability; that satisfactory evidence is not possible to such a creature as man; and that the evidence of religion is the same in kind and degree as that upon which we proceed in other investigations and in all the affairs of life. "What men require," he says, with something like scorn, "is to have all difficulties cleared, which is the same as requiring to comprehend the divine nature, and the whole plan of Providence from everlasting to everlasting."

Yes, the Analogy may be a logical failure to those who will believe nothing until you can prove everything.

## Metaphysical Deficiencies.

The metaphysical deficiencies which have been alleged are felt only by a certain class of metaphysical minds. It is not surprising that the German divine, Tholuck, familiar with the efforts of his countrymen to solve the problem of the universe by sheer speculation, such as the Theodicy of Leibnitz, should remark upon the jejune, commonplace reflections of the Analogy and complain of the reading of it as "a perpetual going afoot over sand." Bishop Fitzgerald aptly rejoins that tiresome as this mode of travelling may be, it is better than for one to mount a hippogriff for an adventurous excursion through the air and find his journey soon ended, not on the sand, but in the sea. Butler himself has shown very clearly that we have no faculties for such speculations, and discarded from the outset "the idle and not very innocent employment of forming imaginary models of the world and schemes of governing it." It is true, that one English philosopher, Mark Pattison, has so far agreed with the German critic as to say that Butler's work "diverts the mind from the great outlines of scientific and philosophic thought and fastens it on petty considerations, being in this respect the converse of Bacon's 'Novum Organum.'" But it is strange that so well read a critic should have forgotten how large a space is filled by religion, both natural and revealed, in the philosophy of Bacon, and how imperiously he would fasten the mind upon the pettiest details at the very opening of his great work. "The capital precept for the whole undertaking is this, that the eye of the mind be never taken off from things themselves, but receive their images truly as they are. And God forbid that ever we should offer the dreams of fancy for a model of the world."

At the same time, it will be found that Butler, while keeping the speculative propensity within due limits, has necessarily glanced at some of the deeper metaphysical problems which underlie both nature and religion, such as the being of a God, the existence of the soul, the freedom of the Will, the nature of Virtue. In his treatment of these problems, he is thought by Leslie Stephen to be a mere child as compared with Hobbes, Hume, or Jonathan Edwards. But the young student at Tewkesbury, who was admitted to the honors of equal combat with the veteran metaphysician of his day, Samuel Clarke, can scarcely be thought wanting in metaphysical ability, had he chosen to exert it. Nor does he suffer in this respect by comparison with his recent critics.

Take, for example, their criticism of his theistic premises. Mr. Arnold tells us that they are so antiquated that he does not care two straws for them. But he gives us no means of estimating his own agnostic premises, not even a marginal reference to Herbert Spencer, nothing but his mere dictum that Butler's conception of an intelligent Author of Nature and moral Governor of the world is anthropomorphic, a quasi-human agent with a will and character. When Butler asks why a tree does not require an intelligent designer as much as a house, he thinks it enough to answer with the agnostic Topsy that it "just grow'd," or has resulted from "a tendency to grow." The theistic proof from necessary being, or essence, he terms puzzling, and would not have religion founded upon a puzzle, but would replace the puzzle with a so-called "stream of tendency making for righteousness," which is no better foundation for religion, or rather no foundation at all. Butler's theism was neither a puzzle nor a metaphor, but based on combined reason and experience. It was enough for his purpose to refer to its "accumulated evidence; from the argument of analogy and final causes, from abstract reasonings, from ancient tradition and testimony, and from the general consent of mankind;" the old ontological, cosmological, teleological, and historical arguments, which have worn so well in time past, and are likely to wear well in time to come.

As another example of his metaphysical presuppositions, take his theory of free-will and immutable morality. Mr. Arnold suggests that Butler's moral government of the world might go on rewarding and punishing men without the annexed notion of an anthropomorphic Governor, and with only the everlasting "stream of tendency" to drive the grinding mill, as it turned out saints or villains with impartial accuracy. But what would then become of man's freedom, and the good or ill desert of actions? Mr. Stephen tells us intrepidly, as a fatalist and an atheist. He says that "Free Will is the device by which most theologians justify God's wrath with the work of His own hands," and exclaims, "How can He judge us after He has made us?" As if anticipating such objections Butler has said: "I have argued upon the principles of the Fatalists, which I do not believe; and have omitted a thing of the utmost importance which I do believe, the moral fitness and unfitness of actions, prior to all will whatever: which I apprehend as certainly to determine the Divine conduct as speculative truth and falsehood necessarily determine the Divine judgment." In other words we can no more imagine God making right wrong than making two and two less than four. And hence He is supremely moral, as well as rational, within the sphere of human freedom.

If, then, it be granted that Butler is deficient in some forms of false metaphysics, and has purposely excluded some metaphysical questions from his argument, yet, so far as he has touched upon them, he has shown the hand of a master, and kept himself in line with the best metaphysical thought of the present day.

### Religious Deficiencies.

The alleged religious deficiencies are the last to be noticed. And they are the most serious. If the Analogy fails to induce religious belief and practice, it fails in its chief aim, and is a total failure. Few critics have gone to so extreme a judgment concerning it, but special objections have been made to it which are of a religious nature. The philosopher Maurice has fancied that Wesley could not find in it his peculiar doctrine of depravity and regeneration. Its tone or spirit has been complained of by some orthodox writers, like Chalmers, Malcolm, and Emory, who have regretted a lack of evangelical savor or sentiment. Mr. Goldwin Smith, as an appreciative critic, speaks of its dry-light of intellectuality as wholly wanting in religious feeling and sympathy. Mr. Matthew Arnold misses in it his "sweet reasonableness," and declares that the total impression left by Butler upon his mind is not exactly that of a saint. The absence of mere saintly phrases is very happily explained by Mr. Gladstone as due to the habit of reserve which characterizes the English type of piety. It may also have been due, in Butler's apologetic, to good sense and good taste, as well as to temperament. At the *symposia* of Queen Caroline, he had seen enough of the loose deism of fashionable circles to know when mere preaching or sermonizing would be misplaced and useless. Addressing philosophers, he used the tone and speech of philosophy.

A lack of convicting or converting power has also been charged, but the charge is not well sustained by the instances cited. The famous saying of Pitt that Butler raised more doubts in his mind than he solved, when traced to its source, proves to have been reported at second hand, and in its authentic form only meant that Butler's abundant candor brought to light many difficulties of which Pitt had never dreamed—which might be said of almost any book of evidences. In the same careless manner it has been reported that the philosopher, James Mill, was made an atheist by reading the Analogy; the fact being that for a while it held him back from atheism until, at length, he lapsed into something like agnosticism. The great Unitarian divine and thinker, Dr. Martineau, declared that he never knew anybody converted by Butler's Analogy, and opened the fiercest of all the attacks upon it in these words: "To question Butler's perfection is in the eyes of churchmen little short of the sin against the Holy Ghost." He was followed by his pupil, Miss Hennel, embodying his objections in an "Essay on the Sceptical Tendency of Butler's Analogy." And two or three other critics have since joined in the refrain, that the Analogy is an incentive to atheism and irreligion. I can give only a few samples of their strictures.

Such censors charge that it undermines the proper evidences of natural religion. Miss Hennel and Mr. Arnold both hint that Butler accepted blindly deistical premises which are discarded in our day, and built all religion on an abstract theistic argument of Clarke which once had currency. But Butler, in accepting the deistical premises, has carefully indicated the sources of their proof, and distinctly asserted that he built up all religion upon solid facts, and not upon abstract reasonings, which he had examined and rejected. Dr. Martineau argues that by importing the difficulties of natural religion into revealed religion Butler laid upon the former a tremendous weight which it cannot bear.  But Butler, before proceeding to the problems of revealed religion, summarized, with masterly fulness and force, the evidences of natural religion, and thus made firm the ground upon which he stands.  Mr. Stephen, commenting upon Butler's argument for reconciling the opinion of necessity with the religion of nature, declares: " No evasion can blind us to the true bearing of his statement.  God made men liable to sin; he placed them where they were certain to sin; he damned them everlastingly for sinning.  This is the road by which the Analogy leads to Atheism."  Now, in his very introduction, Butler has maintained that the end of the Creator is the virtue and happiness of his creatures, though it may not be possible to accomplish this end without something of hazard, suffering, and sin on their part; and in one of his most powerful chapters he has shown that the unfolding scheme of Nature and Providence affords ever-increasing evidence of the wisdom and goodness of the Creator in promoting the virtue and happiness of his creatures.  This is the road by which the Analogy leads away from Atheism.

The censors have also charged that Butler has obscured the peculiar evidences of revealed religion as well as natural religion.  Dr. Martineau declares that the darkness, the negation, the sorrows of natural religion are made, not simply to reappear in Butler's Christianity, but to constitute it and be the only soul it has.  On the contrary, Butler has shown that the difficulties of religion are inherent in the pre-existing constitution of man and nature, that they necessarily reappear in Christianity, no longer, however, as distressing enigmas, but as problems in solution, as evils of sin to be remedied by grace, as marks of Divine justice to be effaced by Divine love.  Mr. Bagehot, like Dr. Martineau, complains of Butler's critique of revelation as antecedently improbable, and maintains that revelation to serve its purpose should be a perfect remedy for human ignorance, should avoid paradoxes and mysteries, and should throw light upon the actual world in which we live.  On the other hand Butler has shown that we are incompetent judges of what a revelation should contain; that to ask for a more perfect revelation would end in demanding omniscience itself; that its mysteries and paradoxes are inherent in the themes of religion; that they are no greater than the riddles of science and common life, and that they often serve as trials of faith. Both Dr. Martineau and Mr. Stephen have bitterly commented upon Butler's view of a vicarious Saviour as the central doctrine of revealed religion, and have denounced it as exhibiting the innocent punished for the guilty and placing injustice upon the very throne of the universe. Against such strictures Butler has shown that the revelation of a vicarious Saviour is in strict analogy with the whole existing constitution of human society—that parents suffer for their children, patriots suffer for their country, philanthropists suffer for their kind; and so, that the Christ crucified as being at once the greatest of sufferers and the greatest of benefactors, the Divine Saviour of a lost world, has placed infinite Love upon the throne of the universe.

I have sketched the merest outline of an argument which is embarrassing in its richness and fulness. It is not enough to read it. It should be studied and pondered. The fault of Butler's censors is that they have not mastered it, whether from inattention or whatever cause. We can admire the genius and culture which have made them eminent in other walks of literature and philosophy where they have achieved deserved fame. Dr. Martineau stands foremost among English philosophic divines, and Mr. Arnold has written poems that will live as long as the language. Nevertheless, the fact remains that these critics plainly show ignorance of certain portions of the Analogy, and as plainly have detached other portions from some needed logical connection. And hence their objections are of no effect. We may accept the judgment of Mr. Gladstone—" The catapult has beaten on the walls of the fortress: it has stood the shock. The tempest has roared around the stately tree, and scarcely a leaf or twig has fallen to the ground. My confidence is strengthened not only in the permanence of Butler's fame, but much more in the permanence and abundance of the services he has yet to render to his country, to his kind, and perhaps to Christendom, as a classic of thought in the greatest of all its domains, the domain of religious philosophy."

This discussion has largely anticipated Butler's apologetic

services, as well as prepared us to appreciate them; and it only remains to set them forth as the results of the inquiry. I shall mention his four principal services:

### The Value of Christian Evidence.

The first relates to the value of Christian evidence. The need of some valuation of it was great in his day, and it is still great in our day. Nothing is more common than for the inquirer into the truth of Christianity to set up some false standard of proof and then demand a kind or degree of evidence of which the case does not admit and which is simply impossible. Butler has enjoined the one true standard as a preliminary study.

In the first place, he has defined the logical value of Christian evidence. It is not demonstrative evidence, but probable evidence. This is the first word and the last word of his apologetic. Demonstrative evidence carries immediate full conviction, while probable evidence admits of degrees from the lowest presumption up to the highest probability or moral certainty. The ebb and flow of the tide, for example, when observed for the first time, would be barely presumable, but, having been repeatedly observed by mankind through many ages, it has become morally certain. Thus it is that the evidences of Christianity are a vast accumulation of presumptions or probabilities which have been amassed by successive generations until they now approach high probability in many minds, and in some of the finest minds of the race have reached moral certainty.

In the second place, he has defined the ethical value of Christian evidence. There is a moral element in our opinions. We are responsible for our belief. If Christianity admitted of demonstrative proof as clear as that two and two make four, disbelief would be an act of insanity for which no one would be responsible. But since Christian Evidence is only probable evidence, there will always be a residuum of doubt in the most believing minds, and therefore always room for faith and the need of faith. As to this deficiency in Christian evidence, be it great or small, Butler has shown: (1) That it is not peculiar to Christianity, but belongs to all matters of opinion; (2) that it is easily explained by the nature of religion and the narrow scope of our faculties; (3) that it is incident to our state of probation and especially needed for the discipline of speculative minds, inquiring into the truth of religion, which otherwise could not be tested and disciplined; (4) that it does not release us from the obligation of continued inquiry; and (5) that after all it may be largely our own fault and part of our highest accountability. No more practical contribution to Christian apologetics has been made in any language than Butler's chapter on the "Supposed Deficiency in the Proof of Christianity;" and none has been more strangely overlooked or misunderstood by his critics.

### The Logic of Christian Evidence.

His second service relates to the logic of Christian evidence. To ascertain the kind of logic or reasoning applicable to the problems of religion is a primary need of the apologete. For the want of it the greatest Christian advocates, in his time as in our time, have tried to chop iron with a wooden axe; to settle religious questions by mere efforts of abstract thought or feats of deductive logic. Discarding all reasoning from ideal premises, Butler has confined the mind to realities, to facts and the relations of facts, by means of that form of inductive logic known as Analogy, which consists in reasoning from known facts to others like them.

He first defines Analogy in general, as used in common life and ordinary inquiries. Its foundation, its measure, and its utility are discussed. As to the foundation of Analogy, it rests upon likelihood. A thing is probable or likely when it is like some other truth already known or some other event hitherto observed: like it, in itself, or in its evidence, or in its circumstances. If the likeness includes its mere circumstances, the likelihood is a rhetorical analogy or simile, as when we speak of the mother country. If it embraces its evidences to the mind, it is a moral analogy, as when the life of Christ is made credible by comparing it with the story of Cæsar. If it extends to its essential properties, it is a strictly inductive or scientific analogy, as when Newton likened the gravitation of the earth toward the sun to the fall of an apple toward the earth. Sometimes all three kinds and grades of analogy may be combined in the same compared objects. Inductively, we may reason that the planets are revolving globes like our earth; morally, we may argue that they are inhabited by angels somewhat resembling men; metaphorically, we may call them sister worlds in the family of heaven. It is evident, however, that a strictly scientific analogy must be based objectively upon observed facts rather than upon our own subjective reasonings and fancies; and that the convincing force of such an analogy will depend upon the frequency and fulness of our observations. It will yield us a presumption or an opinion or a full assurance that an event will happen, according as like events have been observed sometimes or commonly or always to happen. We thus become assured that a child in twenty years will reach the stature of a man, because we have observed that children always grow to manhood. We form opinions as to the manner in which different persons will act in given circumstances because we have observed how they commonly act and with what motives. We acquire presumptions for or against natural events according as we have observed nature extensively or partially. In the climate of England we presume from analogy that there will be frost next January and ice some time in the winter. In the climate of Siam, however, the King presumed from analogy that water must always be soft and yielding, and denounced the Dutch Ambassador as a liar for telling him that it became so hard in Holland that an elephant might walk upon it. Sir Walter Scott in the "Talisman" represents Kenneth as reasoning from the wider analogy of both climates in order to persuade Saladin that a hundred knights had ridden for miles upon a lake as if it were crystal. "Heat," said he, "in your country often converts the soil into something as unstable as water; and so in my land cold often converts the water itself into a substance as hard as rock." It is by thus correcting and completing our observations of phenomena that our analogical reasoning becomes sound and conclusive.

As to the measure of Analogy, we may now see that it relates to finite beings and yields only imperfect information. To an infinite intelligence, able to embrace the past, the present, and the future within its scope, everything must be absolutely certain, and nothing could be merely probable. But to us, probability is the very guide of life. At every step we act upon such evidence. If we waited for demonstration or certainty, we could not act at all, but would be literally distracted with doubt and uncertainty. In many instances we must act upon a bare presumption and sometimes only upon an even chance or balance of presumptions. In our speculative pursuits, also, we must form our opinions by weighing probabilities and ascertaining resemblances to truth. Our whole lives thus proceed, more or less consciously, upon observed analogies. He must be simply omniscient and omnipotent who could dispense with analogical reasoning.

Several questions may here arise which, if settled, would be more interesting than practical. We may inquire into the metaphysical ground of analogy and base it in some profound correlation of subject with object, of mind with nature, ultimately of nature with God. As to its psychical process, we may distinguish it from the intuition which seizes demonstrable truth, and describe it as a subtle mental habit of generalizing our observations and storing them in unconscious memory. As to its logical method, we may trace it as an inductive reasoning from facts to principles rather than a deductive reasoning from principles to facts. Butler starts such questions only to waive them as irrelevant, difficult, and unessential. Certainly they are not essential in practice. As the farmer need not be a chemist, nor the artisan a physicist, though proceeding respectively upon chemical and physical principles, so common men may and do reason analogically in all the affairs of life without being logicians, psychologists, or metaphysicians. Not fully conscious of this latent reasoning in our minds, we do not always appreciate its force and utility. But could we stop and retrace it, divested of all present impressions, so familiar a certainty as sunrise and sunset would appear to have been but one long elaborate accumulation of probabilities. Beattie, in his "Essay on Truth," illustrates this by supposing "a man brought into being at maturity and placed on a desert island. He would abandon himself to despair when he first saw the sun set and the night come on, for he would have no expectation that ever the day would be renewed. But he is transported with joy when he again beholds the glorious orb appearing in the east and the heavens illuminated as before. The second night is less dismal than the first, but is still very uncomfortable on account of the weakness of the probability produced by one favorable instance. As the instances grow more numerous the probability becomes stronger and stronger, yet it may be questioned whether a man in these circumstances would ever arrive at so high a degree of moral certainty in this matter as we experience, who know not only that the sun has arisen every day since we began to exist, but also that the same phenomenon has happened regularly for five thousand years without failing in a single instance."

It is no fair objection to the use of Analogy that it is sometimes abused by rhetoricians in imparting verisimilitude to error and falsehood. The orator Quintilian spoke of it as making the doubtful resemble the unquestioned and proving things uncertain by means of the certain. And because Butler adorns his title-page with this motto, it has been absurdly imagined that he meant to offer his whole treatise as a mere artificial discourse without much regard to its essential validity, even when thus employed in the art of rhetoric. Analogy has its uses in repelling captious objections, in allaying honest doubts, and in predisposing the mind to faith and knowledge by assimilating new and strange truths to those which are old and familiar, and by collecting probabilities where demonstration in the nature of the case is not possible. For purposes of illustration, proof, and conviction it has ever been a potent instrument. But Analogy has much higher uses, as employed in the art of logic, and especially in the logic of the sciences. Through the whole inductive procedure it aids the mind in classifying facts, in generalizing their laws, and in advancing to near and remote discoveries. It has been well termed the soul of induction. Without it no amount of mere observation and experience could ever yield us true science.

Nor can it be justly objected that this art of logic as yet is too imperfect to enable us to discriminate between mere rhetorical and strictly scientific analogy. There are at least a few simple rules for testing analogies, such as the following: That our knowledge of the objects compared should be sufficient or that their ascertained properties should exceed their unascertained properties; that they should be of the same species, their resemblances exceeding their differences; that the judgment should be founded upon the resemblances alone; that the resemblances taken together should afford cumulative probability; that the anticipations of the analogy should be verified by experience; that there should be a concurrence of other relevant analogies. When several of these rules apply, the analogy is sound and valuable; when they all apply, it will amount to a strict induction and carry probability toward moral certainty. Moreover, in default of these or any other rules, it should be remembered that the most practical scientists, like men in common life, often reason better than they know, without being able to give a philosophical account of the logical process by which they have reached their grandest discoveries. Indeed, even if the whole logic of science be pronounced obscure and inscrutable, its actual fabric, together with all popular knowledge, would still remain founded upon analogical reasoning.

Now, since religion no less than science deals very largely with facts, and since analogy is a reasoning from facts to others like them, it follows that analogy may be as applicable to the problems of religion as to those of science. Certainly there is nothing in religious facts themselves to forbid its application. Rather may they be deemed more accessible than other facts, since they lie within the scope of consciousness as well as observation and have been accumulating through ages of recorded history. Nor can there be any presumable obstacle in the mere analogical process of tracing uniformities and resemblances among facts. It would be strange if the most intimate and intelligible phenomena with which we can deal, the phenomena of religion, should prove wholly inscrutable and anomalous; while physical phenomena around us, even the most remote and recondite, are exhibiting law and order. That our wills and passions, like the personal equation of the astronomer, may disturb a religious investigation, is a mere circumstance not in the facts themselves as detached from our personality. All prepossessions aside, it will be found, as we proceed through the realms of nature and of religion, that the one is no more a medley or a chaos than the other. Professor Drummond has even argued that the laws of the spiritual world are not simply homogeneous, but identical with the laws of the natural world, the same in theology as in physiology, in the saint as in the reptile. This, however, may be loading analogy with more than it can carry. To prove the reign of law in religion as well as in nature, it is not necessary to identify their respective laws, any more than it would be necessary to identify the laws of mechanics and chemistry or the laws of chemistry and ethics in order to vindicate their logical correspondence. All that strict analogy requires is that in both cases the laws should be found suitable to the special phenomena observed. Though religious laws be wholly unique, they might yet be correlated with psychical laws, as psychical laws are already correlated with physical laws; and thus render the most varied phenomena analogous throughout the universe.

Religious analogy, in an unscientific form, dates from very ancient times. As artlessly practiced, it might be claimed for some of the Psalms of David and the Proverbs of Solomon, as well as the Parables of our Lord. As a philosophical method its first crude attempt may be discerned in the scriptural allegories of the Greek Church fathers concerning the works of Creation. Origen, for example, sagaciously remarked that one might well expect to find the like difficulties in Scripture and Nature, if both have proceeded from the same author. The later schoolmen, also, sought for endless correspondences between the two volumes of Creation and Revelation. With the rise of the inductive method, devout naturalists began to unfold the analogical argument for theism in the physical sciences. But it was reserved for Bishop Butler to pursue that argument with logical precision and fulness throughout the entire realm of the sciences, psychical as well as physical. Starting with the current theism of his day, he essayed to bring the whole system of natural religion into logical correspondence with the known constitution and course of nature, rendering the doctrine of a divine government, future state, and present probation as scientifically probable as received theories in physics, physiology, and ethics. Then, advancing from these premises, he proceeded in like manner to bring the whole scheme of revealed religion into analogy with the constitution and course of humanity, exhibiting the peculiar doctrines of sin and redemption as but the logical sequel and complement of the whole previous argument. At length, having thus unfolded a harmonious system of nature and religion, by the same analogical reasoning he indicated its cumulative evidences as not less obligatory in ethics than conclusive in philosophy.

The superiority of religious analogy may be shown by comparing it with mere religious speculation upon the origin and object of the universe. In regard to the origin of the universe, there have been endless attempts to build the world upon hypothesis, upon assumed principles, which are themselves false or, if true, are misapplied in defiance, sometimes in ignorance, of the actual structure and course of nature. From the time that Descartes endeavored to show how God might have made the world out of vortices, the history of philosophy has been filled with nebulous cosmogonies and ideal universes, mere creations of fancy, vanishing one after another like brilliant bubbles amid the solid pyramids of our empirical knowledge. In place of such hypothetical constructions, Analogy takes the world as it finds it, combines reasoning with observation, proceeds from facts to principles, and from that portion of the divine government which is near and visible infers that which is remote in space or time. Instead of receding from religion to nature, it would advance from nature to religion, as Laplace advanced from the terrestrial to the celestial mechanics, as Bunsen advanced from the terrestrial to the celestial chemistry, as Chalmers advanced from the terrestrial to the celestial ethics, and as Butler, before them all, advanced from the known scheme of creation to the revealed scheme of redemption.

There has also been much religious speculation upon the object or design of the universe, with which religious analogy stands in contrast. Ever since Leibnitz set the fashion in his "Theodicy," philosophers have been busy imagining a world better or worse than the world with which we are acquainted, and thus charging upon the Creator an optimism or a pessimism alike inconsistent with the virtue and happiness of His creatures. Butler declares that we have no faculties for this kind of speculation; that if we should take the happiness or virtue of creatures to have been the worthy end of their creation, we could not imagine either attained without the other; that if we should assume both ends to have been included in the plan of a wise and good Creator, we could form no judgment as to the fittest means for accomplishing such ends; in short, that the best world which the wisest man might devise would be full of absurdities and miseries not found in the world which exists and with which alone we have to do.

Having thus defined Analogy as applicable to religious problems, and shown the superiority of such Religious Analogy to all forms of religious speculation which would desert the actual world as we find it, and wander off into vague imaginations concerning the origin and object of the infinite universe, and having used it strictly throughout his treatise, he finally defends it from those who would object to it as meagre, inconclusive, and unsatisfactory.

Naïvely, without pretence of logical terms and methods (for logic had not been perfected in his day), Butler has originated a definition and use of what is now called inductive logic, within the religious domain of philosophy, which, after the lapse of a hundred and sixty years, remains unimpaired and unsurpassed.

### The Problems of Christian Evidence.

His third service relates to the problems of apologetics. Besides seeking probable evidence by analogical reasoning, we need to take up the problems of religion in their due logical order and connection. Otherwise we shall ever be going back upon our own path to prove over again what we have assumed as proved, or perpetually tearing up the foundations while building the superstructure of our argument. Many an objection has been fancied to exist on one page of Butler, which has been found answered on another page before or after it. He has precluded such criticism by the exact method with which he arranged and treated the entire series of actual and possible problems of religion.

In the first place, he has clearly distinguished the empirical or inductive problems from the metaphysical; those which emerge in the region of fact and experience from those which lie largely in the region of thought and speculation. He has even relegated some of the latter to an Appendix of Dissertations on Personal Identity and the Nature of Virtue. He has made the distinction so sharp that much of his reasoning holds equally with an atheist or a theist, a materialist or a spiritualist, a fatalist or a libertarian, a deist or a Christian, an infidel agnostic or a Christian gnostic. And he has thus kept for himself a pathway clear and firm through the regions of probable evidence.

In the second place, he has taken up the inductive problems in a series, each problem preceding and supporting the next following: the problem of theism preceding and supporting the problems of all religion; the problem of a future life preceding and supporting the problem of a divine government; the problem of a revelation in general preceding and supporting the problem of the Christian revelation in particular—and so on, in one concatenated course of reasoning.

Had he been versed in the distinctions of modern metaphysics and the rules of strict logic, he could not have projected more clearly and fully the problems of apologetics, through all coming time and all possible stages of intellectual progress.

### The New Scientific Evidence.

His fourth and crowning service relates to the new scientific evidence beginning to appear in our day. As every age has its own form of incredulity, so it has its peculiar form of evidence growing out of the conflict of Christianity with such incredulity. The conflicts of Christianity in past ages with Judaism, with Paganism, with Greek Philosophy, with Northern Barbarism, with Mohammedanism, with modern Rationalism, have yielded vast masses of evidence, much of which is still extant and influential, but some has already been stored away as antique trophies in the arsenal of Christian Apologetics. Now, in the present age of science, the so-called conflict of religion with science, as it issues in their growing harmony, is yielding a new class of scientific evidences of Christianity to be added to the miraculous, the prophetic, the historical evidences of former ages. To this new class of evidence Butler has led the way as a forerunner and even as a master builder.

First. He has conceived religious problems in a thoroughly scientific spirit. Though living at the dawn of that scientific age which is shedding upon us its meridian light, he imbibed its method and committed himself, albeit unconsciously, to its inductive process in the sphere of religion, as Bacon did in the sphere of nature. Like Bacon he announced his intention to study " the conduct of nature with respect to intelligent creatures; which may be resolved into general laws or rules of administration, in the same way as many of the laws of nature respecting inanimate matter may be collected from experiments." And the pages of Bacon do not afford a more scientific conception of the course of nature as governed by general laws, ascertained and yet ascertainable, than do Butler's chapters on the schemes of nature and of Christianity.

Second. He has treated religious problems, if implicitly, yet in a most scientific manner by applying to them the inductive logic. Though never using the technical terms of science, he has in fact discussed the questions of immortality, divine government, and probation as questions of physiology and psychology, of ethical and social science. A few devout naturalists had begun to unfold the analogical argument in the physical sciences; but it was reserved for Butler to pursue that argument with logical precision and fulness throughout the entire series of sciences, mental as well as physical.

Third. By establishing the analogy of nature and religion he has laid a logical foundation for the harmony of science and revelation considered as the human and divine factors in producing our knowledge. The second part of his treatise is pregnant with principles of biblical criticism yet to be developed and applied to the problems emerging between science and the Bible. For example, the primary principle that Scripture, though non-scientific, is not anti-scientific; that it neither teaches science nor anything contrary to science; that its popular and phenomenalistic language, whether in the sphere of theology and ethics or in the sphere of astronomy and physics, cannot impair its revealed truth when fully ascertained—this principle has been set forth with as much clearness as caution—

"And therefore, neither obscurity, nor seeming inaccuracy of style, nor various readings, nor early disputes about the authors of poetical parts, nor any other things of the like kind, though they have been much more considerable in degree than they are, could overthrow the authority of the Scriptures; unless the Prophets, Apostles or our Lord had promised that the book containing the Divine revelation should be secure from those things."

Again, the principle that the so-called conflict of religion and science is only a conflict of the dogmas of the one with the hypotheses of the other; that our knowledge of Scripture may still be as imperfect as our knowledge of nature; and that we must look for their growing harmony in their gradual completion—this momentous principle is set forth with as much courage as clearness—

"As the whole scheme of Scripture is not yet understood, so if it ever comes to be understood, before the restitution of all things, and without miraculous interpositions, it must be in the same way as natural knowledge is come at—by the progress of learning and liberty. . . . . Nor is it at all incredible that a book which has been so long in the possession of mankind should contain many truths as yet undiscovered. For, all the same phenomena, and the same faculties of investigation from which such great discoveries in natural knowledge have been made in the present and last age, were equally in the possession of mankind, several thousand years before. And possibly it might be intended that events as they come to pass, should open and ascertain the several parts of Scripture."

Once more, the principle that in the sphere of revelation, as in the sphere of science, we must accept facts as we find them, whether we like them or not, and that we can no more object to the revealed system than to the solar system, on *a priori* grounds—this scientific principle of Christian evidence has been enjoined with discriminating rigor:

"Though objections against the reasonableness of the system of religion cannot indeed be answered without entering into consideration of its reasonableness: Yet objections against the credibility or truth of it may. Because the system of it is reducible into what is properly matter-of-fact; and the truth, the probable truth of facts may be shown without consideration of their reasonableness."

"And therefore, though objections against the evidence of Christianity are most seriously to be considered, yet objections against Christianity are, in a great measure, frivolous."

"But this is urged, as I hope it will be understood, with great caution of not vilifying the faculty of reason, which is the candle of the Lord within us; though it can afford no light where it does not shine; nor judge where it has no principle to judge upon."

Fourth. He has given prescient hints, albeit unwittingly, of a coming harmony of science and religion and consequent growing proof of Christianity. They lie scattered through his work, like chiselled stones yet to be set in the temple of knowledge. They may be found in the region of every science. In astronomy, he has remarked upon the scientific exactness of our knowledge of the heavenly bodies as compared with our knowledge of our own bodies. In geology, he hinted at a predominance of brute creatures in some other globe which we now know existed in our own globe during its prehistoric period. In biology, a hundred years ago he discerned that law of development throughout living nature evolving embryos into animals, even animals into moral agents, which evolutionists are now verifying. In psychology, he traced the mental habits and moral affections with a precision which has not since been surpassed. In sociology, he projected on an inductive basis that ideal reign of virtue of which speculative philanthropists are still dreaming. In theology, the science of religions, he has exhibited that consensus and dissensus of revealed religion with all natural religions, which divines and philosophers are only beginning to apprehend. There is scarcely a great scientist with whom he might not be compared in scientific rigor. Newton did not more inductively argue from the analogy of the falling bodies to the law of universal gravitation than did Butler from the inherent prevalence of virtue over vice to a universal law of rectitude. Darwin did not more cautiously trace the combined effect of organism and environment in the past evolution of animal species than did Butler the correlation of character and condition in the moral education of the immortal spirit. Huxley has not more strenuously maintained a strict necessitarianism in the laws of nature than has Butler striven to reconcile such necessitarianism with the obligations of religion. A few years since Tyndall delighted the scientific world by depicting the whole course of nature, strata, floræ, faunæ, human races, all as the orderly evolution of a fiery cloud; but Butler long ago proclaimed from the height of his great argument that the whole course of Christianity itself, from its genesis to its apocalypse, may appear in the view of superior intelligences but one majestic unfolding of divine wisdom as much regulated by general laws as the roh of the seasons or the growth of a flower. In a word, the system of religion as conceived and indicated by him is as thoroughly scientific both in its outline and in its evidence as the Copernican system of astronomy or any other theory of exact science.

Lastly, besides thus exhibiting Christian evidence as scientific evidence, Butler, building better than he knew, has constructed a substantial portion of Philosophy itself, considered as the science of knowledge or the science of the sciences. His Analogy serves as a logical buttress on the religious side of philosophy corresponding to the Organum of Bacon on the physical side of philosophy. Viewed together they are opposite segments of that ascending arch of human and divine knowledge, whose keystone is yet to support the Cross as at once the consummation of philosophy and the full illustration of Christianity.

# CHAPTER II.

## *PROBLEM OF THEISM.*

METAPHYSIC THEISM, or Metaphysic Theology as it may be termed when reduced to a system, comprises that theistic theory of the universe which is afforded by general metaphysic science. Having already largely treated it in previous chapters, we need here only recapitulate its elements as preliminary to a clear understanding of the whole logical task before us. These refer to the idea and the nature of God, together with his relation to the world.

As to the idea of God, we may hold it to be innate or traditional or both as combined. If it be innate, we may look for its germs in the human constitution everywhere, especially in the spontaneous feeling of dependence upon an eternal Somewhat which becomes an object of fear and worship, whether it be an idol or an ideal, the fetich of the savage or the Absolute of the philosopher, or howsoever it may be conceived. If it be traditional we may trace it back to a primitive revelation, as part of the divine image which was impressed upon man at his creation but which among pagan and savage races has been defaced and lost, whilst among Hebrew and Christian nations it has been restored and purified. If both views be combined, we need find nothing absurd or irreverent in the hypothesis, that the divine image or true idea of God has been produced in man by an evolutionary process rather than by a creative fiat. Some anthropologists are now endeavoring to develop the psychical as well as physical characteristics of mankind from the animal species during long pre-adamite time, through the various stages of ghost worship, devil worship, angel worship, nature worship, toward the worship of one national deity or supreme ruler of gods and men. Such religious germs in the favored race of Adam may have been quickened and unfolded into the divine likeness by an objective revelation from which other co-adamite races have lapsed into idolatry and animality. We may even suppose this evolution meanwhile to have gone forward historically under that divine revelation, differentiating the God of Israel from the God of the heathen and at length manifesting that pure Christian idea of God in comparison with which the gross anthropopathy of the Old Testament, seems now but little removed from that of the higher Gentile religions. Be all this as it may, the idea itself as now extant, however it may have been produced, even if at first it be taken as a mere fiction or abstraction, is at least susceptible of close study and will bear the strictest tests of logical definition. As we have hitherto shown, the theistic conception instead of involving any of the contradictions charged upon it, is the strongest, clearest and most consistent conception of which the human mind is capable.

As to the nature of God, we may maintain that it is like or unlike or but partly like the nature of man. If our idea of deity corresponds to any reality, we can cognize that reality as a spirit or person like ourselves, having the personal attributes of will, intelligence and consciousness. If there be no such correspondence we can only cognize some vague Power or Principle or Being wholly unlike ourselves and devoid of all the personal attributes as we know them. But if there be at least a partial correspondence we can then cognize the divine personality as somewhat like the human in kind, though unlike in degree; as having the personal attributes but having them without defect and limitation. A sound agnosticism may thus concur with a pure anthropomorphism in recognizing beyond our conditioned will a Will that is absolute, beyond our finite intelligence an Intelligence that is infinite, beyond our bounded consciousness a Consciousness that embraces the universe. In other words, on the supposition that there is such a Divine Person, so intimate and homogeneous a reality cannot be wholly unknowable. As we have elsewhere argued, the nature of God, though incomprehensible, is yet cognizable in greater or less degree.

As to the relation of God to the world, we must weigh the claims of deism and pantheism. According to the former, the divine personality is wholly distinct from the universe and ever remains independent of its development. According to the latter it is merged in the universe and even shares its development. Between such extremes we may endeavor to reconcile the transcendence with the immanence of God in the idea of his independence. The highest and best thinking of all ages has ever thus sought to conserve the truth of pantheism in distinction from the error of deism; to conceive the Creator as inhabiting yet controlling his own creation; and to admit Him capable of making, unmaking and remaking creation after creation with the power of absolute will and the ease of infinite thought. Speculative and paradoxical as such a view may appear, it has its analogy and miniature in our own finite consciousness of the Infinite. As we have already maintained, the phenomenal universe is not a necessary but a voluntary manifestation of the divine personality.

Let it be observed that as yet we have not endeavored to prove Theism, but only to define it and to state the conditions of the problem. We have simply premised that the idea of God, however obtained, is thinkable; that, if there be a God, his nature as a person is more or less knowable; and that He is to be thought and known as in the world yet not of it. With these definitions in mind we are now ready for a logical estimate of the theistic proofs, both in general and in detail. In general, they are depreciated by the atheist, the agnostic and sometimes by the theist himself. The atheist of course opposes them with his own different theory of the universe. The ancient materialism of Democritus, Epicurus and Lucretius thus resisted even polytheism with the notion of a fatalistic or fortuitous origin of the world. The modern materialism of Helvetius, D'Holbach and La Mettrie in like manner substituted mere physical nature for a personal deity. The more scientific materialism of Haeckel, Buchner and Vogt bases even physical nature in a godless eternity of maker and force. The crude pantheism of ancient times was little better than nature worship. The pantheism of Bruno was the mere deification of a materialistic universe. The more refined pantheism of German idealists, like that of the Hindoos, often aimed to obliterate the distinction between God and the world and at length to render the creation an abortion. At such an extreme, the pessimism of Schopenhauer boasts of having destroyed the last vestige of theism. The positivism of Comte and Harrison, and the secularism of Holyoke and Bradlaugh are maintained by avowed atheists who glory in the name. There is no end to the systems of thought which may be found practically associated with atheism. The single fact, however, that all of them may also be found more logically associated with theism by Christian thinkers renders their detailed examination unnecessary at this point in the argument.

The agnostic would preclude the proof of theism by a sceptical theory of knowledge. A line of philosophers from Hume to Huxley has sought to ignore the whole region of theism as inaccessible to our faculties. Mr. Herbert Spencer at length brought the tendency to a crisis by maintaining that the idea of the God Absolute is logically inconceivable and the correspondent reality a mere inscrutable force devoid of all personal attributes. At the same time such sceptics resent the charge of atheism and lay claim to a species of morality and religion, based upon a feeling or apprehension of the Unknowable Infinite. Without questioning their honesty, we need here only refer to the fact that the negative truth of agnosticism as maintained by thinkers like Hamilton is held by divines like Mansel to be consistent with the positive truth of theism and even of revealed theology.

There are two classes of theists that disparage the proof of theism on logical grounds. According to one class, such proof is inapplicable and superfluous. The existence of God can neither be proved nor denied, but must simply be assumed as an intuitive truth having the marks of spontaneity, necessity and universality. Atheism as a theoretical conviction of the understanding is impossible. It only appears as a practical godlessness of the fool who saith in his heart, There is no God. Against this view several objections may be urged: First. If it be an intuitive truth, it may at least be ascertained as such and become confirmed and illustrated. The primary belief in the reality of an external world is thus excogitated and defended against sceptical idealists. Second. The natural cognition of God, at least in a full form, cannot claim the three marks of an intuitive truth. It does not spring up in all minds without reflection as an overpowering reality; it is wanting in many savage tribes not otherwise deficient in human faculties; and it is honestly doubted by some sane intellects. Third. The vast accumulation of theistic arguments in Pagan and Christian literature shows that mankind has not ranked a belief in God with self-evident truths and mathematical axioms.

On this account, another class of theists has been inclined to treat the proof of theism as practically worthless. Their contention is, that since it falls short of demonstration it cannot carry conviction to all minds, but in some minds may only raise doubts without solving them. Belief in God is not a product of reasoning, but a moral sentiment or inspired impulse, like virtue or love, which cannot be enforced by mere logic. There are several answers to this objection. First. Although the proof of theism be not demonstrative, yet demonstrative proof can be claimed for scarcely any of our opinions, and is forbidden by the very nature of religious faith, which must always imply more or less doubt. Were it otherwise, atheism could not be sin or even folly, but mere imbecility or dementia. Second. If unsophisticated believers do not need the proofs of theism, yet speculative inquirers crave them for the satisfaction of their own intellectual wants as well as to repel the cavils of sceptics. Third. Whatever may be said of their practical value, they are at least logically important in a system of theology founded upon natural theism and constructed out of other related truths and doctrines. Fourth. They are, also, philosophically important in that ultimate system of knowledge which must be based upon a theory of revelation as well as of cognition and embrace religious or metaphysical together with empirical science in a rational harmony. It is in this latter point of view, as an essential part of the logic of the sciences, that we are here concerned with them, and shall now proceed to examine them in detail.

It is usual to distinguish two kinds of sources of theistic proofs; the *a priori*, derived from intuition and speculation, and the *a posteriori*, derived from experience and observation. The former by reason of their refined and subtle nature have always had a fascination for contemplative spirits and gifted intellects, enamored of the ideal and the perfect; but have seldom figured in serious controversy with atheists. They have rather been discussed among theists themselves as in a sort of spiritual tournament for the recreation of their own faith. Theologians also sometimes use them in confirmation of plainer, more practical proofs, and metaphysicians value them as postulates in their systems of thought. They merit attention here not so much for their probative force as for their power of logical definition in separating weak from strong arguments and in affording the full conception together with the full proof of God as the Supreme Reason of the world. Naturally, they will fall into three groups, the ontological, the cosmological and the psychological, corresponding to the three chief provinces of general metaphysics. They are often found mixed together in the same argument; but it is desirable to treat them as distinctly as possible.

The Ontological argument is based upon the idea of reality and the relation of God to existence. It claims that God is the essence of reality. He exists necessarily. We cannot even conceive Him fully without assuming his existence. His peculiar perfection is self-existence. Of all beings He alone is absolute, infinite and eternal. Such reasoning might be historically traced from its germs in Greek philosophy to its full flower in modern thought. Plato thus argued for God as the one perfect archetype, or ideal True and Good and Fair, more real than any of his approximate images in the actual world. Augustine, in the same spirit, held God to be that one absolute truth of which in men we can find only dim and broken reflections; and declared that He exists more truly than He is thought. Boethius from our knowledge of the imperfect inferred the reality of God as absolute perfection. At length Anselm, in his Proslogion, cast the reasoning into syllogistic form, maintaining that our idea of God as a perfect being includes his necessary existence as his most unique perfection, and that we cannot even conceive of his non-existence without a logical contradiction. After the Reformation the argument was re-stated and enriched with new features yielded by the new speculative thought of the time. Descartes argued that the Anselmic idea of a Perfect Being existent in thought not only requires his corresponding existence in fact, but is involved in our consciousness of imperfection and could only have been produced by a Perfect Being in our minds. Spinoza with geometrical technicality elaborated the conception of God as the one infinite substance of which all finite existences are but modifications. Samuel Clarke, in his Demonstration of the Divine Being, maintained that both space and time must be necessary and infinite because not inconceivable and that they can only be conceived as predicates of one infinite and necessary substance, the self-existent God. Christian Wolf based his demonstrated theism upon the idea of one absolute substance; and a line of German thinkers, such as Schelling, Hegel, Baeder, Krause, from the same postulate proceeded to unfold elaborate systems of theistic ontology.

At the same time, the ontological reasoning has been eagerly discussed at every stage of its development. On the one hand is has been treated as a mere sophism or logical fallacy. The Platonic proof was neglected by the schoolmen, as only a profane speculation. The argument of Anselm was assailed by his contemporary, Gaunilo, who, in a treatise entitled "A Plea for the Fool" (or Atheist), ridiculed it as of no more force than if one should maintain the existence of a perfect island because he could imagine such an island. Duns, Scotus, Occam, and afterwards Leibnitz objected to the Anselmic and Cartesian proof that it presupposes and assumes the feasibility of the Perfect Being whose existence is to be proved. Locke as a materialist held that the universal substance of Descartes and Spinoza could only lead out to the eternity of matter rather than of mind. Kant, in his critique of the Wolfian argument, sought to render it not only inconsequent but self-contradictory by maintaining that the mere subjective idea of an infinite and absolute God cannot necessitate the fact of his objective existence, but is itself a negative generalization from the finite and conditioned. Coleridge adopted the former part of this criticism; and Hamilton and Mansel, pursuing the latter part of it, argued that the very effort to frame such an idea of God, though it may not affect his reality, transgresses the logical laws of the understanding and whelms it in impotences of thought. Reid, in like manner, had suggested that the ontological reasonings of the school of Clarke, though the speculations of men of superior genius, may have been only the wanderings of imagination beyond the limits of the human understanding. Brown, with more boldness, characterized them as relics of the mere verbal logic of the schools, and as absolutely void of force except for their tacit assumption of the physical argument, without which they would have led us to doubt rather than to believe the existence of a God; even Chalmers, always unwilling to support a good cause with weak arguments, maintained that Clarke had confounded a logical with a physical necessity of existence and failed to prove his main thesis of the non-eternity of matter. And Thomson, in his Burnet essay, declared that one must have been equal with God to possess an *a priori* demonstration of his necessary existence. Some American divines, like Edwards, Hodge, Strong and Bowne, view the ontological argument as more specious than valid and in practice of little force or value.

On the other side, it has been sometimes claimed as a truism or logical demonstration. Anselm himself so stated it in syllogistic form and pleasantly replied to his friend Gaunilo, that the idea of an island does not, like the idea of God, include the elements of absolute perfection and necessary existence, and that if he could conceive of an island involving such elements he would make him a present of it. Aquinas added the Augustinian to the Anselmic proof. After the Reformation Herbert of Cherbury revived the Platonic proof in support of his mystical deism. The Cambridge Platonists blended it with the Cartesian proof. Cudworth argued not only that all finite minds and truths are but ectypal reflections of one archetypal Mind and Truth, but that the idea of such a perfect being could never have been feigned by politicians, poets or philosophers and must only have been produced by that divine logos who enlighteneth every man that cometh into the world. Stillingfleet added that the clearness of the idea in conception is one of the strongest evidences of its reality. Howe approved it as a strict demonstration. The Cartesian proof also with variations figured in the works of Malebranche, Fenelon and Bossuet. The logical consistency of the divine perfections was claimed by Mendelsohn as proof of their reality. The more positive argument of Samuel Clarke was widely accepted and defended among English and Scottish theists. Newton evidently agreed with it, as in one of his scholia, he formally stated that God is not eternity and infinity but eternal and infinite, not duration or space but endures and is present, and by existing always and everywhere constitutes time and space, eternity and infinity. Wollaston, in his Religion of Nature, argued ingeniously that matter cannot, like God, be eternally self-existent, since it is more or less restrained in space and time. Richard Fiddes, in his Speculative Theology, argued that all actual existence implies God as a necessary existence. Moses Lowman, in his Argument for the Perfection of God A Priori, maintained that necessary existence by its very definition cannot but be actual existence, always and everywhere, and therefore can only belong to the one absolute and eternal God. Dean Hamilton attempted to demonstrate the existence of one Supreme Unoriginated Being whose non-existence is impossible because not contingent and all whose attributes are eternal and immutable. In our own time, Gillespie, in his Argument A Priori, has maintained the premises of Clarke, that infinite space and time, as necessarily existent, imply the necessary existence of an infinite and eternal Being. As to the Hegelian proof of absolute deity it need only be said that it has been used in support of the strictest theism by German thinkers, like the younger Fichte, Ulrici and Weisse. Dorner rated it with the highest proof, averring that an absolute Being cannot but be thought as existent and potential with all being and thought. Cousin blended it with the Cartesian proof by arguing that the finite reason must be correlate with an Infinite Reason, as a positive and objective reality. Among American divines, Buel and Winchel have favorably stated the different ontological arguments, whilst Shedd has not only vindicated the Anselmic proof clearly and strongly, but declared it to be of uncommon importance in the present age of materialism and physical science.

Between the extremes are the devout thinkers who have sought more carefully to sift the truth from the error of the reasoning. Dugald Stewart very justly observed that the sublime conceptions of immensity, eternity, and necessary existence as set forth in the ontological argument may at least yield an earnest of our immortality and animate us in the pursuit of wisdom and virtue by affording us the prospect of an indefinite progression. Chalmers, mediating between the modesty of Reid and the rashness of Brown, whilst depreciating the transcendental generalities of the argument, still recommended it as at least worthy of study and having for a certain class of minds the force of conviction. Bishop Littlejohn, without claiming for it the effect of demonstration, suggests that it establishes the antecedent probability of other and less pretentious lines of reasoning, that it shows at least the tendency of human thought towards God; and presents the idea of God as consistent with the loftiest exercise of reason. Professor Flint has forcibly shown that the *a priori* reasoning not only has logical validity, but in its essence leaves to the Atheist the only alternative of absolute scepticism. Lotze, without admitting that such proof of a God is a strictly logical deduction of the intellect, maintains that it must ever carry with it a spontaneous feeling or apprehension of his irresistible reality. As the result of the whole discussion we now have before us the fact that all parties of thinkers, atheists as well as theists, unite in admitting the existence of some absolute and infinite Being, however widely they may differ as to the essential properties of such a Being.

The Cosmological or Ætiological argument is based upon the intuition of causality and the relation of God to the world. It claims that God is the First Cause of the universe. As alone self-existent he must be the source and ground of all other existence. The world, as an effect or event, can only find in him its efficient cause and sufficient reason. Such argumentation in a crude form is of ancient date. Some of the early Greek cosmologists speculated upon the universe as ever changing, transient and contingent. Aristotle may be styled the founder of the cosmological argument. Among the fathers Diodorus of Tarsus argued that the world as variable and mutable must have had one original immutable cause. John of Damascus formulated the reasoning, drew the distinction between the created and uncreated and from the ever varying creation inferred the one unchangeable Creator. Hugh of St. Victor reasoned that the soul must have been created; could not have been created out of matter, but out of nothing; and must have been created by an independent and eternal Creator. Thomas Aquinas included in the cosmological argument the Aristotelian notion of a Prime Mover, the idea of an efficient First Cause, and that of its intrinsic necessity or independence of the world. After the Reformation the reasoning acquired new and more speculative features. The school of Descartes indulged in cosmical speculation on the assumption of Deity as a first cause ever operating through all secondary and occasional causes by sustaining or concurring with them. Leibnitz and Wolff enhanced the reasoning with the idea of a sufficient cause or adequate reason such as can only be found in God as a necessarily existent being, the one absolute and eternal ground of the whole changing universe. The causal argument was a favorite with the early English physicists and natural theologians. According to Bacon God is the highest cause of all second causes, as the chain of nature was tied to Jupiter's chair. Newton, Wollaston, Grew, Charnock, Foster, Boyle, Locke, argued that the entire series of contingent causes without an independent First Cause would be without rational support and consistency, as Sterling has said, like a stark serpent hanging by a hook in the dark. The Scottish thinkers and divines reinforced the argument for a First Cause of the world with the ideas of efficiency, potency, originating force, creative energy; and such reasoning ever since has figured largely in the natural philosophy and theology of our time.

During the latter part of its history the cosmological proof has been keenly criticised, chiefly on metaphysical ground. At the head of its assailants was David Hume, who objected first, that it is a mere begging of the question, the contingency of the world being the very thing to be proved; second, that its axiom of causation is only observed sequence, since for anything we could tell *a priori* the fall of an apple might extinguish the sun or the wish of a man control the planets; third, that if the world be due to a series of efficient causes, they simply produce one another, and it would be absurd to demand any other efficiency of a supposed First Cause; fourth, that the material universe itself may be the eternal and necessarily existent being which is demanded for the argument. After Hume, and stimulated by him, came "the all-demolishing" Kant, who maintained that the cosmological proof is only a masked form of the ontological, since it reasons from the vague idea of general existence as contingent to that of necessary existence, and from the mere idea of necessary existence to that of an absolutely real and perfect Being; second, that the causal judgment is a purely subjective process in the mind with no basis in the objective world of phenomena; third, that the alleged impossibility of an infinite series of contingent causes is a pure assumption easily met by the denial of the alleged necessary first cause of the series; in a word, that the entire reasoning is a mere nest of dialectical assumptions, inconsistent with the Kantian idealism. Following Hamilton as he followed Kant, Herbert Spencer (and John Fiske) has admitted the reality of a First Cause only to pronounce it logically unthinkable. This criticism of Hume and Kant has been resumed and carried farther on physical as well as metaphysical grounds. The younger Mill has objected that the cosmological argument though largely metaphysical can only be a conclusion from experience; that experience suggests an infinite series of causes as more probable than a first cause; that science has disclosed permanent as well as changeable elements in nature, such as indestructible matter, continuous motion, persistent force which may be eternal and uncreated, and consequently that no first cause is needed for a world which has no beginning. The Rev. Stanley Gibson, in his *Religion and Science*, seems to have conceded to such critics that the material universe with all its store of energy may be infinite or if finite may involve a reconcentration of its diffused energy, and in either case its present condition may have been produced by unknown natural forces and laws, operating through an indefinite past. Professor Wundt has argued against the theory of a limitation or creation of the universe that it would interfere with the scientific principle of physical causation and make room for the miraculous as well as anomalous. Indeed, many physicists with more or less avowed atheism, have abandoned the idea that the world is contingent and represent the universe as eternal, though subject to endless evolutions and dissolutions in its history.

The cosmological argument has been defended on the same grounds where it was assailed. The metaphysical objections of Hume and Kant have been met by Reid, Stewart, Calderwood and McCosh, who maintained that efficient causation is based upon intuition as well as observation; that an infinite regress of second causes with no all-powerful First Cause imparting to them efficiency would hang the world upon nothing by a rope of sand; and that the alleged contradictions in the conception of such an absolute First Cause are the mere fictions of a false idealism. Dr. Sterling, in his Gifford Lectures against the Kantian criticism, vigorously maintains that the ideas as well as the facts in the cosmological argument are independent of the ontological argument and combine to render the contingent universe a mere footstool to the absolute necessity of God. Dr. Row also enforces the reasoning from a premise of Herbert Spencer that the assumption of a First Cause of the Universe is a necessity of thought. Among American divines Prof. Diman has forcibly argued against Hume and Mill that all changes imply causal agency as well as observed coincidence and demand an efficient First Cause of the otherwise baseless and disconnected phenomena of nature. Dr. Shedd defends the argument on the ground that every finite object implies original non-existence and therefore creative power in the cause of the whole finite universe. Dr. Mahan, in his Natural Theology, has maintained that the order and arrangement of nature, having had a beginning in time, imply a cause thereof which is out of nature and above nature as well as adequate to produce nature together with all its order and arrangement. Dr. Charles Hodge has assailed the sceptical principles of Hume, Brown and Mill; maintained the axiom of causation to be as self-evident as personal identity or any external reality; and from the contingency of the world as geologically and historically proved to be an effect in time, has inferred an extra mundane First Cause. In like manner the physical objections to the cosmological argument have been met on their own ground and with their own weapons. The recent doctrines of matter and force as held by Clerk Maxwell, Thomson and Reid, have been used against Stuart Mill, Tyndall and Wundt, to prove that the visible and temporal universe must have an invisible and eternal cause as the source of all its stores of varied energy. Flint, though content to leave the argument on its metaphysical premises, reasons from the molecules as manufactured articles, from the vortex rings as impelled atoms, and from spent energies as once potential, in short from all nature as a transient effect, to the necessity of one omnipotent, self-existent, extra mundane cause. Dr. Archibald Hodge, in like manner, cites the same physicists to prove that the material universe cannot be eternal and self-existent and holds that even the primeval fire-mist of the evolutionist logically requires for itself an adequate pre-existing cause. Indeed, the mass of theologians still maintain that a Creative Cause, if not inconsistent with evolution, is at least an antecedent necessity to it, as well as to the universe of which it is predicated.

The grains of truth in the cosmological argument have been carefully sought for by a few discriminating thinkers. Chalmers, in his Natural Theology, warily bringing the Scotch verdict of not proven, maintained that if the matter of the world be eternal the order of the world is temporal, thus requiring a Fashioner of the latter and therefore a Creator of the former. Dorner considered the argument inconclusive as applied externally to the relation of God to the world, but valuable as applied internally to the relation of the world to God who originates and produces the world within the sphere of his own activity. Dr. Martineau, in his Study of Religion, after metaphysically defending causality in God as universal and omnipotent, maintains not only his total immanence in the universe, but also his partial transcendence as being capable of producing an infinite variety of other universes. Flint also holds that the First Cause must be not only in and all through the universe, but also out of, anterior to, and above the universe. Prof. Bowne, in his Philosophy of Theism, though far from claiming the cosmological argument as demonstrative, takes a causative world-ground to be the universal postulate which cannot be denied without undermining all reality in man as well as nature. Prof. Schurman, in his Wakely lectures at Andover, carefully rejects the creational form of argument, but retains for its kernel the idea of an eternal dependence of the world upon God as its intra mundane cause in distinction from the popular conception of an extra mundane Creator. Without citing more authorities we may now conclude that deists and pantheists, atheists and theists, can agree that there is some one eternal cause of the world, however much they may differ as to the proper attributes of such a Cause.

The Psychological proof, sometimes called Anthropological, is based upon the intuition of personality and the relation of God to the soul. It presents God as the one absolute person, the source and ground of the human spirit, the necessary complement of our finite reason, will and consciousness, the embodiment of all mental and moral excellence. Man at his best and highest estate is but the shadow, the image, the epitome of God. We may sooner doubt our own existence than doubt his existence. Such reasoning has its roots deep down in human nature, as well as far back in human history, though its full flower has appeared only in the later metaphysical thought of our time. Springing from a spontaneous tendency to personify external objects, it has struggled upward from the grossest fetichism of savage tribes to the refined anthropomorphism of philosophers and divines. The ancient polytheism was but a varied personification of human powers and passions which for ages had the form of actual personality. Xenophanes said, that if the animals could think they would conceive a deity in their own likeness; and it would seem that the gods and goddesses of the Greeks and Romans could not have been thought less real to them than their own virtues and vices. Even the Epicureans depicted the gods in human forms though without human relations; and while the Stoics represented deity as the universal force and reason, yet they arrayed him in an ethereal robe of humanity. After the purer conceptions of Christian theology became prevalent, theistic proofs and illustrations were still drawn from a crude psychology by Melito of Sardes, who wrote a treatise on the Body of Deity; by Tertullian, who held to a refined corporeity of God as well as man; and by Audæus, who found a divine image in the human frame. Among the schoolmen some of the higher psychological arguments were derived by Hugo St. Victor from the spiritual nature of man; by Abelard from the monitions of conscience; and by Raimund, from the moral necessity for a Supreme Judge of human actions. Since the Reformation the reasoning has been enriched by the growth of psychologic science. The English physicists and divines, who have already been noticed, attributed psychical volition as well as mechanical energy to the First Cause and deduced all the other divine attributes both mental and moral as corollaries of the ontological proof. By the German thinkers a basis for theism has been sought in the ideals of an absolute Ego or infinite Mind or primordial Will or supreme Reason, which have not only been treated as metaphysic entities, but maintained as divine realities, having their reflection in our own reason, will and consciousness. In this manner the conception of God as an infinite and absolute person has at length been reached as the very goal of speculative thought.

Like the other arguments the Anthropological has been keenly discussed, especially during its recent history. By its assailants the whole theistic conception has been gradually stripped of every element of personality. Kant, as a metaphysician, challenged Natural theologians to name a divine attribute which is anything but a name, apart from anthropomorphism. Comte, who led the assault in the name of physical science, simply ignored a personal God as a mere anthropomorphic fetich or myth and even rejected the notion of a First Cause as a metaphysic fiction. Herbert Spencer, whilst assuming a First Cause, argued from the premises of Hamilton that its infinity and absoluteness are inconsistent with the limitations of personality. And John Fiske, in his Cosmic Theism combining the reasonings of Comte and Spencer, claims that the deanthropomorphizing process of science has left us the conception of God only as an absolute Being or Persistent Force devoid of anything like human volition or consciousness. "Physicus," in his Candid Examination of Theism, argues that the First Cause cannot be volitional, but must be mechanical, since our notion of volition is derived from muscular energy, which is only a form of physical force. Among German metaphysicians in the schools of Kant and Hegel, Schopenhauer has maintained that the Absolute will is mere irrational force, and von Hartmann has associated it with mere unconscious reason. Dr. Paul Carus, in the Open Court, ingeniously describes the Infinite as a mere mathematical abstraction or material quality, which has no religious significance, and cannot be attributed to a personal God, conceived as an individual being, or great world-ego swayed by interests and passions in the government of the universe, like a powerful monarch. Many other thinkers of the present day might be cited as showing the same subtle tendency to retain the personal names of Deity, whilst depriving him of all personal attributes or resolving them into mere psychical illusions. Their view is expressed by Barret in his Physical Ethics, when he stigmatizes the anthropomorphic theism as worse than the idolatry of wood and stone since it is the worshipping of a mere creation of our own minds as if it were the creator.

At the same time, however, the argument has been maintained by its defenders on the very grounds where it is assailed. We confess, said Jacobi, to an anthropomorphism inseparable from the conviction that man bears the image of God; and maintain that besides, this anthropomorphism, which has always been called Theism, is nothing but atheism or fetichism. As we have seen on previous pages, the so-called religion of humanity devised by Comte may be viewed as itself but a caricature of the true anthropomorphism. From the same Hamiltonian premises taken by Spencer it was argued by Mansel that it is our duty to think of God as a person, while inconsistently believing Him to be infinite; and by Alexander Hodge that we may positively know God to be infinite, though we can only conceive his personality as indefinitely great. Against the deanthropomorphizing process of science alleged by Fiske, it has been urged by Cocker, Diman and Schurman that its votaries are still personifying nature as God and reasoning back to a potential First Cause which is but a disguised form of an old theistic argument. If our idea of a volitional First Cause be derived from that of our own physical or muscular energy, Dr. Row replies that it also carries with it the inseparable idea of a permanent self or conscious personality in every act of origination. While some German metaphysicians have been treating the absolute will and reason of the world as mere impersonal entities, others like Schelling and Krause from the same premises have virtually anthropomorphized the universe itself as an Absolute Ego of whom they have evidence by direct intuition, or through the very process of self-consciousness or in the commonest acts of cognition. Nor have the speculations of monists and agnostics availed to refine away this divine idea into a mere human idol of the popular theology. It lives in practical connection with the most daring anthropopathy. Many divines and Old Testament preachers of the day, though defining God as infinite and absolute in all his perfections, still attribute to Him mere human passions and frailties and at times seem to depict Him as little more than an absolute monster of anger, jealousy and cruelty.

From both extremes of absurdity, the argument has been rescued by the judicious theists who carefully sifted its truth from its error. Dr. Charles Hodge, whilst admitting with Mansel that anthropomorphism is the indispensable condition of all human theology, still maintains that it is as true in philosophy as in divinity; because the anthropomorphizing tendency is original and universal in fetichism and polytheism as well as monotheism; because the reality of a personal God is as much required by the veracity of consciousness as the reality of an external world; because we are constitutionally forced to attribute to Him personality as well as infinity, and psychical as well as mere physical perfections; and because we everywhere read his personality in the works of nature as well as in the words of Scripture. Professor Flint guards the anthropomorphic principle by showing that man is the image, but not the measure of God, since man is like God in the kind of attributes which are possessed but unlike in the degree in which they are possessed; and since his utmost knowledge of God must ever fall short of a full comprehension. As to our apprehension of God as an infinite and absolute power Professor Calderwood takes the ground taken in these volumes, that our conception of his personality, though inadequate, involves no contradictions, and our cognition of Him, though partial, is real as far as it extends. Such theism is very ably protected on its pantheistic side by Professor J. McBride Sterret in his " Study of Hegel," on the assumption of a self-conscious Absolute person before the world-process, in whom nature and man appear, not as discordant and irreconcilable with God, but as forming one organic whole without losing their relative dependent reality. On the deistical side, Lotze has argued that the divine personality, unlike the human, is not subject to the limitations of a non-ego and does not need the contact and stimulus of the cosmic whole of which it is a part; but is ever self-sufficing and self-knowing. Dorner also represents the Absolute Being as Absolute Life, at once factor and product in the universe. Accepting the ultimate generalizations of the physicist, Dr. Martineau reasons metaphysically that the first psychological source of theism is the recognition of a living Will as the cause of all phenomena, and that to that psychical Will must be ascribed the physical unity and wisdom of universal nature. Professor Schurman argues that such intelligent and volitional Being would account for the phenomena of the material rather than the moral world, and predicts that the cosmic theism of secular science will yet coalesce with the anthropic ideals of Judaism and Christianity in a new anthropocosmic theism exhibiting God as at once spirit and love. Upon such grounds, Professor Purinton, in his Christian Theism, maintains that without personality God would be inferior to man, however mighty his cosmical power may be; and as the human reason calls for a Perfect Reason, and the human conscience for a Perfect Righteousness, so the human heart calls for a Perfect Love. Indeed, it would not be difficult to show that the Christian ideal of divine philanthropy in the redemption of mankind fills up our highest conception of an infinite and absolute Being, whose love, like his power and wisdom, is devoid of all human limitations, infirmities and passions. But without anticipating later arguments, we may here conclude that the most opposite schools of thought, deistical and pantheistical, even atheistical and theistical, can unite in recognizing through and beyond the human consciousness an Absolute Will or Reason, to be treated either as a mere personification or as a true personality.

If now we bring together the three classes of *a priori* proofs we shall find that their strength is in their union. Take each of them by itself, and it will seem weak and inconclusive. The ontological argument alone will yield only the empty notion of an infinite Being without causal relation to the world and without personal relation to man. [The cosmological argument alone will prove the existence of a single eternal cause, whatever may be the attributes of that cause. The psychological argument concludes that the single Absolute Will is either a personality or at least a personification.—ED.]

# CHAPTER III.

## THE MIRACULOUS EVIDENCE. THE MYTHICAL THEORY OF REVEALED RELIGION.

When Infidelity denounced Christianity as an imposture, neither her philosophic probability nor her historic credibility was seriously invaded. Such an hypothesis was inconsistent both with Reason and with Fact. When it attempted to strip away from her the seal of miracles, her historic credibility alone was invaded, but the structure was left still reposing upon a philosophic basis. The problem remained how that which was so true in philosophy should yet be so false in history. And to have solved this problem by a subtle compromise seems to be the peculiar boast of our modern metaphysical era. That compromise is, no longer to deny that anything has happened, but in the glare of modern science to reveal what could not have happened and to throw uncertainty over what may have happened. In other words, the contention is, that there is in the sacred narratives an historic portion, that there is also a non-historic portion, and that, taken together, they form a mythic medley of incidental facts and popular legends. The voice of Infidelity now is, not that Christianity is a fabrication (that would outrage all history), not that she is a true history (that would outrage philosophy), but (the sole remaining hypothesis) that she is only a gorgeous mythology, descending to us from the twilight eras of time, and gathering around it in its solemn progress through the ages her group of gray-haired shepherds, her priests and kings and prophets, her Messiah and Apostles. The Infidelity of Voltaire and of Hume stood aside from Christianity—the one, from the seat of the scorner, reviling her; the other, from the imagined height of Philosophy, gracefully compassionating her. The Infidelity of Strauss would fain stand at her very altars, in the garb of a modern Plato whose insight has reached beyond existing superstitions and fables to an airy and thoughtful system of which they are but the gross and vulgar expression. When the two former assailed us, the one with its scoffs, and the other with its subtleties, we could lay our hand upon the open Bible and feel safe, returning only grief and pity. But when the latter would banish that book to the upper shelf with Hesiod and Homer and lead us back into the peopled gloom of antiquity, so twining the horrid visage of error with an alarming semblance of truth that for the time we are at a loss to distinguish our Jehovah from a Hebrew Jupiter, our Moses from a Hebrew Solon, our Jesus from a Jewish Socrates, it is hard to say whether indignation or dismay is the predominant feeling.

### Subtle Dangers of the Mythical Theory.

It would, perhaps, be difficult to exaggerate the dangers which are to be apprehended from this latest form of Infidelity. One of them, appearing at first sight, is its logical consistency. Unlike the illogical systems which have preceded it, it is based upon a philosophy which is legitimately consequent in all its conclusions, and which seems to conduct to the inevitable results of all true metaphysics. Accordingly, we do not find in the work of Strauss any of that partiality and inconsequence and confusion of a man who scarcely knows what he believes, but is blindly struggling against what he is unwilling to believe, but there is everywhere that calm, unostentatious consciousness of power, that high philosophic candor and confidence, belonging to one who has swept the whole field of conjecture and settled his conditions of belief beyond recall.

Another source of apprehension is to be seen in the appalling analogies which it so cunningly detects between Christianity and the contemporary mythologies. It has ever been the main effort of infidelity to confound her with the false systems of religion that have prevailed in the world—and no species of error is so formidable as that which appears as a counterfeit of truth, for "the similarity," to quote another distinguished

German, "is that caricature resemblance the ape bears to man and which has led so many naturalists into error—a resemblance founded upon no real affinity, upon no internal sympathy of organic conformation, but which is merely the likeness of a spiteful parody, such as we may suppose an evil spirit to have devised to mock the image of God, the masterpiece of creation." But the chief cause of alarm is to be found in the fascinating scientific garb in which it descends from the heights of learning, masking its latent hostility under honest pretensions and even under a Christian name. It offers such a ready solution of the internal difficulties that perplex even the believer, and would bridge over by such an airy and graceful structure that painful chasm which has been so long widening between the disclosures of modern Science and the simple revelations of the ancient Book which contains our faith. It does not, therefore, professedly aim at the entire demolition of Christianity as an objective system of belief and practice, as a public religion for the State, a gospel for the pulpit and the cottage. It would considerately leave the historic and miraculous Jesus to the people—perhaps they need such—but the true and proper Christianity it would reserve in the form of a certain Esoteric System of Doctrine for philosophers.

### Origin of the Mythical Theory.

The mythical theory of interpretation primarily owes its origin to the prevailing philosophy in Germany. When that philosophy had become widely diffused and developed itself in its true character, it became necessary either to avow some sort of coincidence with real Christianity, or to deny historical Christianity altogether. That division of the school who expressed their infidel sentiments undisguisedly both by profession and conduct could have resort to the latter expedient. That section, however, who are more moral in their conduct and who couched their belief under a refined and abstruse phraseology could combine both expedients, resolving the gospel narratives into mere historical or symbolical envelopes of the ideas of their own peculiar system. In this exigency neither of the two existing methods of interpretation could serve them.

On the one hand was that of the orthodox, or Supernaturalists, those who explained the sacred writings literally, admitting both inspiration and miracles. This plainly controverted not only their philosophy but also the discoveries of science. On the other hand was that of the Rationalists or Naturalists, those who though they denied miracles and inspiration, yet attempted by the most ingenious exegetical devices to accommodate Scripture to the discoveries of science in order to preserve the historic form. This involved too many evident absurdities to afford a permanent ground of conviction. The mythical method of explication was all that was left—that which would sacrifice the historic form in order to preserve absolute truth. This system had already been to some extent in application. At first only the primitive history of the Hebrews was abandoned as mythic, that being deemed a just and valuable concession to all antiquity, sacred and profane. Gradually the mythic element was admitted into the whole Old Testament in order, as it was thought, to enhance the dignity and value of the New. In like manner by successive concessions the Gospels suffered a similar process of mutilation. At first only the youth and infancy of Jesus were admitted to be legendary. The narratives of that period of his history, it was maintained, could not have been written contemporaneously, as He had not then excited sufficient attention, neither could they have been written during the later portion of His history, as they plainly have in view Christ not as suffering and struggling but as glorified. They were therefore composed after the resurrection; but at that period their author could have no resource but tradition which was colored by the Messianic fictions generally prevalent. In making this concession, the historical integrity of the narratives relating to Christ's public life was intended to be left unmolested, and that portion continued to be interpreted according to the principles of the Naturalists. Soon, however, the conclusion of the history suffered encroachment for like reasons, and the Ascension into heaven was granted to be fabulous, the interval between the Baptism and Resurrection alone being declared of true historic worth. Thus, as expressed by one critic, "men entered into the history of the Evangelists by the triumphal arch of the myth, and went out by a like door, but for all the intermediate space they were compelled to content themselves with the crooked and hard road of the Natural Explication." When we consider what that Natural Explication was, which was applied to the uninvaded portion, with what ineffective ingenuity it labored to resolve miracles and apparitions of angels, and demoniacal possessions, etc., into mere natural phenomena superstitiously misinterpreted by the wonder-loving populace, it would seem that Strauss only perfected the incomplete work of his predecessors when he made that declaration, so welcome to all expectant Germany, that Christianity is mythology. He claims the admission of the mythic element into the whole of the Gospel history—and his critique of the life of Jesus is an ingenious effort to separate the non-historic portion and detect the various forms which it has assumed. The plan of his work is first to vindicate the possibility of myths in the New Testament from extrinsic and intrinsic sources; then to state the distinctive characters of the myth and directions for detecting it; and then to apply these to the special incidents recorded in the life of Christ, aiming against the Orthodox interpretation on the one hand by a laborious compilation of all the internal critical objections, and against the Naturalist on the other by an ingenious exposure of the hollowness of their artifices. We shall endeavor to give a sketch of his theory, a statement of its defences, and some of the methods of refutation—premising that it will be necessary to use language sometimes more novel than reverent.

### *Definition of the Myth.*

The myth is variously defined, and distinguishable into various sorts. It is not to be confounded with voluntary and fraudulent fiction. All idea of premeditation or invention is to be excluded from the process of its formation, as it is the gradual production, not of an individual, but of entire societies and of successive generations, or if it be the conception and expression of an individual he is only the interpreter of a far more general popular conception, and acts in obedience to vast national impulses that have long moved and are moving simultaneously upon all. That such fables should have been believed in ancient times seems strange to us only because the faculty of producing them has nothing analogous to it in modern intelligence. With regard to the different kinds of myths, they are said to be such as involve the exposition of a fact, or of an idea under the historic form. When the basis of a narrative is fact, *i. e.*, real events embellished and colored by prevailing opinions with regard to the divine and supernatural, it is called historic mythos; when the basis is a simple thought or a novel idea it is philosophic mythos—the latter is the invention of a fact by the aid of an idea, the former is the intuition of an idea in a fact and by the aid of a fact. The Grecian Hercules and the Hebrew Samson may have had their origin in some real character, and may therefore be considered historic myths. The apparitions of the pagan mythology and those which occur in biblical history are classed as philosophic myths. These two species of myth are often complicated together so as almost to elude analysis—as, for example, the account of the transfiguration, the historical substance of which was the extraordinary impression made by Jesus upon his contemporaries and upon the following generations; and the philosophic portion of which was that the Messiah was expected to resemble Moses and Eli, and as a consequence the illumination of his face—an expectation which in his time had its cause in the writings partly mythic and partly historic of the Old Testament.

### *Negative Characters of the Myth.*

A brief summary of the directions which are given by Strauss for discriminating between the ideal and historical element will aid our conceptions. The myth, then, has a negative and a positive character. (1) It is not history, (2) it is fiction, a product of the intellectual tendency of a certain society. It is not history when the events related are incompatible with the known universal laws which regulate the order of events. Of these laws several may be mentioned. One is that it is held to be inconsistent with all just philosophical ideas and all experience worthy of faith that the Absolute Cause should interfere with second causes; all celestial voices, all divine apparitions, human miracles or prophecies, or acts of angels or demons are to be deemed as violation of this and therefore fabulous. A second law is that there should be some natural order of development in the succession of events narrated. The sudden transition of the partisans of a great man, after his death, from the most profound discouragement to the most lively enthusiasm is cited as a violation of this. A third law is that the psychological features of men then were identical with those of men now—they could not have felt, thought, and acted in any other way than we ordinarily think, feel, and act. The bargain of the Sanhedrin Jew with the guard at the tomb whom he knew to be faithless, or the incapacity of the human memory to retain and reproduce discourses such as those in the Gospel of John, are ranged in this category. These last two laws, however, Strauss observes, are to be used prudently, as subordinate to the first only and conjointly with other criteria.

But, secondly, a narrative is not to be held as history, when it not only fails to agree with the laws which regulate events, but to harmonize with itself and with other narratives. It is alleged that there are sometimes positive contradictions; sometimes important discrepancies as to time, place, number of persons, name, and basis of the narrative; sometimes the re-occurrence of scenes and discourses that could scarcely have happened with such slight variations. Sometimes, too, in cases when there is what we deem a silence rather than disagreement, it is asserted that it can be proved the second narrator would have written of such things had he known them, and would have known them had they happened. Such are a few of the negative characters of a myth.

### Positive Characters of the Myth.

The positive characters of the myth—*i. e.*, that it is fiction—appear (1) in the form or (2) in the basis. If the form is poetic, the actors in it exchanging discourses of a hymn-like character, lengthy, and with a kind of inspiration not to be expected from their situation and ignorance, we are warranted in suspecting its historic worth, remembering that legendary poetry loves the most simple form and an appearance completely historic. But the chief criterion is to be sought in the basis of the narration. If that remarkably accord with certain ideas prevalent when the narration is born, and which seem rather to be the product of preconceived opinions than the results of experience, a mythic origin is to be ascribed. Taken separately, Strauss would regard these indications of a non-historic character as scarcely satisfactory. They must be made to concur in a particular case. Thus the history of the Magi, and the Massacre of the Innocents at Bethlehem, agree in a striking manner with the Jewish idea with regard to the star of the Messiah predicted by Balaam, and with the precedent of the sanguinary order given by Pharaoh. But that alone would not suffice to convince us of its mythic character. When to it is joined, however, that what is there said of the star contradicts natural laws; that what is attributed to Herod contradicts psychical laws; that Josephus, who gives so many details concerning Herod, preserves, with all other historical documents, perfect silence touching the massacre at Bethlehem, and that the visit of the Magi with the flight into Egypt according to one Evangelist, and the presentation of the infant in the Temple according to the other, reciprocally exclude each other—but little room is left for doubt.

### An Example of a Supposed Christian Myth.

This is a sufficient exposition of the elaborate rules which have governed Strauss in his interpretations. A single instance, the first one in his book, of his method of applying them, will be given—the Annunciation and Birth of John the Baptist. He first attempts to undermine the literal explication of the Supernaturalists. The apparition of the angel to Zacharias, he says, shocks all modern conceptions. The whole doctrine of angelology seems to vanish before him like mist. The names and ranks of celestial spirits, he attempts to prove, are neither of Mosaic, nor of any pure Hebraic origin, being first mentioned explicitly in Daniel, and plainly derivable from the Religion of Zoroaster as the Jewish rabbins themselves confess. The whole belief in angels is now a dead tradition, belonging, first, to the idea which all early antiquity formed of the relation of God to the world, that of a Monarch surrounded by his court of ministers, which idea is obsolete, and, second, to the desire and necessity of those primitive times to account for natural phenomena by the intervention of supernatural causes and agents, which desire and necessity modern research has dissipated. The discourse and conduct of the celestial apparition he deems equally shocking to reason. Zacharias's natural incredulity is punished with dumbness, whilst Abraham's in the Old Testament, which is far more heinous, is left unnoticed, and whilst Mary, too, puts the same question to Zacharias that Sarah did to him. This inconsistency then cannot belong to God, nor to the celestial being, if there be such; nor to a wilful fraud of the narrator, but to the great national preconceptions of the Jews. If, then, the account be not a literal history, what idea must be substituted in place of the one thus destroyed? will the natural explication suffice? Strauss then exhibits the absurdity of the artifices of the Naturalist, such as that Zacharias whilst engaged in the Temple service was brooding, in a dreaming state, over his childless condition, and this subjective image in his mind combining with some optical illusion in the cloud of incense threw him into a trance in which he saw the apparition and heard the voice, and from the stupor occasioned by which he never recovered until the marvellous coincidence of the birth of John with the incidents of his dream produced a reaction into his natural state, etc. If, then, these occurrences be neither supernatural nor natural, what are they? Strauss then attempts to show that the mythic explication is the only consistent and satisfactory one. He reminds his readers that the Jews delighted to represent great men as the sons of mothers long sterile [*e.g.*, Isaac, Samuel, Samson, etc.]; to prescribe a name for them and a Nazarite regimen; to herald their birth by an angelic apparition and to represent them as precursors and types of their long-expected Messiah. Hence the barrenness of John's mother, the celestial messenger Gabriel, the prescribing the name John, the abstinence from strong drink, his mission as forerunner, the hymn of Zacharias in the Temple after the circumcision of his son, similar to that of the mother of Samuel when she committed her son to the high-priests, etc. The only important deviation from the Jewish herotype is the dumbness of the priest. This, however, is easily disposed of. To ask for a sign and guarantee of any prediction was common among the ancient prophets, as was also the temporary loss of a sense inflicted as extraordinary punishment by a celestial apparition. Saul lost his vision until Ananias restored it, and Daniel the power of speech until the angel touched his lips. But we need not enter further into the details of this appalling dissection. " To sum up [remarks this subtle critic, with a quiet effrontery that after a while becomes characteristic and familiar], we are here upon a ground purely mythico-poetic and all the historic reality which can support or conserve itself with certainty is reduced to this; John the Baptist by his subsequent works and by their relationship with the works of Jesus made an impression so powerful that the Christian legend was written to glorify in this manner his birth, and connect it with that of Jesus."

### *Mythical Explanation of Judaism.*

Such is a specimen of the formidable bearing of modern criticism in its infidel form. Jesus was only a Jewish Socrates. By the unexampled grandeur of his teachings and his acts he persuaded a class of his compatriots that he was the Messiah; and that vast mass of national fictions and popular legends, which had been accumulating by ages of fruitless expectation, gathered around him and his history, the one modifying the other. Christ did not fulfil prophecy—he fulfilled tradition. Prophecy was but that natural desire to discern futurity which was common to all antiquity, but which among the Hebrew people was modified by a sort of Chinese deep-rooted national vanity and by a specialty and separateness from other nations, of which it had for ages felt conscious, and which led it not only ever to project over the whole future the disk of its own vast self, begetting hope and expectation by the successive accretions of centuries, but also obstinately to exclude what might have tended to dissipate all this, the light of contemporaneous civilization. Hence when the first Christian community, with a few recruits from its own soil, wheeled off to the Gentiles, carrying with them all its golden cloud of glorious old myths and legends, it was left desolate amidst the ruins of its grandeur; its national hope was frustrated; that vast hidden power of moral cohesion, which was its life, was almost lost, and with no centre of political interest and glory around which to rally it wandered abroad, scattered and peeled, clinging feebly to its ancient traditions, yet from both internal and external repulsion ever refusing to amalgamate. It became the wonder and scorn of the nations.

### Mythical Explanation of Christianity.

In vain do we appeal from the theory to that mighty historical experience which the world has had of the efficacy and truth of Christianity for eighteen centuries. We receive, in cool and confident reply, some such jargon as this: Religion differs from Philosophy by giving to the conscience the same formation of absolute Truth, but under the form of an image, and not under the form of an idea. A myth then is absolutely necessary to mediate between the two, to give the idea life and permanent subsistence in the minds of the ignorant and sensuous—hence all religion is associated with mythos. Now that vast spirit which animates universal humanity is perpetually engaged in the development of ideas in individual and concrete forms—the infinite in the form of the finite. In Grecian Humanity it developed itself mainly in forms of the ideas of the True and the Beautiful. Hence Homer, Plato, and Phidias; hence, too, those inseparable philosophic myths of Jupiter and Hercules and Apollo. And has the world outgrown its historical experience of these—are they not still enthroned in our literature, transformed into our mighty poems and orations, visibly embodied in our pictures and statues and temples? Can we emancipate ourselves from them? Turn now to Hebrew humanity. Its mission was the sterner task of developing the great ideas of the Just and Holy. Hence, the exalted conception of Jehovah, immutable and timeless, I-am-that-I-am—external to man and history. Hence Moses and the Law issued from Sinai. Hence the idea of the race in the concrete form of one individual whose fate and personality should be the occasion of awakening in the consciousness of men the conceptions and motives of the holy Jesus, sinless and humble, suffering, struggling, triumphant. Hence, too, the inseparable historic myths connected with all this—the necessary intervention of angelic apparitions, messengers of a God distinct from the world. Hence prophecies and miracles and signs and wonders. Neither has the world yet cast off its historical experience of all these. The pure law that lived in the mythical and poetic envelopes of the Hebrew book has passed into our constitutions and social corporations; and the grandeur and holiness of the true Christ is still worshipped under its old sensuous images and primitive legends. And can we, need we, emancipate ourselves from all these? We will have our Homer and our Apollo, and we will let the people have their historical and miraculous Christ. They may worship the son of God in the form of a single man; we will worship universal man as the son of God, the infinite race as sinless—sinful only in the finite individual.

### Mythical Explanation of Biblical Morality.

Do we further object that the Biblical history is essentially distinguished from all profane mythology by its high moral worth, and by its superior credibility? With regard to morality, they have their answer ready. After a few remarks concerning the modern misconception of pagan fables, and the amount of pure ethics to be found in pagan literature, and a running allusion to the divine orders given to the Israelites to steal and carry away the jewels of the Egyptians, Strauss concedes superior moral worth to the New Testament. Nevertheless—what then? If an immoral divine narrative is necessarily false, a divine narrative the most moral is not necessarily true. With regard to its credibility, the argument is also exceedingly ingenious. As an offset to the absurd myths of the Greeks and Brahmins, the plagues of Egypt, the burning bush, and the marvellous histories of Balaam, Joshua, and Samson, are adduced—and the result of the comparison is that Biblical fable is removed from Greek and Indian fable only by a slight degree in point of extravagance, and that granting their superior worth does not prove Biblical history necessarily true, nor exclude from it the mixture of inventions. Moreover, it is asserted that this very superior credibility can be accounted for philosophically. That which at once shocks our belief in the character of the Greek gods is that they are clothed with attributes incompatible with our idea of what is truly divine. They themselves have a history, are born, married, beget children, perform great exploits, endure the evils of labor, triumph and are conquered. In the Old Testament Biblical history, however, there is no history of God—His people only have a history. But still this furnishes no guarantee of its historic worth—for though the Hebrew conception of God is less gross than that of other nations, yet that conception itself is not perfect inasmuch as it represents God as distinct from the universe, an artist, at best limited and finite; and it does violence to a true philosophic conception of the world, whose chain of causes and effects are made to suffer interventions of the Deity, by miracles and supernatural appearances. Strauss labors most ingeniously to establish this point. The belief of it, he says, is so "firmly rooted in the conscience of the modern world, that in actual every-day life to think or to maintain that the Divine Actor has manifested himself in an immediate manner is to earn the reputation of a fool or an impostor."

Such is the way in which the intrinsic objections to the possibility of Christian myths are disposed of by this subtle critic. The extrinsic objections are met with like ingenuity. The belief of the Christian that his religion is historic and not mythologic is balanced by the like belief of the faithful Mussulman in Mahomet, and of the Jew in Moses; and the authenticity of the evangelical books, by a laborious investigation of the early writings of the Church, is left shrouded in uncertainty.

### The Theory Sophisticating.

We have now given a sketch of this insidious system of interpretation. When we recover from the temporary shock of doubt and alarm and rescue our Bible from its rude handling and endless mutilations; when we sit down in the quiet mood of true devotion and read the simple, unaffected life-like narratives of the fisherman of Galilee, and notice the effect which they have had and have upon our hearts and the hearts of others, with what readiness does the mountain of mist vanish! If, therefore, an Infidel, after such perusals and observations, should deliberately and habitually regard Christianity as only one of the world's mythologies, it would be almost useless to argue with him. Error has had the same effect on him that an ingenious counterfeit of a true coin might be supposed to have upon one who refused to apply, or was incapable of applying, all the possible tests of its genuineness; who saw only the external form, the image and the superscription, but who had not taken it into his hand and felt the weight of the living ore, nor penetrated it by the searching ordeal of experience, and who would not receive the witness of those who had thus tested it. Or if, like Strauss, he profess to have attained to a sort of philosophic Christianity without miracles and inspiration (to continue the metaphor of the coin), he is like one who would mutilate its marvellous form and divine image, because there were skilful counterfeits that bore a very exact resemblance, or who would entirely melt it down, and remould it into a new shape, thereby not only mixing it with base alloy, but frustrating the very design of its circulation among the people. The very fact that all the false religions of antiquity claim a miraculous attestation, if it does itself presuppose a true miraculous religion, of which they are the counterfeit, is at least explicable upon the hypothesis of such a religion.

### Pagan Mythologies Mere Counterfeits.

From this point of view the mythologies of profane antiquity may be regarded as so many brilliant distortions of those floating traditions of the true God, which were carried away from a period beyond the reach of all profane written history, when the race was dispersed into its great family branches. And contemporaneous with early Christianity emerging from the twilight of her own types and symbols, they may be considered as dwelling around her like misshapen golden mists, that begirt the rising orb as it ascends to the zenith of its unclouded effulgence. That zenith was the associated grandeur of godhood and humanity in the person of our Lord. Then all type and symbol vanished—then all visible manifestation of Jehovah in form of angel, priest, or prophet was ended, receiving its completion in the true Angel that came down from heaven, in the true Prophet of God, and the Priest with his true sacrifice—then, too, all miracle died with that last great miracle. Meanwhile there are whole peoples that still dwell in the twilight of cast-off mythologies, deluded by shadowy systems of false angels and priests and prophets and miracles, unmindful that the great orb has already arisen; but the time shall come when they shall all melt away before it, when the nations of the whole earth shall sun themselves in its glory. Thus not only does Christianity present herself as true history, but she vindicates her claim to it, in that she alone offers a true science of all history, in that all history is else but a splendid chaos. What would this riddle of six thousand years of human existence be without the revealed key to its solution? What would this world be, past and to come, without Christ as a sustaining keystone, in the arch of universal history, spanning the gulf of time from the Apostasy to the Restoration?*

### Christianity Self-Vindicatory.

This theory of Strauss, at best only teaches us not to rely exclusively, or with too much confidence, upon the empirical proofs of Christianity—not to loiter in the outer court, the open area of its external evidences, where there is so much common ground for Infidel and Christian, but to point within to the high mysteries and sovereign truths there enshrined; to make men feel the need of Christianity rather than to amuse them with speculations about its origin. Many of the saints in heaven knew naught of the historical proofs of Christianity. They believed in miracles because they believed in Christ, and not in Christ on account of His miracles. No man was ever led to Christ by the evidences of Christianity. No man cometh except the Father draw him, neither will they be persuaded though one rose from the dead. The testimony of miracles is complete in itself and conclusive, but the true ground of all rational conviction is in the truth as self-vindicatory, as testified in us by the Holy Spirit, and as perpetually re-established by the most endearing witnesses from our own experience. So long as we take this ground we are safe. Armed with this faith we can enter the domain of history fearlessly, prepared to find Christianity in the form of accredited facts, both deeds of God and deeds of men, miracle or narrative. But when we present ourselves in that field devoid of such armor we are liable to be vanquished; with that armor miracles themselves become an

---

*This argument is more fully unfolded in the next chapter, that on the Historical Evidence of Revealed Religion.

all-conquering weapon in our hands. The whole case simply stated is this: We believe in the Christian faith, because it manifests itself to us now as real, and because also in all the past we find it in the form of actual historic phenomena, duly accredited—it is time then to show that it accords with all sound philosophic speculation.

## Summary of Refutation.

The refutation may be thus summarized:

In the first place, this mythical theory is incompatible with the known character of Christ and His apostles and the integrity of their biographers, the authors of the Gospels. We might more easily believe that they were impostors, fabricating miraculous stories as cunningly devised fables, than that they had deluded themselves into believing mere legends as miracles.

In the second place, the mythical theory is incompatible with the historic stage of development which had been reached by Jew and Gentile, at the time when the supposed Christian legends were formed. Such legends or myths only arise in the credulous infancy or childhood of nations. The Jews had already become sceptical as to the alleged miracles of Christ and His apostles, and the Greeks had passed beyond the mythmaking period into that of Philosophy, denying even the supernatural origin of their own national mythology.

In the third place, it is incompatible with all the circumstances attending the origin of Christianity. There was too short an interval between the death of Christ and the proclamation of His Gospel for such a mass of myths to have been developed, much less sincerely accepted. It is simply incredible that in the space of a few months or even years a Christian mythology should have grown up such as only centuries or ages could produce. Moreover, it was but a small body of disciples consciously accepting doctrines and miracles of recent origin and opposed to popular beliefs, and not a vast nation unconsciously forming legendary miracles and doctrines which had been bequeathed from one generation to another, in accordance with traditional faith and popular fancy.

Finally. The time in the world's history when Christ appeared was too enlightened to admit of the formation of a current mythology. It was at the highest epoch of Greek culture and of Roman power that the Christian religion emerged from an obscure province of the empire upon the stage of Gentile civilization. Not only was the jealous Jew denouncing Christ as a false Messiah, but the sceptical Greek and the indifferent Roman were in no mood to accept Him as a new incarnate deity. Such a thing as the formation of Christian legends, if it could have taken place in a corner, could not have occurred in the view of the whole civilized world. Christianity openly challenged universal scrutiny and was at length accepted in its supernatural character, even by its adversaries and persecutors. It was only two or three centuries afterward that infidel attempts were made to compare it with the mythical religions which it had superseded. And in that first encounter with the mythical theory it came off victorious, and for centuries afterward has maintained its supremacy. It is too late now to class Christianity with the pagan mythologies which it once encountered and over which it long since triumphed, logically as well as morally, on their own chosen field and with their own weapons.

# CHAPTER IV.

## THE HISTORICAL EVIDENCE OF REVEALED RELIGION.

UNIVERSAL history is the circumstantial evidence of revealed religion. It has all the cogent qualities of circumstantial evidence. It is the evidence of facts which cannot be falsified, and of facts innumerable, cumulative, and convergent in their significance. It at once explains revealed religion and is explained by it.

### The Four Great Historical Facts.

On a general review of human history four universal facts become conspicuous. First, the existence of evil in the world. Second, of a plurality of races and nations. Third, of different forms of civilization. Fourth, of diverse systems of religion. This condition of mankind finds its only adequate explanation in the early histories of Holy Scripture. There, with an hieroglyphical brevity suggestive of the omniscience which it veils, clews to the whole complex enigma of history are furnished the inquirer.

The first fact, this moral and physical disorder, this abounding crime and disaster, this tragic hue in the whole drama of human existence, is traced back to the first tragedy in the Garden of Eden. Whether interpreted literally or allegorically that tragedy presents all history as scarred with the traces of a demon of evil who first effected the fall of man and nature. History, in the light of this revelation, is but the arena of a foretold struggle between the seed of the serpent and the seed of the woman.*

*Throughout this paper historical phenomena are presented in the

The second fact, the assemblage of nations, which appears upon that arena, emerging all from a fabulous antiquity and darkening the whole retrospect with a mass of extravagant fiction, is explained as but the scattered family of one original progenitor; and their generic likeness, amid endless specific diversity, is reconciled by the record of their early dispersion at the Tower of Babel, a miraculous confusion of tongues by which it was effected being still an accompaniment and explanation of the phenomenon.

The third fact, the subsequent appearance of the race in different states of barbarism and civilization, is represented as a divinely ordered result. That portion of mankind which by the primitive impulse was scattered in a migration of ages, gradually lost both the memory and the intellectual heritage of their early ancestry or else sank naturally into historical insignificance. But that portion of mankind who were not destined to practise this nomadic habit, coalesced into states and empires, or modifying the original civilization which they carried away with them in the dispersion, formed new civilizations in their new social circumstances.

The last of the four facts, the existence of idolatry and superstition, is then easily explained. That primitive revelation or natural formation of conscience, which among the Jews was preserved pure and perfected in Christianity, in the Gentile world either spread out and was lost in vast putrefaction, as among savage tribes, or in co-existence with its various forms of civilization gave birth to mighty and progressive systems of error—a growth of diseased and monstrous strength, as if in huge demoniacal caricature. The literal interpreter finds in them all the satirical intent of the primal deceiver. To such an interpreter it is no marvel that our modern philosophy has been so cunning in the detection of these congenial analogies—no marvel that in its profane attempt to scale the heavens whence it looked down from the height of speculation upon history conjured up as a diabolic panorama of all the kingdoms of the

---

Scriptural language appropriate to the religious point of view which is supposed to be taken. Such language is often more or less metaphorical; but, as we have seen in our discussion of Anthropology, it is quite reconcilable with scientific facts and theories as to the physical origin and moral evolution of the human race.

world, it saw the visage of error so strangely blended with a semblance of truth; it saw Jehovah but as an Israelitish Jupiter, Moses but as a Hebrew Solon, Jesus as but a Jewish Socrates, without miracle and without deity. These superficial resemblances are only such as denote a counterfeit, and they are accompanied with dissimilarities which indicate the absence of the genuine. Confessedly without any national art, the corrective of poetical absurdity, the Jewish religion was not only devoid of any Brahminical monsters, not only devoid of any such popular conceptions, but it was possessed of religious symbols infinitely more consistent than those of the fanciful Greeks. Confessedly without science or philosophy, its sacred books contained doctrines which the most profound metaphysics of other nations never equalled, and records of facts without which all other history falls into chaos. The pure supernaturalism of the Hebrews and its mythical correspondent were not both "the product of a certain intellectual direction of society." The latter was a product of Satan, wrought out of the corrupt material of human nature; the other was a product of Divine Providence wrought in spite of that material.

### *The Biblical Scheme of Human Redemption.*

But the Bible furnishes something more than a mere explanation of the great conspicuous facts of human history. It does something more than account for the present moral and intellectual condition of the divided race of mankind. It contains also a revelation of that "mystery which from the beginning of the world has been hid in God, who created all things by Jesus Christ, to the intent that now unto the principalities and powers in heavenly places might be made known by the Church His manifold wisdom according to the eternal purpose which He purposed in Christ Jesus our Lord." To that eternal purpose each of the four universal facts of history bears intelligible relation. The first fact, the apostasy, though antecedent to all history, was that which determined its whole subsequent course and aspect. What the career and destiny of man might have been in his pristine state is, of course, a purely hypothetical question. What they are, however, in consequence of the apostasy the Scriptures clearly reveal to us—a vast judgment to end in mercy and a long process of restoration through divine love. Apart from the personal significance of Christ crucified to the individual, which is excluded from our present inquiries, that greatest event of all time had also a wider social significance, a relation to the whole race in all its eras. It was that which made its end consistent with its beginning—the sustaining keystone in that arch of divine purpose spanning the gulf of time from the Apostasy to the Restoration, from the Creation to the Judgment.

The course of Divine Providence throughout history does not therefore present itself to us as a series of occasional gracious interferences in the life of an abandoned race, nor yet as a mere systematic display of vindictive justice, but as a consistent whole, connected in its outline and details with the work of human redemption—as the gradual fulfilment of that promise blended with the primal curse in Paradise. Why its fulfilment should have been so protracted, can only be explained by a scriptural view of the divine justice and mercy, though even here lowly conjecture might not be wholly at fault. Why the particular plan devised for its accomplishment should have been selected, is not our concern, but that plan as revealed to us in the Bible, and as realized in history, we may reverently inspect for the encouragement of our faith. Its outline is indicated by the three remaining facts which have been enumerated, viz., The division of the fallen race into tribes and nations, their subsequent career through various stages of civilization, and their appearance under diverse religious systems. These are existing historical problems which originated in the earlier eras of time. They receive their solution in its later eras. They are intimately related to the scheme of human redemption during the pre-Christian period and during the post-Christian period.

Here let the eye assist the mind by means of a tabular view of the chronological eras, the divine dispensations, and the social stages embraced in the vast scheme of human redemption.

| *Chronological Eras.* | *Divine Dispensations.* | *Social Stages.* |
|---|---|---|
| The Pre-Diluvian. | Justice (J). | Experiment. |
| The Pre-Christian. | Forbearance (J-M). | Preparation. |
| The Christian. | Mercy (M-J). | Appropriation |
| The Millennial. | Love (M). | Fulfilment. |

Without seeking numerical accuracy we may divide the Biblical history into four great eras: the pre-diluvian era, extending from the Apostasy to the Deluge; the pre-Christian era, extending from the Deluge to the Incarnation; the Christian era, extending from the Incarnation to the Millennium; the Millennial era, extending from the Millennium to the Judgment. As Divine Providence in human history displays the attributes of Justice and Mercy, there are four dispensations corresponding to the four eras: a dispensation of absolute Justice without Mercy; a dispensation of Justice with increasing Mercy; a dispensation of Mercy with decreasing Justice; a dispensation of absolute Mercy or Love. And since human society has been constituted with capacities for religion, politics, science, and art, in a word for civilization, there are four social stages corresponding to the four divine dispensations: a stage of experiment ending in failure; a stage of preparation for Christianity; a stage of appropriation of Christianity; and a stage of fulfilment in a perfected Christian civilization.

The pre-diluvian civilization is depicted briefly in the sacred narrative as an abortive experiment. Glimpses are afforded us of the origin of the arts, of religions, and of cities. A few historic figures are named, flitting like colossal phantasms across the scene, and then it closes in darkness. The first murder has borne its fruits. The intermarriage of the descendants of Seth and Cain, the children of God with the children of men, has issued in a giant progeny of sin and debauchery, requiring the cleaning baptism of the deluge. "And God looked upon the earth, and behold, it was corrupt, for all flesh had corrupted His way upon the earth. And God said unto Noah, the end of all flesh is come before me; for the earth is filled with violence through them; and behold, I will destroy them with the earth."

During the pre-Christian era, however, the world was made ready for the present Christian era by means of divine dispensations and through social stages of culture, all having a preparatory relation to the Christian Religion.

### The Pre-Christian Dispersion of Nations.

The primitive separation of mankind during the pre-Christian period was such a preparatory dispensation. Like many other divine dispensations, it had indeed a proximate as well as a prospective design. Proximately in its relation to the men of that age, it was a mixed mercy and judgment, both a just punishment of their impiety and the frustration of a demoniacal intent of renewing the primeval disorder. Prospectively, in its relation to Christianity and to future ages, it was an indication of what would thereafter be the mode of the divine conduct of the race. To speak in the style of the Scripture narrative itself, it was the result of that compassionate soliloquy uttered over the new-born earth after the frustrated experiment of the antediluvian world: "And the Lord said in His heart, I will not any more curse the earth for man's sake." It was the scheme adopted by infinite wisdom in this exigency. The ungodly portion of the race was not again to be destroyed, nor was the heterogeneous mass as a united body to be elevated to the reception of the promised blessings. It was to be separated, sundered, and its several portions to pass through a vast historical ordeal, ultimately receiving the promised blessings, but only after long preparations, by fragments, and during successive periods of probation. The divided races and nations were still to be detained in their tedious banishment under a providence of divine mercy and judgment, by their own mutual collisions chastising and being chastised. Jehovah was to select one of them which by a supernatural course of means and processes He should employ as an instrument for perfecting that form of saving truth which He designed should be the ultimate possession of all. With the others He was to deal contemporaneously after His ordinary methods; so adjusting them as to territory, condition, and period that they should subsequently appear at the right historical juncture prepared for the then impending task.

### The Pre-Christian Civilizations.

The forms of civilization developed by the dispersed nations during the pre-Christian period were also a Providential preparation for Christianity. To afford an intellectual preparation for Christianity might be regarded as the particular work assigned to the Gentile world, to that portion of it which was not reserved in a barbaric and savage state with other and more remote designs. The Jewish nation in contradistinction does not seem to have inherited any dowry from the primitive civilization or to have formed any national civilization of its own. In its passage from Sinai to Zion it was too busy with sterner tasks to rear temples and frame philosophies. It was given to it to lay the foundations of that imperishable structure into which all the gathered nations were to bring their glory and honor. For the completion of that structure, however, for the reception and diffusion of Christianity the Jewish people were disqualified both by their inveterate religious beliefs and by their national vanity. Whilst, therefore, it was a just judgment which wrested from them their ancient heritage of divine truth, it was an expedient of infinite wisdom which had prepared an adequate Gentile civilization for the emergency—which had elevated certain Gentile nations to such an intellectual condition as had already in its reaction effected the destruction of much superstition and error and at the same time prepared the world for the pure spiritual system now entering upon its mission of mercy.

### The Pre-Christian Religions.

The growth of false religion during the pre-Christian period was also prospective in its bearing upon Christianity. Whilst the Jews under a supernatural economy were slowly elaborating that true religion which was yet to be the inheritance of the whole world, other contemporaneous nations, possessing higher civilization, indeed, but struggling against infernal might, only exhibited abortive attempts, strewing the pathway of time with the monuments of their baffled strength—melancholy failures over which the angelic spectators of human history might bend with shadowing wings in compassion and awe. These were the incidental but necessary aggravations of their mysterious judgment, the wild and piteous bewilderment of the instincts of a fallen humanity struggling bravely forth for its lost Creator if haply it might feel after Him and find Him. To every age, to every people were propounded the same dread problems which within the sphere of revelation were in course of slow solution, the same consciousness of guilt, the same longing for divine help, the same fearful looking for of judgment. Each has striven with these problems in its own way and left them unsolved; each has had its own method of shrouding their fearful import, its art to give them some practical expression in the myth and the legend, or some architectural embodiment in the temple and the tomb, its philosophy to weave them into some airy and thoughtful metaphysics behind the grosser popular faith, its government to subordinate them to some species of political idolatry.

At the head of the nations, hoary with wisdom, appeared Egypt, the first of them called to the task, but overpowered and yielding in patient agony beneath it. The priest of the Nile as he wandered amidst avenues of frowning sphinxes felt the burden of mysteries which puzzled the patient man of Uz and his comforters. But what diverse solutions are left us as recorded in the inspired Hebrew poem and as wrought in the Egyptian tomb. In the one perplexity at the anomalies of Providence is relieved by some faint hope of an ultimate adjustment, disgust with life ennobled and sanctified, and awe of death dispelled by some dim prospect of after glories. In the other these feelings having no such support upon which to reach forth and fasten, ineffectually baffled on all sides, seem to have quietly exhausted themselves in a mighty despair. Forests of colossal statues, solemn groups of gigantic sphinxes, bewildered the awed worshipper in that dark religion, each looking down upon him as the stern keeper of the riddles which it was not for him to solve. The abodes of the dead received the architectural glories belonging to the palaces of the living.

From Egypt the same problems in the course of Providence passed to Greece, and were in like manner left unsolved in her philosophy as well as in her mythology. The goal of all her elaborate speculation was an altar to the Unknown God which the apostle to the Gentiles found in the midst of her temples and statues. The same problems as transmitted in Roman civilization were treated as insoluble with only a more practical form of scepticism. When Jesus presented Himself as an incarnation of truth, the Roman governor, Pilate, could only turn away with the incredulous sneer—What is truth? And after the Roman arms had been carried triumphantly throughout the known world, the mythical gods of the provinces were stored in the Pantheon as mere trophies of Cæsar.

### *Unconscious Prophecies of Paganism.*

Paganism, however, besides being thus incidentally a melancholy experiment and failure, was also in its prospective bearing upon Christianity a vast unconscious prophecy. Built upon the same essential wants in human nature, possessed perhaps of some heritage of the primitive revelation, it could not be entirely without confused presentiments, instinctive pre-assurances of the coming glory. Truth was there, traditional and innate and prophetic, though in putrefaction and hideous caricature. It gleamed in brilliant distortion through the most splendid mythologies, it lay in spectral fragments beneath the darkest superstitions. In spite of fiendish malice the Jehovah of the Jews was in some way the God of the Gentiles. The kingly Messiah of the chosen people was still the desire of the nations, and that Providence which illumined its future with His prophetic image did not fail to project some faint halo of it over the deeper gloom of theirs. They, too, in a distorted form had their religious symbolism, their imagined revelations from Deity by priest and oracle, their monstrous avatars, their writhing Prometheus, their sacrifices, animal and human—instincts perverted by infernal satire as they reached helplessly forth toward Golgotha and Calvary. They were the satanic distortions of God's image as reflected in man yet to be restored to unity in the perfect humanity of his divine son, the anomalies of a dispensation of judgment yet to be solved by a dispensation of grace. Regarded as contemporaneous with Christianity emerging from the twilight of her own types and symbols, they were the huge golden clouds which begirt the rising orb as it went up through a world of darkness to its meridian splendor. Then all types and symbols were to vanish. Then while heathenism sat exhausted with the riddle of the world unsolved, in unconscious expectation of its solution, while philosophy was already in the melancholy twilight yearning for the day-spring,

> "Holy with power
> He on the thought-benighted sceptic beamed,
> Manifest Godhead, melting into day
> What floating mists of dark idolatry
> Broke and misshaped the Omnipresent Sire."

### The Epoch of the Incarnation.

At this central epoch of history its whole aspect in the eyes of witnessing principalities and powers may be said to have changed. Infinite love had stooped into the abyss of time and reconciled the world to God. God had so loved the world that He gave His only begotten Son that the world might have everlasting life. And now heathenism though still so widespread, civilization though still feeble, the nations though still severed and hostile, humanity though still corrupt, and nature though still disordered, sustained a different relation to the Divine reconciler, the Father as represented by the Son. The enigmatical prophecy of past providence was to evolve its slow fulfilment in the providence of the future. That vast hidden current of divine purpose, upon which the scattered race had so long floated in divergence from the origin of history, now began its slow convergence toward the issue of history. The ages of experiment and preparation with reference to Christianity were to be succeeded by the ages of appropriation and realization.

This, too, was to be a tardy and gradational process, not by a simultaneous movement of the body of mankind, but in predestined portions, through successive stages and during long eras. The judgment of the nations was not yet complete, nor was the whole world ready for mercy. Christianity herself was not yet prepared for her ultimate work of social as well as individual regeneration. She had come forth from Judea a fragmentary mass of doctrines and institutions, needing both internal consolidation and external naturalization. These two objects were to be attained both contemporaneously and successively, the one helping forward the other.

### External History of Christianity.

As to the external naturalization of Christianity among the nations, this object could not be fully attained by the first Gentile civilization which she appropriated. It was largely composed of the rubbish of ancient error, and sank beneath her more massive spiritual forces. The admixture of a sterner ingredient was needed in order that civilization might be fitted to receive Christianity. "He that hath made of one blood all nations of men to dwell on all the face of the earth, and hath determined the times afore appointed and the bounds of their habitation," from the primeval summits of history had foreseen the exigency and prepared the requisite expedient. It was then, with the fall of the Roman Empire, that the hardy nomadic portion of mankind in northern Europe, so long reserved in a savage state, casting off after a brief struggle its cumbrous mythology as but the extravagant dreams of its youth and infancy, was moved by a divine impulse to invade southern Europe and became the rightful heir of that Grecian and Roman civilization under a Christian form which might else have languished in imbecility and decay.

Let it be here observed, in passing, how wonderfully the sovereign Father of mankind conducts a system of specific dispensation among the various tribes and kindreds which compose His human family. We have seen His great primitive act of territorial adjustment in regard to the whole race at the outset of its history. At that early period He is represented as having sundered the race into different nations and scattered them abroad over the world, in plain fulfilment of His design that they should dwell on all the face of the earth. The process of their division and dispersion is described as due to miraculous dispensations. He had confounded their language at the Tower of Babel, and by this expedient at once frustrated their tendency to concentrate and sent them forth under the impulse of a migratory habit which adheres to them for ages, until such time as the earth shall have been sufficiently covered with population. But this species of divine supervision did not cease with the great primitive act of territorial adjustment. As He dealt at the outset with the race as a whole, so did He thenceforward continue to deal with its several portions during all their subsequent dispersion and progress. He conducted each to its destined locality and enclosed it within its own physical environment. He determined the bounds of their habitation. With respect to one particular nation, the chosen people, He had carried out this process of colonization in a miraculous manner. He had violently extricated them from their Egyptian bondage; designated prophetically the land which they were to inhabit; conducted them thither by a pillar of cloud and fire; extirpated the original owners of the soil and established them in its secure and permanent possession.

### History of American Christianity.

In like manner the dispensations of Divine Providence toward the American people indicate the same prescience. It appears in the circumstances attending their settlement upon this continent. The remaining hemisphere of the world was discovered at the time appointed and ordered as the bounds of their habitation. It may be regarded as a pre-destined theatre for the later acts of history. It emerges into the view of mankind, if not with the same supernatural aspect as the miraculous land of promise, yet with equally marvellous signs of Divine Providence. No train of direful plagues opened the way for the liberation of the American colonists like those which loosened the fetters of Egyptian bondage. No celestial prodigy heralded their passage through the wide waste of waters like that which guided the emigrating tribes of Israel through the wilderness— no extraordinary interpositions attended the removal of the savage tribes of North America such as attended the extermination of the Canaanitish aborigines. Yet the facts which have resulted are as remarkable as if they had been thus miraculously produced. The fugitives from European oppression enter a domain which has evidently been held in reserve for their use, and the primitive inhabitants vanishing before their superior prowess, leave them in undisturbed possession. Nowhere else in modern history do we find the Ruler of nations conducting a people to a territory which has not been already pre-occupied for some important purpose, and where the pre-occupants have not at length settled down into joint and peaceable possession with their conquerers and finally given birth to an amalgamated civilization.

As Christian Europe became the heir of Greek and Roman culture, so Christian America has become the heir of Christian Europe. By such far-reaching and world-wide dispensations has Divine Providence led to the external establishment of Christianity among the nations of the modern world.

### *The Internal History of Christianity.*

Meanwhile the other preliminary mentioned, the internal consolidation of Christianity as a doctrinal system, she was destined to attain through a long refining ordeal of persecution and dissension. Her faith and worship were to come to her as the distilled issue of the errors of thousands of decayed systems. But as she emerged from that ordeal into purity of doctrine and form at the Reformation, she gave release to the intellectual and political powers so long joined to her in unnatural bondage. They started at once into rapid and flourishing growth, so that now she appears upon the broad stage of the world in a young and vigorous civilization, astir with vast preparations for her final task. That task is the bestowment of salvation upon the rest of the Gentiles according to primeval promise. The ancient realm of heathenism, where the god of this world has so long reigned in gloomy grandeur, is now for the first time appearing upon the arena of general history, though still covered with the outworn myths and superstitions which linger as the morning clouds of that Sun of Righteousness so far above them and beyond them. The religious aspect of our era presents the two phases of Christianity and heathenism, the one possessed of all the moral, intellectual, and political forces of the world, the other superannuated, decaying, and powerless. All mankind are at length visibly marshalled as if for the triumph of Christianity, presenting a void of practical atheism through which it may pass unobstructed, as in Africa, or a mass of ancient superstitions already yielding to its pressure, as in western and southern Asia, or a corrupt Christianity still in the ordeal of persecution, as in eastern Asia, or within the bounds of Christendom held in check by a Protestant civilization, as in Europe and

America. In other words, the lines of general history, from its middle epoch, seem to be converging toward a solution of the first of its primitive problems. In the approaching destruction of idolatry and superstition, Christianity as the one absolute and universal religion seems marching towards its triumph over all false religions, resuming their truths while it rejects their errors, according to scriptural promise.

### *The Prospects of Christian Civilization.*

But the removal of religious error from the world will also affect, as well during its process as at its issue, the solution of the next problem of general history—the destination of the different civilizations of mankind. Viewed as disconnected from Christianity, civilization is itself an embodiment of interests which intimately concern her in her earthly state as organized in the Church. It was that pure adjunct to heathenism which she inherited from it and by which she shall yet overcome and possess it. During the earlier Christian eras she suffered the accompanying civilization to have a false unhallowed alliance; worship was resolved into mere art; revelation was drawn as a veil of superstitious reverence over the eye of science; the State was made the powerless instrument of the Church; but now in the present era these several earthly powers are in a state of greater or less indifference and antagonism. The question arises, is this to be the intellectual and political condition of the world when Christianity has her destined prevalence? Is art always to be but a prostitution of beauty to error and superstition? Is science still to widen the gulf between the revelations of the Scriptures and the revelations of nature? Is geology ever to wander like a busy gnome exulting over the mistakes of Genesis? Is biology to destroy the divine image in man and reduce him to the image of an ape? Is philosophy to swallow up the divine knowledge in her speculative cosmogonies and theogonies or leave it to vanish in sheer nescience? Is the State always to protect and tolerate the Church? Is government to be but a necessary barrier against invasion? Are the nations to exhaust their resources in a system of costly armaments and waste them in destructive warfare? In a word, is all civilization to continue but a mighty assemblage of misdirected powers?—or rather may we not say that all these are only the rightful ministers and co-workers of Christianity, emancipated indeed from her present control, yet still held in safe abeyance and moving with perverted potency within the lesser sphere of which her own grander sphere is but inclusive. Shall she not yet reappropriate them and transfuse them with her own spirit? May we not look for the time, however distant, when art shall be resolved into worship; when this widening gulf between science and revelation shall be bridged over by increasing knowledge and faith; when the State shall be merged and lost in the Church, and the nations no longer held in antagonism of mutual repulsion shall be tranquillized by a reign of universal love and peace; when the pure socialism of the early Christians shall no more be presented only in hideous caricature, and that diffuse philanthropy, which is now but an aimless instinct, shall be elevated into a feeling definite and self-knowing, clothed with intelligence and beauty? Indeed, can we not already discern vast social tendencies which must sooner or later issue in the triumph of a Christian science over error, of a Christian art over nature, of a Christian state over slavery, of a Christian civilization over heathen barbarism throughout the earth?

### *The Predicted Triumph of Christianity.*

The transition of prophecy into history, it may be, is miraculous only in prospect. We look forward to the Second Advent of Christ, the Millennial Reign of Peace, and the Judgment of the World as a pageant of rapidly succeeding events, depicted upon the prophetic canvas as

" ——foreshortened in the tract of time."

But the regeneration of mankind, like the creation of the world, may be a long evolutionary process through successive stages and periods of civilization. Be this as it may, call it a pageant or a process, or a process issuing in a pageant, the time must come when the goal of history shall be reached in the universal triumph of Christ as the Saviour of the World.

# PART SECOND.

## SCIENTIFIC EVIDENCES OF RELIGION.

# CHAPTER I.

## THE LOGICAL NATURE OF THE SCIENTIFIC EVIDENCE.

AFTER the lapse of nineteen centuries the Christian religion is again on the defensive. In the present instance it has been driven to its defences by an assault more desperate than any it has ever before sustained. It is an assault made falsely in the name of Science and with scientific weapons. The assailants have arrayed against it those bodies of human knowledge which are most certain in their nature and popular in their impression. Astronomy, they tell us, now declares no other glory in the heavens than that of Newton, Laplace, and other discoverers of their laws. Geology has shown us that the earth was not created in six days, but has been self-evolved through unmeasured time. Anthropology is teaching us that man was not made in the image of God, but emerged in the likeness of an ape. The other, higher sciences, psychology, sociology, comparative religion, they assure us, are taking a like offensive bearing against the ethical and religious teaching of the Bible. And to all these successive attacks, it is claimed that the Christian religion has offered but a feeble and ineffectual resistance; that it has hitherto retreated before every advance of science; that its miraculous evidences have already been reduced to mere myths and legends; that its most essential doctrines are being steadily undermined by scientific research; and that it is only a question of time when it shall be left without any defence and without anything worth defending.

*Present Scientific Crisis.*

At such a crisis it would be idle to disguise the fact that the defenders of the Faith are not presenting an unbroken front to its assailants. The line of defence may be firm at the centre, but at the extremes it is unequal. At the extreme left appears the new school of biblical critics, conceding, step by step, the ground invaded in the name of science. For the avowed interest of Christian truth they are admitting that the Bible teaches false astronomy, false geology, false anthropology, even defective ethics and theology, and now that all that remains to be contended for in Holy Scripture is a certain essential faith to be somehow distilled from its errors by means of learned criticism, or perhaps new dogmatic definitions by the Church. At the extreme right remains the elder school of biblical students, denouncing such concession as weakness or treachery. Taking their stand on the Canonical Scriptures with the doctrine of plenary inspiration they are insisting that the teaching of the Bible is to be held true in astronomy, in geology, in anthropology, no less than in ethics and theology, and that the whole book, without a show of compromise, must be maintained as containing and being the very Word of God written. Meanwhile, those who stand at the centre between these extremes, can see that, if the right wing has been too rashly advanced, yet the left wing has already wavered and broken away, with banners trailing in the dust, amid the exultation and derision of their foes and the indignation and dismay of their friends.

### Duty of United Defence.

Now while it is our duty to repel all assailants of revealed religion, it is also plainly our duty, as far as possible, to make common cause with all its defenders. We should endeavor to stand with and stand by even those apologetes who may seem to us mistaken or misguided. If we may, if we can, we should rally them back to positions which perhaps they have too hastily deserted. For the sake of that Book which is the source of our common Christianity and civilization, and for the sake of that Church which originally produced it and has faithfully kept it through the ages and triumphantly borne it as a standard never lowered before any foe, we cannot but beg them to keep in line as true defenders and not as mere critics of the Word of God. To this end, speaking for myself, I would hope to complement their opinions instead of antagonizing them, and seek to conserve all that is just and sound in their authorities and methods. If they have read with admiration Dr. Draper's "History of the Conflict between Science and Religion," I would remind them that there is another counterpart history, which Dr. Draper did not write, of that true religion and true science, between which there never has been and never can be any conflict. If they have been charmed with the scholarly pages of Dr. Andrew White's "Warfare of Science with Theology," I would remind them that Dr. White does not show that science has ever waged warfare with revealed religion, but only with some theological dogma or tenet which has usurped the authority of revelation or invaded the sphere of science. If they have followed our learned brother Dr. Briggs in his luminous "Biblical Studies" so far as to look for scientific errors in the Bible, I would remind them that Dr. Briggs himself has found some scientific truths in the Bible, and that it is not even thinkable that its divine Author could have revealed anything contrary to the most advanced human science. In a word, if they are beginning to fear that modern science casts some doubt or discredit upon the traditional Christian Evidences, as they figure in our standard treatises, I would invite them to consider another class of evidences, which modern science itself is affording, and which, in the strictest sense, deserves to be called pre-eminently the Scientific Evidences of Revealed Religion.

### The New Scientific Evidence.

The general evidences of Revealed Religion date from its very origin, and have been accumulating for thousands of years. Before the Christian era, they served practically to distinguish the true revealed religion from the false natural religions of the ancient world. Since the Christian era, after coming in contact with Gentile culture, they have assumed logical form as a growing body of truth, handed down from generation to generation through nearly twenty centuries of time. It will be found that each age or critical period of civilization has had some peculiar conflict with Christianity, and as the result some issuing contribution to its evidences. Its successive conflicts—first with Judaism in the life of our Lord; then with Paganism in the age of the Apostles; then with philosophy in the age of the Church fathers; then with Mohammedanism in the age of the schoolmen; then with Italian naturalism, English deism, French atheism, and German rationalism since the age of the Reformers—have yielded vast masses of evidence, much of which is stowed away in its apologetic literature as the logical trophies of its conquering march through the centuries. In like manner in this pre-eminently scientific age we are involved in a seeming conflict between Science and the Bible, with its issuing contribution of Scientific Evidence.

The origin of the Scientific Evidence, as we know it, dates from the time of the Reformation, which included a revival of Science as well as of Religion. It is true that in the first Christian age there were some prelusive strifes between Greek philosophy and the theology of the Church fathers, but the issue was a mere conquered peace which was false and premature. It is true, also, that in the middle ages a few enlightened schoolmen asserted the rights of free scientific inquiry, but their efforts seemed only to strengthen an ecclesiastical and dogmatic bondage which was becoming intolerable. It was not until the Reformation had liberated both religion and science that they both sprang at once into new relations, sometimes hostile, sometimes indifferent, but often friendly and fruitful. Pre-eminent among the forerunners and leaders of the last named harmonizing movement, stands the great apologete, Bishop Butler. In a former chapter I claimed for Bishop Butler the singular merit of having contributed to the General Evidence of Revealed Religion the beginnings of that Scientific Evidence which is peculiar to our epoch. It was shown that he made this contribution by conceiving religious problems in a thoroughly scientific spirit; by applying to them the scientific method known as the inductive logic; by laying a logical foundation for the harmony of Science and revelation in the analogy of nature and religion; by enunciating principles applicable in the Scientific interpretation of the Bible; by giving prescient hints of a coming agreement of the Bible with Science and consequent growing proof of Christianity; and by building up, albeit unconsciously, a substantial part of the philosophic structure of Science itself. Without renewing these discussions I pass at once to our next topic, the logical nature of the Scientific Evidence.

### Its Logical Premises.

As all reasonable evidence involves facts or principles upon which it is based and from which it proceeds, we need to define clearly, if but briefly, the premises of Christian Evidence in general, but especially the evidence before us. In the first place, since there could be no revelation without a God to reveal, we must assume, not indeed as unproved, but as at least provable, some theistic theory of the world as affording the conditions of intelligent communication between the absolute reason of God and the finite reason of man. The sceptical philosopher who regards Jehovah as a mere mythical personage, like Jupiter, or a bare abstraction termed the Unknowable, would simply make a revelation metaphysically impossible or logically inconceivable. But, as a matter of fact, nearly all schools of thinkers, even some agnostics, allow a theory of absolute being, more or less consistent with the idea of revelation. Theism in some form underlies the best thought and belief of mankind, and in starting with theism we take ground common alike to philosophy and religion.

Besides this universal tenet, we must still further assume, as in the process of proof, the existence of a divine revelation in the Holy Scriptures. The evidence of this revelation, as we have said, has been accumulating for ages until now it amounts to the highest probability in many minds, and in some minds to moral certainty itself. It has been tested by the searching criticism of each successive generation; and it equals the best-reasoned science in the kind if not in the degree of its certitude. The burden of disproving it rests upon the objector to it. If it is to be hereafter called in question at every step of this inquiry, we shall only be ever returning upon our own path and make little or no progress toward any good result. Rather let it be our aim to advance with and beyond the Miraculous, Prophetical, and Historical evidences of former ages, to the new Scientific evidence of our own day.

As a third premise, it is quite logical to assume the integrity of the canonical Scriptures as containing divine revelation in distinction from all other sacred writings. It is more than twenty centuries since the Old Testament Canon was closed, and about fifteen centuries since the completion of the New Testament Canon. During all that time the consent of Christendom in them both has been practically unanimous. The genuineness of the sacred books would seem fairly presumable. While free discussions of the canonicity of each book may still be allowable and of the highest importance among expert scholars and divines, who are specially fitted and called to purge the Canon from spurious ingredients, yet if we admit them rashly and crudely into our popular lectures and treatises we shall only be perpetually tearing up the foundations upon which we are trying to build. As an oriental scholar, you may endeavor to trace all the sacred books of the East, including the Bible, to a primitive tradition or universal revelation, but it is still a fact that the maxims of Confucius or the Zend-Avesta were not included within the Canon. As a Church antiquarian, you may value highly the apocryphal and patristic writings which were discarded after full trial; but the Book of Tobit or the Epistle of Barnabas has not been restored to the Canon. As a Christian thinker, you may believe that devout genius differs only in degree from divine inspiration; but the Imitation of Christ or the Paradise Lost has not yet been exalted into the Canon. As a Biblical critic, you may doubt the inspiration of some of the Sacred Books, but the Song of Solomon or the Epistle of Saint James has not been ruled out of the Canon. Whatever may be your private opinions on such points, yet as a loyal churchman, to say the least, you will accept the Canon as it stands and find in it the written Word of God. Some things may be considered as settled by the wisdom of the Christian ages and the general consent of the Catholic Church.

### *Popular Fallacies.*

After thus defining the premises of the new Evidence as including theism, a revelation, and the Canon, it becomes important next to repel certain fallacies which assail it at the present time and may thwart its direct and full effect upon the mind. These fallacies should be challenged at the threshold, not, as I have said, with the view of offending any apologists who may practice them, but simply to clear away all rubbish from the common ground where we are to stand together in defence of the Faith. I shall state them in the popular form under which they have become current.

The first fallacy relates to the aim and scope of revelation. It is expressed in the dictum, "The Bible was designed to teach nothing but religion and morals." This is a specious sophism. That the Scriptures principally teach matters of faith and duty lying within the realm of theology is obvious enough; but it does not follow that they may not also, incidentally and secondarily, teach some other matters lying within the realm of other sciences. The fallacy is false in its premise, false in its process, and false in its product.

### The Bible as Prejudged.

Its premise is a masked form of rationalistic prejudgment. Bishop Butler, while ever commending reason as our only faculty for judging anything, even revelation itself, is careful to make reason a critic only of the evidences of revelation, not of its contents; and he has a masterly chapter on "Our incapacity of judging what were to be expected in a Revelation." In the nature of the case, the aims and topics of any divine communication lie beyond the reach of human faculties. A Revelation, in any proper sense of the word, implies our previous ignorance of its whole purpose and purport. If we could know *a priori* what the Bible should teach us and how it should teach us, we should need no Bible at all, and we might soon prove that the one we have is not worth having if we approach it in this spirit. Such prejudgment, moreover, may become not merely irreverent, but irrational. It is as unphilosophical to prejudge the phenomena of Scripture as the phenomena of Nature; to prescribe the course of revelation as the course of science. Experience has shown, as Butler proves, that in either case we are liable to infinite mistakes; and especially in the latter case, that we could not even furnish a good inventory of the wants which a revelation should supply. Men have absurdly hoped to find in the Bible exact rules of life and business, full political codes, elaborate systems of divinity, precise information concerning the future life, a panacea for bodily ills, a talisman against harm, a fortune-book to conjure with, in short almost anything that it does not contain. And we are quite as likely to preclude from it what it does contain. It is but a truism to say that the Bible was designed to teach simply what it is found to teach. And if it is found to teach geological truth in the first chapter of Genesis, as well as theological truth in the first chapter of St. John, we can only infer that it was designed to teach such truth in each instance. In a word, the design and full purport of Holy Scripture are not the proper problems of Introductory Criticism, but are simply questions of devout Exegesis; and the very last questions rather than the first. Not until we have thoroughly studied the Bible in all its actual contents and possible relations can we affirm that it was never designed to teach scientific as well as religious facts and truths.

### The Bible as Mutilated.

But the sophism before us is as fallacious in its procedure as in its premise. Sometimes, instead of starting as a prejudgment, it claims to have been a sort of generalization on the face of the Bible, to the effect that it is manifestly a book of religion and morals, and therefore teaches nothing else. Very soon, however, this mere crude generalization becomes a foregone conclusion, to which all the contents of Scripture are thenceforth to be adjusted. As superficial investigators will choose the facts of Nature, so they will choose the texts of Scripture, to suit their favorite hypothesis, while ignoring or distorting all the rest. And the worst of the mistake is, that the hypothesis often contains a large amount of truth with its error, and explains many of the relevant facts, though not all of them. In this way, good men, from the best motives, in order to exalt the religious teaching of the Bible, will wholly neglect or reject its physical teaching as connected therewith. Selecting certain portions of Scripture supposed to be purely ethical and theological in their purport, they will disparage all remaining portions as unimportant or quite worthless, because astronomical, geological, or historical in their bearing. And having thus exscinded scientific truths, they will go on to mutilate religious truths, culling proof texts around their favorite tenets, Calvinistic or Arminian, Baptist or Methodist, Presbyterian or Episcopalian, Protestant or Catholic, until the only divine standard of unity is made a source of endless dissension throughout Christendom.

> "This is the Book where each his dogma seeks,
> And this the Book where each his dogma finds."

In short, the fallacy before us, as applied in the study of the Bible, tends to narrow its scope even as a book of religion and morals.

### The Bible as Ignored.

A mutilated Bible can only bring cumulative evils in its train. It is not strange therefore that reasoning so false in its premise and in its process should be also false in its product. Not only are the Holy Scriptures marred and wrested by its unscientific treatment of their phenomena; but it engenders a growing breach between divine knowledge and human knowledge, with an issuing conflict of opinions and interests in every region of civilization. History shows us that if we may err by seeking too much in the Bible, we may also err by finding too little in it. Time was when the former error prevailed. Revelation was claimed as the ancient fountain of all knowledge both in Pagan and in Christian philosophy. The whole cyclopædia of the natural sciences was derived from Genesis, the Book of Job, and the Psalms, with their so-called Mosaical Mathematics, Scripture Geology, Biblical Physics, Sacred Zoology, and all the rest. And by consequence religion itself became allied with superstition and conceit, while science was enslaved and philosophy degraded. But ever since the Reformation we have been reacting toward the other extreme of finding too little in the Bible. The springs of all philosophy are now sought outside of revelation in the mere human reason alone. Great Christian thinkers in our day no longer feel their intellectual need of a revelation in framing their theories of knowledge and systems of science as they may still feel their spiritual need of it in moulding their faith and practice. Imagine such thinkers standing with St. Paul before the Athenian altar to the Unknown God! Then, imagine his trenchant challenge, "Whom ye ignorantly worship, him declare I unto you!"

And the result is that the natural sciences are now openly detached from Holy Scripture, if not arrayed against it, as no longer consistent with its teachings. It is to be held as important in its theology and ethics, but worthless in its astronomy, geology, and physics. Even the higher psychical sciences are beginning to assert a like independence in the form of a naturalistic ethic, and a comparative theology or science of religions divested of miracle and prophecy and discharged of all Scriptural ideas. Let the breach go on, and the whole circle of the sciences will break into mere splendid fragments of knowledge, philosophy will sink into hopeless nescience and unbelief, and the discredited Bible will become the jest of the pulpit as well as of the club and the newspaper; no better than was the derided oracle, or augury, amid the decaying culture of Greece and Rome.

### The True Scope of Revelation.

It is plain that such evils can be checked only by taking a new point of departure and changing the entire mode of procedure; by approaching Holy Scripture as containing an attested and accepted revelation; by submitting our human reason to the dictates of the divine reason in the divine Word, with at least as much docility, patience, and candor as we practise in a scientific inquiry in the realm of Nature; by laying aside all prepossessions as to its aims and uses, and keeping ourselves within its own divinely prescribed limits; and there awaiting a full inductive investigation of its contents. Such an investigation will show that, while the Bible mainly traverses the realm of the mental and moral sciences with its revelations, yet it also extends into the realm of the natural sciences, and includes more or less of their ground and material within the scope of its teaching. It thus includes astronomy in connection with its revealed doctrine of creation and the angels; geology in connection with its revealed doctrine of the Sabbath and of the old and the new earth; anthropology in connection with its revealed doctrine of the First and the Second Adam; psychology in connection with its revealed doctrine of regeneration and resurrection; sociology in connection with its revealed doctrine of Christian brotherhood and the Church; and the science of comparative religion in connection with its most peculiar doctrines, the incarnation, the trinity, and the atonement. There is, in fact, no science which is not more or less included within the scope of revelation as found in the Scriptures.

### *Alleged Scientific Errors.*

Another popular fallacy relates to the content of revelation. We now hear it said on all sides, "The Bible contains scientific errors in distinction from its religious truths." The dictum, as often joined to the before-mentioned fallacy, becomes mere reasoning in a circle and begging of the question. At one time it is assumed, as a sort of axiom, that the Bible was not designed to teach scientific truth, and thence inferred that its scientific teaching is erroneous. At another time it is assumed, as a matter of fact, that its scientific teaching is erroneous, and thence inferred that it was never designed to teach scientific truth. And so with each turn of the circle the fallacy grows, that the Bible contains scientific errors. We can only escape from the vicious circle by thoroughly testing its covert assumptions.*

### *A Questionable Theory.*

At the first glance, it will be seen that it is based upon a questionable theory of inspiration. It assumes that the divine guidance of the sacred writers was limited and variable, so limited as to make them inerrant only in religious matters, but in all other matters, especially scientific matters, to leave them exposed to their own erring faculties and to the errors of the unscientific ages in which they lived and wrote. This theory of inspiration is held by reverent minds from the best motives. It would loyally exalt religious truth over all scientific truth in importance, and judiciously separate the essential Word of God from a supposed erroneous book which merely envelops and contains it. Unfortunately, however, it not only prejudges the purport of revelation, but proposes a false discrimination between scientific Scripture and religious

---

* This question is more fully discussed hereafter in the chapter on The Alleged Scientific Errors of the Bible.

Scripture which is simply impossible, if only for the reason that all religious truths involve some scientific facts, and all scientific facts involve some religious truths, in endless complexity. Moreover the inspired writers themselves never thus discriminate between the divine teaching in different spheres of human interest. Nor can such discrimination be made by any devout exegete. Logically, if not morally, we are as much bound by the geological writings of Moses as by the theological writings of St. Paul, even though we should like neither or think one less important than the other. In point of fact, as will hereafter be more fully shown, each kind of truth is important in its own time and place, and both are so implicated and combined in the Biblical system that they must stand or fall together as in a massive arch which, if any segment be removed, would tumble into ruins.

### The Fallacy Proves too Little.

But besides thus sheathing a mere assumption the fallacy before us is a sword which will cut both ways. It will prove too little or too much according to the strictness with which it is applied. It will prove too little, if the meaning merely be that the Bible does not teach science, nor use the technical phrase of science, but couches its revelations in the language of appearance common to all men in all ages, though not always scientifically accurate. Its astronomy thus speaks of a sunrise and sunset. Its geology describes the earth as made in six days, each with a morning and an evening. Its anthropology depicts man as formed out of the ground like a clay image. Its historiography has seeming discrepancies as to events, dates, and numbers. And it also contains allegories, parables, and other literary forms which lack scientific exactness. Let such inaccuracies or discrepancies be accounted as errors, and every scientific text-book will be found full of them. In fact no book could possibly be written without them. The Bible, considering its antiquity, is remarkably free from them. Many of them can be readily explained. But even granting all of them, any list of them that has ever been made would appear as mere specks in the pure marble of its shrine or spots upon its sun of truth.

### The Catholic Doctrine.

It may be well to observe, in passing, that this is no mere Protestant invention or new Presbyterian tenet; it is Catholic doctrine. Fifteen centuries ago said St. Augustine: " To those books which are already styled canonical I have learned to pay such reverence and honor as most firmly to believe that none of their authors has committed any error in writing. If in that literature I meet with anything that seems contrary to truth, I will have no doubt that it is only the manuscript which is faulty, or the translator who has not hit the sense, or my own failure to understand it." The Greek Church fathers, as well as the Latin schoolmen, emphatically deny the possibility of errors in the Canonical Scriptures. The Roman Church has simply exalted the Pope as an infallible interpreter of the infallible Bible. The Anglican Articles admit that Churches have erred, but not that the Scriptures have erred, leaving that point undefined. And though it be true, that the first Protestants held the Bible to be infallible, yet it is also true that the fallibility of the Bible is largely a notion of Protestant growth; and has become one of the extreme issues of the Reformation. In opposition to all past catholic teaching, some Christian writers in our day are maintaining, not only that the Church is fallible, but that the Bible is fallible, and that the individual reason is practically an infallible interpreter and judge both of the Bible and of the Church. The result is that certain textual and literary difficulties which have long been known within the circle of Christian scholars are now bruited abroad in the Church as proofs of a general errancy of the inspired writings.*

### The Fallacy May Prove too Much.

We have seen that the fallacy before us proves so little of Biblical error, in one view, as to prove scarcely any at all, at least none of a scientific nature. But it will prove entirely too much, if it is consistently and thoroughly applied, and the lack of scientific phrase and accuracy is not confined to the physical realm of revelation, but as rigorously extended throughout its

* The different forms of infallibilism are more fully presented and discussed in my Philosophia Ultima, vol. ii., pp. 372-91.

spiritual realm. The Bible no more teaches the science of theology than any other science, and its anthropomorphism in the one sphere is quite as unscientific as its phenomenalism in the other. If it be an error to say that the sun rises and sets, then it is an error to say that Jehovah hath his throne in the heavens and thundereth marvellously with his voice. If it be an error to say that in six days Jehovah made heaven and earth, then it is an error to say that one day is with Jehovah as a thousand years, and a thousand years as one day. If it be an error to say that Jehovah formed man out of the ground, in the image of God, then it is an error to say that Jehovah repented that He had made man and cursed the ground for his sake. And such theological errors are much more flagrant than such astronomical or geological errors. In the light of modern culture, what were the Biblical pictures of the curtained heavens, or of the dramatic week of creation, as compared with the Biblical picture of Jehovah as countenancing slaughter and slavery and polygamy, or as a jealous God, angry with the wicked every day, and holding aloft a cup of wrath from which to pour out famines and wars and pestilences over the earth?

### *Approximate Truths.*

It need scarcely be said that the whole fallacy lies in admitting that there is any error whatever in either class of statements. The so-called errors are simply approximate truths or partial revelations adapted to a rude age and people, and yet to be completed and explained by later revelation or scientific research. The gross anthropomorphism of the Old Testament was thus explained by our Lord and his Apostles consistently with the purer and fuller theism of the New Testament. And the crude phenomenalism of the same Scriptures has been likewise explained, and is now used consistently with the more exact and complete science of our day. In neither case was any error once committed; in neither case is any error now conveyed. Men still speak truthfully, as they always have spoken truthfully, and always will speak truthfully of a sunset and a sunrise which are apparent physical motions, no less than of a wrath and a love of God, which are seeming human passions.

As to all the alleged errors of the Bible within the domain of religion or science, it is enough to say in general that they appear as errors only when detached from their proper connection in the Holy Scriptures considered as a gradual revelation, by means of which the chosen races of mankind have been educated and developed, from the rudiments of Judaism to the doctrines of Christianity, and from primitive barbarism to modern civilization. And as to the alleged scientific errors in particular, it should further be said that they seem precluded by the fact that the Author of Scripture is also the Author of Nature, and any seeming contradiction between them must be due either to some false induction from Nature or to some wrong exegesis of Scripture.

### A Dangerous Fallacy.

It will be seen that I have not assumed any existing doctrine of inspiration, plenary or limited, verbal or ideal; and that I am not now advocating any special theory of the errancy or inerrancy of Holy Scripture. I am simply maintaining, for the purpose of this discussion, that those who do hold an extreme theory of scientific errancy should hold it consistently and take the consequences. They must be prepared to hear of error in the religion of the Bible as well as in its science; in fact, of worse error in its religion than in its science; and, also, much greater evidence of its religious error than of its scientific error. Such has been the actual, as well as logical result in some schools of Christian learning. For this reason it is very unfortunate that the word "error" has become so current in connection with the sacred writings. As applied to their mere literary imperfections, or seeming inconsistencies, or typical rites and obsolete precepts, it is misleading. As used in Biblical study it opens the door to destructive criticism; and in common life it leads to irreverence and unbelief. Begin by admitting error into the written Word of God, in any strict sense of the word "error," and the book might continue interesting as a body of Hebrew and Greek literature, beautiful as "a well of English undefiled," perhaps instructive as a thesaurus of pious themes and mottoes, but as a Canon, as an authoritative rule of Christian faith and practice, as a criterion of any essential truth, it would become, sooner or later, not worth the paper on which it is printed. Nor will an intelligent public long listen to preachers who declare their very texts to be erroneous.

### The Key-note.

The only just, wise, and safe position for us to take is, that while our human interpretation of the Scriptures is always fallible and often errant, as we know to our cost, yet the divine revelation contained in the Scriptures, so far as ascertained and ascertainable, cannot but be infallible and inerrant, the very Word of God.

And this is especially the true position to take in regard to the relations of science and revealed religion. The Bible is neither a scientific book nor an antiscientific book. It does not teach science, nor does it teach anything contrary to science. It does not teach any theories in astronomy, geology, and other sciences; nor does it teach any errors in astronomy, geology, and other sciences. On the contrary, as will hereafter be shown, it does teach some astronomical, geological, and other scientific facts, both natural and supernatural, and also certain extra-scientific truths or revealed doctrines which are logically essential to the sciences themselves in any complete philosophy or system of perfect knowledge. This is the key-note of all our discussion; and the proofs of it will accumulate as we proceed.

The whole question has a practical side which should not be forgotten. As "the witness and keeper of Holy Writ," the Episcopal Church is distinguished by the abundance of Holy Scripture which she provides in her liturgy. The lessons, psalms, epistles, and gospels read in a single day sometimes exceed the amount read in a whole week in other communions. And this is in accordance with apostolic precept and divine command. St. Paul reminded a young divinity student that from a child he had known the Holy Scriptures which are able to make him wise unto Salvation and to render the man of God perfect, thoroughly furnished unto all good works. The same Apostle warned him as a custodian of the Faith to avoid oppositions of science falsely so called, and to beware of such philosophy as is vain and deceitful, after the rudiments of this world and not after Christ.

# CHAPTER II.

## THE LOGICAL VALUE OF THE SCIENTIFIC EVIDENCE.

WE approach the last and most serious of the popular fallacies which are now hindering the appreciation and reception of the scientific evidence of revealed religion. I shall crave the liberty of discussing it without reserve and with that directness which the importance of the subjects demands. If I do not carry with me the full consent of all minds, I may at least hope to stimulate inquiry and to present some aspects of the Biblical question which seem to have been forgotten or undervalued at the present juncture and yet are needed before coming to a final judgment.

The two fallacies already noticed refer to the scope and to the content of revelation, the one excluding scientific truth from its scope, the other including scientific error in its content. The fallacy now to come before us refers to the form of revelation and tends to depreciate its value. We meet with it in a current phrase everywhere repeated as if it were an axiom: "The Bible is literature, to be studied as we study other literature." Having been charged with error by some of its own friends, perhaps it is not surprising that it should sink toward the level of mere human writings, or that, in the literary excess of our times, it should be overrun with a species of criticism which is largely æsthetic, sometimes rhetorical in its aim and spirit. We seem threatened with "a book religion," in a new sense of the phrase. A fresh literary interest in the Bible pervades even the secular press. One might almost fancy the Book had lost its unique sacredness as he hears applied to it the technical terms once confined to the productions of ordinary literature, and reads in his morning paper of Hebraic myths and legends and Biblical dramas and lyrics and idyls and the rest. I am not about to say that there is anything positively false in this phase of Biblical study or that it is not in itself deserving of unstinted praise or that it may not even be a healthy symptom in the present diseased state of opinion. I would simply give it its due place and importance, as it bears upon the question of connecting the Sciences with the Bible as evidences of revealed religion.

### The Bible More than Mere Literature.

The assertion that the Bible is literature is true—but it is not the whole truth. The Bible is more than mere literature. It is divinely inspired literature as collected within the sacred Canon in distinction from all other literature, ancient and modern. In a limited though not the most important sense it is a literary product or rather a collection of literary products, resembling in some respects the productions of the masters of literary art. Its chronicles, proverbs, psalms, prophecies, gospels, and epistles may be likened, as they have been often very favorably likened to certain corresponding literary types with which it is now the fashion to class them and sometimes to confound them. But at that point the superficial resemblance ends. It does not extend to the revealed content enveloped in these literary forms, the divine purport of the human language. There is still a fundamental difference between literature and Scripture. In distinction from all other books, this volume contains the accredited mind and will of God, otherwise unknown and unknowable by any unaided genius of man. While the poet and the philosopher only voice the common human heart and conscience, the prophet and the apostle claim to bring us divine ideas in inspired words; and, if we admit the evidence of their claim, it becomes not merely undevout, but illogical, to read the prophet Isaiah as we would read the poet Virgil, or the apostle John as we would read the philosopher Plato. As I have elsewhere said, when St. Paul stood among the masterpieces of Greek art and literature at Athens, he quoted a saying of Aratus and Cleanthes with the polite acknowledgment, " As certain of your own poets have said ";

but when he cites a text from Moses and David, it is with the devout preamble, "As the Holy Ghost saith."

### The Bible no Mere Ancient Classic.

If the literary forms of the Bible suffer in comparison with those of the ancient classics, it is because they were produced by a somewhat rude people whose government was a theocracy, whose art, so far as they had any, was subordinated to religion, and whose literature was made a vehicle of divine revelation. There is no evidence that prophets and apostles studied mere rhetorical effect, like poets and orators. And, therefore, the two cannot be classed together. As to content and purport, the Genesis of Moses is not to be named with the Theogony of Hesiod; nor the prophecies of Isaiah with the Iliad of Homer; nor the story of Jonah with the adventures of Ulysses; nor the psalms of David with the Odes of Horace; nor the parables of our Lord with the fables of Æsop. Under greater beauty of form there is an essential difference in matter which stamps the classical writings as merely human works. While Greek sages and Roman poets fancifully claimed the aid of the Muses, Hebrew prophets and Christian apostles spoke as they were moved by the Holy Ghost.

### The Bible Free from Pagan Science.

And this divine import of the Holy Scriptures, in contrast with all other ancient writings, appears even in the sphere of science as well as in the sphere of religion. Although the Hebrew prophets may have been, and doubtless were, greatly inferior to the Assyrian, Egyptian, and Greek sages in scientific knowledge, yet their expressions betray none of the grotesque absurdity which disfigures the astronomy or geology of their contemporaries as found in the sacred books of the East, or even in the more artistic mythology of the Greeks. Compare the confused and trivial cosmogony of the Chaldean tablets with the lucid and stately method of Genesis. Compare the gross Egyptian picture of the earth as a chaotic egg conceived by the sable-winged bird of Night, with the simple statement of the Divine Spirit's agency in creation. Compare the fanciful feats of Hellenic gods and goddesses in producing plants, animals, and men, with the sublime fiats of the one Creator of heaven and earth. Compare the trivial fables of Prometheus and Pandora with the profound teaching of the story of Adam and Eve. Why is it that the Books of Moses have outlived scientific discovery and criticism, while those of Orpheus, Hesiod, and Thales have long since lost all scientific interest and value? How comes it that these "semi-barbarous Hebrews," as they have been contemptuously styled, have so exceeded the science of their own time, and even their own personal knowledge, that they have written what is still true for our time, and is likely to be true for all time to come? It is simply because they were under divine guidance even when moving in the realm of natural science, and spake as the Spirit gave them utterance.

### Personal Errancy of Inspired Writers.

In thus accepting the sacred writers as organs of the Holy Spirit we do not need to palliate any of their faults and vices as committed outside of the divine communications. Why should we doubt the inspiration of sinning David or erring Peter, when we behold a Bacon or a Shakespeare, notwithstanding their personal failings, made the Providential instrument of conveying immortal truth and benefit to mankind? Their personal errancy is quite apart from their official teaching, and, instead of tingeing Holy Scripture with errors, sometimes only enhances its truthfulness by contrast, as when a royal psalmist so freely confesses his own sins and the shameful lapse of an apostle is so fully portrayed by an evangelist. Even if the author of Genesis shared the geological errors of his age, as he may have done, yet there is no trace of them imparted in the revealed history of creation as we can now read and interpret it in the light of modern science.

### Personal Freedom of Inspired Writers.

Nor need we imagine any loss of the individuality and freedom of the inspired writers as exercised within the divine communications. Was Isaiah less fervid or Paul less logical because filled with the Holy Ghost? Do we not sometimes see ordinary minds inspired and governed by some superior mind, yet acting as freely and characteristically as if their own masters? We could not, if we would, conceive of prophets and apostles as mere machines or automatons without thought and volition; and never, even while receiving their divinest messages, do we lose sight of their human peculiarities, whether it be an austere reformer who is proclaiming the vengeance of Jehovah, or a well-bred scholar who is reasoning out the mysteries of godliness. Though we accept Genesis as a work of the Holy Spirit, we are not blind to the dramatic form of the divine story of creation or to the allegorical drapery in the inspired picture of primeval man.

### Divine Unity of the Scriptures.

Still less may we find any difficulty in the varied idiosyncrasies of the inspired writers, their diversities of idiom, style, diction, purpose, temperament, and environment; in short, the manifold human element which appears on the face of Holy Scripture. As a collection of writings by different authors, in different ages, under different circumstances, the Bible has been called "a library." But it is a library selected by divine wisdom, preserved by divine Providence, animated by divine intelligence, organized and unified by divine purpose, and unfolding one divine scheme of individual and social regeneration from the primeval promise of redemption to the fulness of millennial glory; from the genesis of the heaven and earth in the ages past to the apocalypse of the new heaven and the new earth through the ages to come. To revere the divine truth and glory of such a book is not bibliolatry. The true bibliolater is your mere litterateur admiring only certain lyric, dramatic, and epic beauties which are but as the jewelled crown, sceptre, and robe of the Spiritual Monarch who wears them whilst reigning in the hearts of mankind.

We have still to consider the inferential fallacy that the Bible should be studied "as we study other literature." This, also, expresses only half of the truth. It is true enough that the student of the Hebrew and Greek Scriptures needs the same literary appliances which are needed in the study of the Greek and Latin classics, such as grammar, lexicon, text-book, critical skill, literary taste, and that linguistic tact which comes as a gift or with long practice—in other words, the furniture of the art of Higher Criticism. But this is not all that he needs. He needs pre-eminently certain other qualifications which are not needed in the study of any other book, ancient or modern.

### Logical Pre-requisites of Biblical Study.

At the outset, he needs logically certain postulates or principles without which his whole literary equipment will be worse than useless. The Bible in its presuppositions is so fundamentally different from all other literature that it cannot be judged by the same literary standards. It assumes the existence of the one true God on every page; it claims to be a miraculously attested revelation to man from the beginning to the end of the world, and it has been set apart by the whole Church as a genuine product of the Holy Spirit. And such premises are not mere traditional prejudices or dogmatic obstructions, but rational presumptions, imbedded in the very phenomena of Scripture itself, and supported by the best historical evidence which the world affords. They are not found in any contemporaneous literature, Assyrian, Egyptian, Grecian, or Roman. A critic repudiating them, an atheist, an agnostic, a denier of miracles, inspiration, and the historic canon, is simply a critic who has already prejudged the whole case. His attitude, to say the least, is illogical and unreasonable. He is ignoring the only true premises of the whole argument. It is as if he were about to discuss a treatise on physics without regard to the mathematical axioms from which it proceeds, and which it everywhere involves. He may be fully competent to criticise classical authors; but he is not fully competent to criticise the Holy Scriptures. And he shows his incompetency as soon as he enters the field of biblical criticism. He brings his sceptical spirit with him, he comes in search of superficial analogies between heathen mythology and revealed religion; and naturally enough he finds in Jehovah only an Israelitish Jupiter, in the prophetic revelations mere Hebrew oracles, in all the Bible stories nothing but Jewish myths, and in the whole miraculous history of revealed religion a purely natural development of universal religion embellished with Syrian conceits and oriental fancies. This is the logical and inevitable result of using the higher criticism without regard to the essential distinction between classical and biblical literature.*

## Misapplied Classical Criticism.

And a like mistake is made by some Christian scholars of the same school, who, though accepting the fundamental principles of biblical literature, will proceed to forget them or even protest continued belief in them while undermining them. When such critics come upon a seeming discrepancy or verbal inaccuracy, instead of endeavoring to explain it or retaining it simply as a still unexplained difficulty, they will straightway proclaim it as an "error," implying incompetency or deceit in an inspired writer. If they regard the story of Eden as a spiritual allegory they do not directly connect it with the Holy Spirit as its real author, but incorrectly style it "a myth" or mere human fable, and sometimes rashly trace it as such to a Persian or Chaldean origin. They seem to handle a sacred book as if it were a literary forgery to be self-convicted by means of its grammatical solecisms and anachronisms, and would, if they might, reconstruct the entire canonical Scriptures as if they were some chance miscellany that has drifted down to us on the stream of profane tradition. While theoretically accepting the Holy Scriptures as inspired of God, they practically treat them as they might treat the works of Homer or of Livy.

The principle that the rules of classical criticism should govern biblical criticism was first judiciously broached by Ernesti, the German Cicero, but pushed to rash extremes by Eichhorn, De Wette, and Herder. It does not follow even on philological or literary grounds that a good critic in one language will be a good critic in another language, and with reference to another class of themes. The great Bentley himself was a striking example to the contrary. After he had vanquished all his opponents in the famous "battle of books" by triumphantly proving that the Epistles of Phalaris and the Fables of Æsop were forgeries, he might have remained the acknowledged master of the critical art, had he not been

* This subject is more fully treated heretofore in the paper on the false Mythical Theory of Revealed Religion.

tempted in a rash moment to try his pen upon the great English epic of Milton. He fancied that there were certain literary blemishes in the Paradise Lost, which must have been interpolated by the amanuensis or the redactor of the blind old poet, and which might be removed by his own critical sagacity and conjecture. What havoc was wrought by such emendation may be shown by one or two specimens. On etymological grounds the infuriate legions of Satan were made to draw their "blades" instead of their "swords," and brandish them toward the "walls of heaven," not toward the "vault of heaven," according to Milton's grander conception. Topographical inaccuracies were found in the scene of Raphael's leave-taking,

> "So parted they; the angel up to heaven,
> From the thick shade; and Adam to his bower."

Bentley argued that Adam could not have left his bower, and substituted the ponderous reading,

> "So parted they; the angel up to heaven:
> *Adam to ruminate on past discourse.*"

The well-known line, suggesting the dim interior of Hell,

> "No light, but rather darkness visible,"

was elucidated so as to read,

> "No light but rather *a transpicuous gloom.*"

Disraeli tells us that there are a thousand such critical emendations in Bentley's Milton; and exclaims, "Let it remain as a gibbet on the high-roads of literature and serve as a terrifying beacon to all conjectural criticism." The school of Bentley, however, still survives in some biblical critics of acknowledged learning, who naïvely think to prove their points by imagining a redactor behind every difficult text, translating the divine name Jehovah as "Jahveh," calling the first section of the canon the "Hexateuch," and ascribing its various portions to the initials of imaginary writers.

### Abuse of the Higher Criticism.

The method of the Higher Criticism is sound enough when rightly used and applied within reasonable limits. Its value, though sometimes exaggerated, is undisputed in determining the date, structure, and authorship of ancient writings, whether sacred or profane; and in this age of light and liberty it is practically as unfettered as the wind. The question of its free use by biblical scholars is a false issue. As a matter of fact, it is already freely used by biblical scholars of all classes, by the most orthodox as well as by the most infidel. But it is also abused and perverted and may lose the essential qualities of Christian scholarship. When it is applied to the Scriptures regardless of their divine origin and claims, it cannot but become fallacious and destructive; and when its crude results are forced into popular sermons to the unsettling of the common faith, it becomes, if not a breach of clerical ethics, yet a strange inconsistency and just cause of offence.

### Scientific Pre-requisites.

In the second place, the biblical student needs scientific aid, scientific in distinction from literary appliances. Unlike all other ancient books the Bible is found to embrace the whole field of the sciences, physical and psychical, in manifold connection with its revealed doctrines; and no mere literary critic is competent by mere literary methods to settle questions lying partly or wholly within the province of any of these sciences. Without astronomical knowledge he cannot tell whether the astronomical scriptures are in accord with the discovery of suns and planets. Without geological knowledge he cannot tell whether the order of the creative days agrees with the order of the earth's strata. Without ethnological knowledge he cannot tell whether the Mosaic genealogies include or exclude pre-Adamite and co-Adamite races of mankind. Without archæological knowledge he cannot tell whether the Mosaic cosmogony was of Hebrew or Chaldean origin, or derived from primeval tradition still more ancient; nor whether the Elohist and Jehovist sections were original writings or compiled documents; nor whether Moses wrote the whole or parts of the books which have always borne his name. Without historical science he cannot tell whether the Mosaic codes formed a logical or chronological series; nor whether they date before or after the Babylonian exile. And without some knowledge of psychology, sociology, and comparative religion he cannot even approach the higher problems of the soul, the Church, and the future of Christianity. In a word, no amount of mere literary criticism, however learned and acute, can settle these and other complex scientific questions connected with the Old and New Testaments, but extending quite outside of Hebrew and Greek literature, into other fields of modern scientific research.

### Unscientific Higher Criticism.

Moreover, though we dare not say that the literary spirit is peculiarly errant, yet it is fair to say that it has hitherto greatly needed more of the scientific spirit to check and guide it. Its vagaries for the last hundred years, especially in the schools of Germany, have made it the scandal of Christian learning as well as of common-sense. Some of us began acquaintance with it nearly fifty years ago, when we were young and eager students of divinity, and we cannot now be charged with ignorance of it by those who are hailing it as a novelty. Nor, indeed, is it necessary for anyone to master all its details, in order to see that it has lacked the inductive method of true science; that it has proceeded from assumed facts, with inadequate hypotheses, to illegitimate conclusions, and that it is largely mere critical conjecture based upon critical conjecture, brilliant erudition without solid knowledge. Upon its polychrome Bible might be written what Bossuet wrote upon a charming treatise of Malebranche, " pulchra, nova, falsa." Its fascinating symbols, E, J, P, and D, howsoever combined, still figure in an unsolved problem, for the simple reason that the personages indicated by them, the Elohist and the Jehovist, the Deuteronomist and the Priestly Codifier, with the ubiquitous Redactor, are purely ideal, without even the despised evidence of tradition to make them real. Indeed, for the sake of such mere modern fancies, it has set aside the historical evidence of the entire Jewish and Christian Church, the direct testimony of the nearest inspired and contemporary writers, and the biblical knowledge of our Lord himself, to say nothing of his divine knowledge. And now, as the result of all this literary guesswork, it offers us, in place of the received canon, a medley of pseudonymous fragments behind which the true authors and editors, it would seem, have been masquerading as inspired prophets and apostles for thousands of years. In all reason and frankness it is time to protest against such speculations among Christian scholars. Not because they are beyond the right and liberty of research (this is a false issue); not because they are necessarily rationalistic or heretical (this some critics deny); not even because they are unwelcome (we might almost wish some of them were true); but simply because they are unscientific; because they are contrary to the literary phenomena and the historical facts; because, even if true, they would add but little to our stock of biblical knowledge; because, in a word, they are either not proved or not worth proving. We take the ground of the Higher Criticism against them. We will believe them when we can believe that Shakespeare did not write the dramas of Shakespeare, or that the Waverley novels had an unknown redactor in Sir Walter's private secretary, or that the Anglican Prayer-book was a post-exilic production of the Pilgrim Fathers.

### *Spiritual Pre-requisites.*

But besides scientific aid, the biblical student also needs spiritual aid before and above all literary requisites. The Bible should not be studied as we study other books, for the eminent reason that unlike any other book, ancient or modern, it claims to be a product of the Holy Spirit and requires for its full comprehension the inward illumination of its divine author. No mere grammatic or literary study can exhaust the infinite mind of the Spirit which the natural mind receiveth not. It is old-fashioned doctrine, but it is doctrine which has been tested, that spiritual discernment rather than æsthetic taste is the primary requisite of biblical study. Having that requisite, a reader of our English Bible, though ignorant of Hebrew and Greek and as devoid of literary culture as a Bunyan or a Moody, may become mighty in the Scriptures, versed in those divine mysteries which were in the bosom of God at the beginning of the world and which our Lord declared had been hidden from philosophers and sages and revealed unto men as unsophisticated as babes. On the other hand, the most accomplished literary critic, if destitute of these primary graces of reverence, docility, and faith, will betray a fatal lack of spiritual insight, and will find in the Scriptures only what he finds in other ancient books, attractive myths and legends, sagas and folk-lore, excellent moral and religious maxims, together with abundant mistakes, absurdities, and errors; in short a Bible without miracle or prophecy or inspiration or authority. Have we not seen him thus invading the shrine of revealed truth unabashed, and taking prophets and apostles by the beard? No wonder that the deep things of the Spirit vanish under his critical dissection of the letter. The Wounded Dove flees from his scalpel. He has cut the divine documents as with the pen-knife of Jehudi. "And it came to pass that when Jehudi had read three or four leaves, he cut it with the pen-knife, and cast it into the fire that was on the hearth, until all the roll was consumed in the fire that was on the hearth." *

### Rationalistic Criticism.

It is not merely naturalism, hostility to the supernatural and miraculous, which must be charged against such critics: it is a false rationalism. It is a rationalism which is itself irrational. It is a rationalism which perverts our God-given reason and will not take the place of right reason, lowly yet exalted, before the One Absolute Reason. It is a rationalism which does not even recognize the limitations of reason, but would attempt transcendental problems, which a revelation alone could solve and has solved. It is a rationalism which refuses to submit the finite mind of man to the infinite mind of God as revealed by his Holy Spirit in his Holy Word. It is a rationalism which reveres neither the inspired Bible nor the illumined Church, but is ever handling the word of God deceitfully and evaporating the creeds and forms of the Catholic Faith. And its mere naturalistic tendency is not so much to be dreaded as its unbelieving spirit. Let it explain away, if it can, the whole supernatural element of the Bible, as now popularly conceived. Let it exhibit, if it will, every miracle as a natural event, and the entire evolution of revealed religion from Genesis to the Apocalypse as a natural process under natural laws, as Bishop Butler long ago conceived it; but let it

* Jeremiah, xxxvi.

not touch with rash hand that divine revelation which the miracles attest, around which the supernatural shines, of which prophets and apostles are the heralds, and before which the tallest seraph in glory reverently bows, alike with the little child at its mother's knee.

### Conservative Higher Criticism.

At this point it is important and only right to discriminate carefully between the Reverent and the Rationalistic schools of biblical study, known as the Conservative and Radical wings of the Higher Criticism. The former disclaim the rash and destructive conclusions of the latter and are fairly distinguishable from them by having the spiritual requisites which we have just noticed. Some of them use the Higher Criticism learnedly in defence of the traditional authorship and historicity of the sacred records, exhibiting their substantial consistency without the aid of hypothetical documents, scribes, and redactors. Others contend that the inspiration and authority of the Scriptures can be conserved, though it be proven that they were largely an accretion or collection of sacred traditions, documents, and codes compiled by pious hands, before and after the time of Moses, to whom they were popularly attributed by our Lord and his apostles. Still others also maintain that revealed religion need lose none of its supernatural character and claims, if it be shown to have had a history or a development since the Exodus, which seems forbidden by literal statements of the sacred narratives, but may be traced in them by a literary expert versed in Hebrew antiquities. Without inquiring how far these views are self-consistent, sound and valuable, I shall endeavor scrupulously to give them due consideration and weight, and be ready to welcome such critics in the ranks of sincere defenders of the faith on the basis of the principles laid down in the previous discussion. These principles are, that the Bible extends its revelations within the realm of the physical sciences as well as the psychical sciences; that it is to be held no more erroneous in the one realm than in the other; and that for its proper study it requires scientific knowledge and spiritual insight no less than literary scholarship. A biblical critic who accepts these principles and stands firmly upon them may speculate as he likes in regard to the historical origin, the editorial arrangement and the literary qualities of the sacred books. He may maintain, if he wishes, that the Pentateuch was a sort of inspired mosaic derived from primeval revelations through Babylonian tablets, Egyptian hieroglyphics and Hebrew documents. He may argue, if he choose, that the Levitical and Deuteronomical codes have been rearranged by inspired redactors with more regard to logical than to chronological order and accuracy, as in modern statute-books. He may hold, if he will, that the prophetical scriptures were restricted by their inspired authors to the environment and foreground of Jewish history with no conscious reference to the future church or the general history of mankind, to which they have been found applicable. He may describe the divine allegories in Scripture as Hebrew myths, the Psalms as oriental lyrics and class the literary forms of Holy Scripture generally with pagan productions to which they bear a vague outward resemblance. In a word he may adopt any critical hypotheses, conjectures and surmises, which seem to him plausible, provided he still accepts the Holy Scriptures as containing an objective revelation from God to man, which is absolutely unique, infallible and authoritative in all its ascertained teaching, whether that teaching be found within the sphere of Science or of Religion and though it be not stated scientifically or technically in either of these spheres.

### *Higher Qualities of the Scientific Evidence.*

Having thus cleared the Scientific Evidence from the current fallacies which hinder its due appreciation, we are now ready to examine its logical qualities more directly. In general, it may be said to share the qualities of science as distinguished from ordinary vague knowledge. First of all, it shares the certitude of science. Like all true science it is founded upon unquestioned facts rather than upon assumed principles. When we argue from the Divine wisdom and goodness, that a revelation should be made, we assume principles which are not generally admitted; and when we argue from miracles and prophecies, that a revelation has been made, we assume facts which are still questioned; but when we show that astronomical facts or geological facts are in agreement with corresponding truths in Holy Scripture, we show that the Author of Scripture is also the Author of Nature, and has made known nothing in the one volume contrary to what has been found in the other. The proof of natural religion is largely a matter of abstract reasoning, and the proof of miracles and prophecies is mainly a matter of historic testimony; but the glory of Jehovah as magnified by astronomy and unfolded by geology is purely a matter of Scientific evidence.

This evidence also shares the impartiality of science. It is a just boast of true science that it is absolutely unprejudiced and disinterested; that in its quest for facts it will not be governed by authorities, traditions, or precedents, however venerable; that it is neither swayed by the passions and infirmities of mortals nor turned back from its course by persecution, torture, or death itself; and that when it reaches its conclusions it seems to have no regard for human interests the most dear or sacred, but becomes impassive as nature and merciless as fate. History shows us that it has often forced its own votaries to abandon their most plausible hypotheses, reverse their cherished opinions, and at length accept the very results from which they had recoiled. History shows us, too, as in the case of Galileo, that it has sometimes compelled even divines, priests, and popes with infallible claims to reconstruct their long-established interpretations of Scripture, but, after seeming to menace Scripture itself, has only opened new and larger views of its meaning and left it like a sun cleared of clouds, to shine with increased radiance and glory. Now when astronomy thus becomes a witness to the truths of revealed religion, it is no interested advocate pleading a cause, no specious apologist defending a claim, but it is Science itself giving evidence at the bar of Omniscience.

This evidence still further shares the cumulative power and fulness of Science. As we study the sciences philosophically we find that they are not mere scattered fragments of knowledge, but a linked series helping one another forward in a general progress toward perfect knowledge. We find also that as thus arranged they have a common ground with the Bible where their own discovered facts become accordant with revealed truth as fast as they attain scientific exactness and clearness. Into this common ground, therefore, they enter not as wrangling disputants with chance testimony, but as competent witnesses with an ever-growing consistency pointing forward to the ultimate demonstration of the whole Word of God by the reason of man and the perfect coincidence of human Science with divine Omniscience.

But the high qualities claimed for the Scientific Evidence may appear more clearly as we now proceed to define its sources and the various forms in which it is afforded. These are fourfold, to be here announced necessarily in general terms, but hereafter to be more specially and fully illustrated:

### The Evidence of Scientific Authorities.

*First.* The chief authorities in each science can be cited in favor of revealed religion. Much of the current evidence of Scientific knowledge rests upon authority and testimony. We are in the position of laymen or learners in respect to the Masters of Science, and accept the results of their researches, sometimes without understanding the processes by which such results have been reached, and often without mastering the details of such processes, even if made intelligible to us. We thus believe the scarcely credible discoveries which have been made in astronomy or in geology, though ourselves unable to verify them. When, therefore, leading men of science declare their discoveries to be not in conflict with the truths of the Bible, and hold their religious faith consistently with their scientific knowledge, this is testimony of the highest authority. If there were any necessary antagonism between science and revealed religion, then such men would be the first to feel and show it and the last to quit the battle against the Faith; but on the contrary, as a class, with exceptions which only prove the rule, they have given their united and unequivocal evidence in support of revealed truths. It will be found that the history of the sciences is full of such personal evidence of scientists themselves.

### The Evidence of Scientific Facts.

*Second.* The ascertained or demonstrated portions of each science can be shown to be already in harmony with revealed religion. After centuries of research and criticism, we possess, especially in the physical sciences, large bodies of exact knowledge, resting upon observed facts, susceptible of demonstrative proof, and no longer challenged as admitting of a doubt. The portion of astronomy known as celestial mechanics rests upon such a certain basis; and the portion of geology known as terrestrial physics is approximating a like certitude. Now if these well-ascertained facts of science stood in glaring contrariety with any revealed truths to which they are directly related, this would tend to show that the author of Scripture is not also the author of Nature, or that the human authors of Scripture had communicated divine knowledge in a form inconsistent with human knowledge. But instead of this result it is found that the two portions of knowledge, the divine and the human, logically require one another, that neither can do without the other, and both together serve at once to support science and illustrate revelation. As we review the sciences we shall find them yielding this species of evidence in proportion to their maturity as bodies of certain knowledge.

### The Evidence of Scientific Theories.

*Third.* The problematical or hypothetical portions of each science can be provisionally adjusted as in sufficient harmony with revealed religion. In distinction from the demonstrated portions of scientific knowledge, the whole field of investigation is covered with masses of unsolved problems for the solution of which men of science have framed various conflicting hypotheses or tentative constructions of fact, all of which cannot be true, though each may have elements of truth. Astronomy and geology, for example, are filled with such problems and hypotheses concerning the origin, the development, and the destiny of the heavens and the earth, and astronomers and geologists are accordingly divided as in hostile camps upon a battle-field. Now it is not "the business of the reconcilers"—as Mr. Huxley is pleased to term us—to reconcile scientists among themselves, nor need we be troubled to reconcile their mere conflicting speculations with any revealed truths which they may seem to menace. All that we need do or can do is to exhibit the problem of opinion, to state the relative agreement or disagreement which would ensue when all the facts are known and the true theory has been obtained. And we shall find, in regard to these conflicting hypotheses, that while some of them would leave existing interpretation of Scripture undisturbed, others would only require that interpretation to be modified favorably, and that, whichever hypothesis may ultimately prevail, the essential truths of revealed religion will remain unimpaired, if not enhanced and illustrated. The history of the more advanced Sciences will show us how a scientific evidence which at first seemed hostile has at length become friendly and all the more conclusive because tried and purged in the fires of controversy.

### The Evidence of Scientific Marvels.

*Fourth.* The marvels of modern science may serve to explain and illustrate the miracles of revealed religion. It would seem that the supernatural signs and wonders by means of which Christianity originally obtained credence in the world have become incredible to some persons who fancy that the Science of our day has demonstrated their intrinsic impossibility or shown that there is nothing analogous to them in modern experience. While it is true that such miracles are no longer wrought because no longer needed to attest the claims of inspired writers, the book of Revelation having been closed and the canon completed, yet it should not be forgotten that science itself is unfolding before us more stupendous marvels than any miracles recorded in the Old or New Testament, and is thus by the achievements of man rendering the wonderful acts of God more easily conceivable and more credible. It is showing us that what is possible with man cannot have been impossible with God. You may have deemed it impossible that iron should swim, as Elisha caused an axe-head to swim in the brook by means of a wooden staff; yet perhaps you crossed the ocean last summer in a huge iron bowl which swam at the rate of twenty miles an hour. You may sometimes have thought it incredible that our Lord should have raised Lazarus from the dead, yet before experience it would have been no more credible that men should talk together across the Atlantic and girdle the globe with their instantaneous thought. Miracles could not have happened? Miracles do happen! In some cases science even helps us to conceive how a miracle may have been wrought through divine knowledge and skill in due consistency with natural laws. In fact, there is no modern science within whose province ancient miracles did not occur, which now have their parallels in its own marvels and achievements. While, then, some sceptics are ever invidiously telling us that the age of miracles is past, science itself is showing us that the age of miracles has come again.

### Valuation of the Scientific Evidence.

It only remains to estimate the value of the Scientific Evidence. And let it first be remarked that its value is imperfect only in so far as science itself is still imperfect. If it consists largely of probable evidence rather than of demonstrative proof, it is because all science rests largely upon such evidence, being mainly an empirical collection of facts; and if it be more complete in some sciences than in others, it is because some sciences are more complete than others, according to their different stages of advancement toward perfect knowledge. These distinctions being always premised, its value will appear in three respects.

It is valuable in relation to other Evidences, the Miraculous and the Prophetical, the External and the Internal. Without it, indeed, other evidences would be weak or worthless. No ancient miracles or prophecies would now have any evidential value if science could falsify them as the myths and legends of a former rude age and people; still less would any external evidence of this dubious kind uphold a supposed revelation containing scientific errors and absurdities, such as appear in the Chaldean tablets or the Book of Mormon. But when science is found to explain miracles and prophecies as quite possible and credible expressions of divine power and knowledge, when astronomy and geology are seen illustrating the divine perfections revealed in Scripture, and when each science appears coming into agreement with revealed doctrines as fast as it approaches scientific completeness, then there will be a convergence and accumulation of all the evidences, both external and internal, toward the highest degree of moral certainty.

It is valuable in relation to the scientist himself. All science is, in one good sense, agnostic toward religion. At the end of its empirical research it comes to a metaphysical void, where its torch goes out, and any further light must be the light of a revelation. Were there no evidence of a revelation, agnosticism might be justified and unbelief become sane and rational. But when such evidence is at hand, evidence strictly scientific in its sources and quality, evidence as scientific as the evidence of the solar system or of the theory of evolution, then there is no longer any room for reasonable doubt and ignorance. Such scientific evidence will have come to the modern scientist craving knowledge, as of old the prophetical or philosophical evidence came to the Greek seeking wisdom, and the miraculous evidence came to the Jew requiring a sign.

It is valuable in relation to all the interests of civilization. We must not forget that our whole civilization is essentially Christian and has its roots deep down and far back in revealed religion. Our art is full of Christian ideals. Our philosophy is saturated with Christian thought. Our jurisprudence is transfused with Christian Ethics. Our States are irradiated with Christian Churches. Our philanthropies are Christian Charities. Kill or sap the roots of this wondrous culture with agnosticism and unbelief, and all its goodly flower and fruitage will wither away. But support it with scientific evidence, animate it with scientific faith, and fresh life will flow from its roots into all the branches. Our art will repent and return from the husks and the swine. Our philosophy will unite revelation with reason in the search for perfect knowledge. Our politics will aim to preserve law with liberty, and social with individual rights. Our Churches will have become united with our States in the one Catholic Faith. And our philanthropy will ever keep its face toward the predicted reign of universal love and peace.

### Timeliness of the Scientific Evidence.

Need it be added that the value of this evidence is timely and practical? We live in an age of science, in the chief epoch of science. During the last three centuries science has made greater progress than in the previous twenty centuries; and during the last fifty years, greater progress than in the previous three hundred years. It is entering the new century like a conqueror with his trophies. It has gained vast possessions in astronomy, in geology, in chemistry, in physics, in the mental sciences, and it has brought with it marvellous inventions—the rail-car, the steamship, the telegraph, the photograph, the spectroscope, the lucifer match, electric lighting, Roentgen rays, anæsthetics, antiseptic surgery. Justly therefore its votaries have become the idols of the people, to be applauded as heroes while living, and when dead to be entombed among kings, nobles, warriors, and poets, as benefactors of the race. Unhappily, however, as if intoxicated with all this success and worship of science, some rash hands are driving her car of triumph as a war-chariot into the sacred domain of religion, across the fair pastures of the Church. And now, in this seeming conflict with science we can only overcome scientific unbelief with scientific evidence. It is a battle which can only be fought with the weapons of Science. And the victory, when it comes, will be a victory of Science, her last and noblest victory. Not the mere physical comforts, which she is multiplying among us; not alone the arts of utility and beauty which she is nourishing; not even the humane charities which she is promoting, will be her crowning achievement, but, over and above these, and as the primal source of them all, will be her own demonstration of the truth, the beneficence, and the glory of the Christian religion.

# CHAPTER III.

## THE ALLEGED SCIENTIFIC ERRORS OF THE BIBLE.

At the threshold of the scientific evidences we meet the general question, Does the Bible contain scientific errors? The question may be treated mainly as a philosophical question, in its bearings upon science as well as upon religion. Unhappily, it has become mixed with several side issues, which should be detached from it and thrown out of the discussion. As it is to be presented here, it will have nothing to do with the current disputes in different churches, or with the definition of any type of orthodoxy, or even with the formal vindication of Christianity itself. These are important issues in their own time and place. But there is a larger, if not higher, view of the main issue which they involve, and which they may even hide from our sight. All schools of philosophy, as well as all churches and denominations, have a common interest in inquiring whether the Bible can yield us any real knowledge within the domain of the various sciences. Indeed, all men everywhere will become practically concerned in that inquiry, if the oldest and most highly prized book in the world is now to be set aside as a mixture of truth and error, obsolete in science, if not also in morals and religion, and of little further use in the progress of civilization.

The way to the question should be cleared by several distinctions and admissions. Let us first distinguish mere literary imperfections from scientific errors, and frankly admit the existence of the former in the inspired authors. They were not trained rhetoricians or even practised writers. They show the greatest variety of culture and of style. The rugged simplicity of the prophet is in contrast with the refined parallelism of the Psalmist. The evangelists did not write pure Greek. It has been said it would be difficult to parse some of the sentences of St. Paul. Many of the Old Testament metaphors seem gross to modern taste, and there are certain didactic portions of Leviticus which are too natural to be read in public worship. Nevertheless, to reject the teaching of inspired writers on such æsthetic grounds would be like denying the mathematics of the "Principia" because Newton wrote bad Latin, or repudiating some medical classic as unfit for the drawing-room. The literary blemishes of Holy Scripture, as seen by fastidious critics, do not touch its revealed content or divine purport, but may even heighten it by the force of contrast.

We may also distinguish and admit certain historiographical defects in the inspired authors. The prophets and evangelists were not versed in the art of historiography, and did not write history philosophically nor even always chronologically. Their narratives have many seeming discrepancies as to events, dates, places, names, and figures. The line of the patriarchs is yet to be traced, amid conflicting chronologies, with historical accuracy. Persons and events do not always appear to synchronize; as when it is stated in the Book of Kings that Ahaziah was forty years old on coming to the throne, and in Chronicles that he was twenty-two years old. The Evangelists Matthew, Mark, and Luke tell the story of the crucifixion of Christ with differing motives and details which have not yet been fully harmonized. Such things are simply unavoidable in all historical composition. At the present date of antiquarian research, neither the dynasties of the Pharaohs, nor of the Cæsars, nor even of the popes have been clearly ascertained. No one can read Bossuet's Universal History, or even Bancroft's History of the United States, without losing himself in chronological puzzles. The English historians, Clarendon, Neal, and Burnett narrate the execution of Charles I. with substantial agreement, but from the most varied dogmatic points of view. There are obvious misprints in some editions of Hallam's Constitutional History, which could not have been in his manuscript. There may be trifling mistakes in some English translations of Neander's Church History, which are not in the German, as well as grave misconceptions in some of his critics, which are neither in the English nor in the German. In like manner, as to any supposed inaccuracies in the Chronicles and the Gospels, the fair presumption is that they are not errors of the inspired text, but mere errors of transcription, or errors of translation, or errors of interpretation, or, simply, still unexplained difficulties. It is the business of historical criticism to harmonize standard historians, not to impeach them; and thus far such criticism, as applied to the sacred historians, instead of impugning the scientific accuracy of Holy Scripture, has only confirmed it by unexpected coincidences and ever-growing certitude.

We should still further distinguish some traditional glosses in the inspired writings. The original autographs, and their first transcripts, have long since been lost, and our existing text of the Hebrew and the Greek must have become corrupt through the negligence or design of copyists and editors. Even the vowels, points, accents, spaces, verses, and chapters, which have been added as aids to the sense, have also proved a source of faults and mistakes, especially in the numeral letters. The Book of Samuel is made to say that the Lord smote fifty thousand men in a village of less than five thousand inhabitants; and the Chronicles seem to state that King Jehosaphat raised more than a million fighting men out of a district not half as large as Rhode Island. King David is said to have saved more silver coin for the decoration of the temple than could have been in circulation. The Trinitarian proof-text, "There are three that bear record in heaven," seems to have been interpolated in some late manuscripts for a purpose. It is even alleged that there are spurious claims of authorship in the titles and contents of the sacred books. David, we know, did not write all the Psalms; and we are now told that Moses did not write the Pentateuch, nor Isaiah the whole Book of Isaiah. In short, the entire Bible gives internal evidence, it is claimed, of anonymous fragments compiled by unknown hands. References are made in it to lost documents, such as the books of Jasher, Nathan, and Gad, the Wars of Jehovah, and the Visions of Iddo. There are two accounts of the creation, two versions of the commandments, three distinct codes in Exodus, Leviticus, and Deuteronomy, besides any number of parallel, detached, and repeated passages throughout the Scriptures, suggesting to some critics a mere patchwork of loose chronicles, proverbs, psalms, prophesies, gospels and epistles.

Certainly all these phenomena have been common enough in secular literature. The Greek and Latin classics, and even standard English authors, are marred with textual corruptions, such as the loss or change of a word or letter, or even part of a letter, sometimes running a single number up into the thousands, and sometimes reversing the meaning of a whole sentence or turning it into nonsense. The text of Xenophon is full of them. The Epistles of Cicero have them by the hundred. The single play of Hamlet fills two large octavos of the Variorum edition of Furness. There have also been some pseudographs more or less innocent. The antique manuscripts of Chatterton deceived the practised eye of Walpole. Literary critics of the last century eagerly discussed the question whether the poems of Ossian had not been forged by their professed editor, James McPherson. It has long been a moot point who wrote the letters of Junius. Moreover, we have had fine examples of literary compilation and reproduction without a taint of forgery or plagiarism. Froissart's Chronicles of Knights, Kings, and Fair Women" were personally collected by him in France, England, Scotland, and Spain, and inscribed upon illuminated parchments, which are still extant. Bishop Percy, the accomplished redactor of the Reliques of Ancient English Poetry, not only recovered many manuscript ballads, but by his skilful emendations of them adapted them to modern taste and fancy. The materials of Froissart and Percy were at length wrought, by the masterly pen of Sir Walter Scott, into poems and novels which are read wherever the English tongue is spoken. And if Judge Holmes or Mr. Ignatius Donnelly could prove that Shakespeare did not write Shakespeare, but only recast and arranged the tragedies, histories, and comedies which bear his name, that incomparable book, with all its archaisms, anachronisms, and solecisms, would remain the masterpiece of genius that it is, and men might still quote Shakespeare, as John Randolph used to say, "to prove anything worth proving."

Perhaps, also, the Bible might be the Bible still in its most essential import, although its long-reputed authorship should now be discredited. It may be conceivable that such a Bible could have survived its own literary errors as a trophy of the most devout scholarship. But if quite conceivable, it is not yet certain, nor very probable. The plain statements of the inspired writers themselves, their apparent indorsement by our Lord and his apostles, and the consistent tradition of three thousand years, still stand opposed to the conjectures of learned criticism. And such conjectures are not sustained by all the literary precedents and analogies. The title of a famous author, like Homer or Shakespeare, represents the judgment of his nearest contemporaries and successors, and grows with the lapse of time until it becomes too certain to be easily set aside.

Such claims for Moses and Isaiah were not even questioned during more than twenty centuries. It would seem rather late now to overthrow all this external testimony by mere internal criticism of their accepted writings. Any traces of compilation in the sacred books need conflict as little with their received authorship as the like use of documents and fragments in acknowledged works of genius. It is as easy to conceive that Moses could compose or compile the Elohistic and Jehovistic records of Genesis with their different names of God, as that Shakespeare composed or compiled both King Lear and Richard III., though the former, quite consistently, has only the pagan names of Jupiter, while the latter is full of the Christian names of our Lord. As yet, there is no more critical demand for two Isaiahs in the Isaianic prophecies than for a dozen Homers in the Homeric poems. In fact, the sacred writers are not half as fragmentary and composite as well-known English historians, poets, and philosophers. Nor do marks of editorship always weaken the genuineness and integrity of a standard treatise. The postscript of Joshua, at the close of the Pentateuch, concerning the death of Moses may have been read by the ancient Hebrew as we now read a biographical note to the works of Bacon. Passing allusions to other books of Kings and Chronicles may have seemed like the conscientious references of a Hume, a Prescott, or a Motley to well-known official records; and explanatory remarks and parenthetical hints, easily distinguishable by their connection, may have been like helpful annotations upon the text of a Milton or a Butler, with the difference that, in Hebrew manuscripts, they could not be put within brackets or in the margin. Indeed, a competent editor, like Ezra the Scribe, might canonize otherwise unknown writers, as a Niebuhr or a Grote could sift crude annals and sanction the most obscure authors, or as some rare genius might detect for us the apocrypha of Shakespeare. Not even such tell-tale signs as new words, late idioms, or local phrases could wholly discredit a renowned author whose writings have come down to us through all the vicissitudes of language and literature. The several codes of Moses, if framed before the conquest of Canaan, would have been no more ideal than the Republic of Plato; and any later Hebraisms or Chaldæisms appearing among them since the Babylonian exile need be no more puzzling than Anglicisms or Americanisms among the feudal forms and Norman phrases of a recent edition of Blackstone. If the first and second parts of Isaiah are in any sense prophetic, to refer them to different authors at different periods, merely because of differences of theme, style, and diction, would be like assigning a double authorship to Paradise Lost and Paradise Regained; or arguing from a modernized version of Chaucer that he could not have written the Canterbury Tales; or claiming Childe Harold as an Elizabethan poem because of its few archaisms and Spenserian stanza. In all Hebrew literature, early, middle, and recent, there is no stumbling-block like that of Lord Tennyson singing in the Yorkshire dialect as well as in the purest English. Sometimes the feats of genius may perplex us even more than the marvels of inspiration. Besides, it should not be forgotten that while the Bible is literature, and very good literature, yet it is not to be treated as uninspired literature, and judged by mere æsthetic rules alone, much less classed with the pseudonymous fragments which have become the puzzle and the scandal of critics. More than forty years ago that prince of biblical scholars, Joseph Addison Alexander, thought that such treatment of Isaiah had already reached its limit, with the promise of "no further invention, unless it be that of reading the book backward or shuffling its chapters like a pack of cards." The higher criticism may have its duties as well as its rights, and it is not one of its rights to impose mere speculative conclusions upon us as scientific verities. Without at all undervaluing any of its assured results, we may still hope, as we watch the brilliant tournament of learning and genius, that the combatants will at length fight their way around the field of conjecture back to the traditional belief from which they started, and which is still the common-sense judgment of mankind. That judgment is, that if there be any evidence at all of inspiration in the sacred writers, such evidence favors their long-established authorship as well as canonicity, and their consequent accuracy, no less than their veracity, as organs of divine revelation.

We are now ready for several conclusions. Neither the literary imperfections, nor the historiographical defects, nor the traditional glosses of Holy Scripture can of themselves, at their worst, impair its scientific integrity or philosophic value, if it have this value. Such mere *errata* may yet be corrected or explained, and prove in no sense permanent errors, much less essential untruths. They are wholly superficial and transient, not of the abiding essence of the revealed Word. They may, indeed, and they often do, raise presumptions against the claim of inspiration in the minds of hostile critics; but they are not the proper pleas of the friendly critics who look for scientific errors in an inspired Bible. Such critics take the dangerous ground that the Bible teaches nothing but religious truth, and may even teach such truth in connection with scientific error. This is dangerous ground: because it is ground lying inside the limits of an accepted revelation; because it involves not so much the mere human form, as the divine content, of that revelation; and because it exhibits that divine content as an amalgam of fact and fiction, truth and error, knowledge and superstition. It is dangerous ground, also, because it opens the way for hostile critics to proceed quite logically from scientific errors to religious errors in the Bible, by arguing that if it teaches false astronomy and crude physics, it no less clearly teaches bad ethics and worse theology. And it is dangerous ground in philosophy as well as in religion, since it would deprive her physical no less than her psychical provinces of their chief source of transcendental knowledge, and abandon her whole metaphysical domain to the empiric, the agnostic, and the sceptic. Literary and textual obscurities there may be upon the surface of Holy Writ, like spots upon the sun, or rather like motes in the eye; but scientific errors in its divine purport would be the sun itself extinguished at noon. Such a Bible could not live in this epoch.

Happily, however, these grave issues are not yet upon us; and it would be very ignoble, as well as unwise, to array mere prejudices or unacceptable consequences against an opposing argument, without squarely facing its logic.

### The Physical Teaching of the Bible.

Let us first clearly distinguish the physical teaching from the spiritual teaching of the Bible, as it may be roughly outlined in its own language. We shall find that while the Scriptures principally teach what man is to believe concerning God and what duty God requires of man, yet they secondarily teach some other matters of human interest lying within the scope of science as well as religion. In other words, although the Bible mainly traverses the realm of the mental and moral sciences with its revelations, yet it also extends into the realm of the physical sciences and includes more or less of their ground and material. In astronomy it teaches that in the beginning God created the heavens and the earth; that wisdom was with Him when He prepared the heavens; that by understanding hath He established them and garnished them by His Spirit; that the heavens declare His power and faithfulness and glory; that He is worshipped by the whole host of heaven in the very heaven of heavens; and that they are the abode of the Father and the angels, unto whom in all heavenly places is now made known His manifold wisdom upon earth. In geology it teaches that in six days Jehovah made the sky and land and sea, plants and animals and man, and saw that all was very good; that He rested on the seventh day to make it the type and pledge of a Sabbath for man; that the whole earth is full of the riches of His wisdom and goodness; that every rainbow betokens His ordained succession of seed-time and harvest, summer and winter, throughout the year; but that, nevertheless, as the earth was once destroyed by water on account of sin, so it will yet be renewed by fire as an abode of righteousness. In anthropology it teaches that God formed man out of the dust of the ground and breathed into him a living soul; that he was created in the image of God, with dominion over the beasts, but a little lower than the angels, in a state of innocence; that mankind became so corrupt as to require the judgment of the flood; that thereafter ensued different races, languages and arts, with one peculiar race chosen for their redemption, and that the degraded humanity of the First Adam, of the earth earthy, is yet to be succeeded by a regenerate humanity of the Second Adam, the Lord from heaven, through the resurrection of a celestial body. Without going on to cite its more spiritual teaching in psychology, in sociology, and in theology, and without answering objections before we meet them, we are to confine our attention to this physical teaching, portions of which are now before us, and to inquire if in any sense, to any degree, it can be regarded as scientifically erroneous.

### *No Teaching of Scripture Erroneous.*

Let it first be observed that the general distinction between errant and inerrant Scripture is not made by Scripture itself. As a theory of inspiration it is modern and extraneous. It has arisen from the supposed need of adjusting an ancient book to the science and culture of our time. Its good motive is not to be questioned nor can its plausibility be denied. That divine truth should have been offered to us in a setting of human error does not seem at first sight wholly without analogy or precedent. If Nature has its flaws and monsters, why may there not be faults and mistakes in Scripture? If the development of science has been mixed with error, why not also the delivery of revelation? There is even a grain of force in such reasoning as applied to any mere textual or literary difficulties yet to be removed or explained. But the moment it is applied to the sacred authors themselves it breaks down. It was not their theory of their own inspiration. If anything is plain in their writings, it is plain that they claim to be making divine communications under an unerring guidance. Our Saviour, too, sanctioned the claim in His own use of the Hebrew Scriptures, and renewed it for the Christian Scriptures. At length the apostles went forth maintaining it amid the masterpieces of Greek and Roman literature. When St. Paul, in an assembly of Athenian philosophers, quotes from Aratus and Cleanthes sentiments also quoted by Cicero and Seneca, it is with the polite acknowledgment, "As certain of your own poets have said," but when he quotes from Moses a sentiment afterward quoted by David, it is with the devout preamble, "As the Holy Ghost saith." Now it is simply impossible to associate such statements with an erroneous communication from God to man in any sphere of truth, physical or spiritual. The only escape from them is to except them from the physical sphere, or limit them to the spiritual sphere. But no such exceptions or limitations can be found. As judged by their own claims, the Scriptures, if inerrant at all, must be accounted inerrant as to their whole revealed content, whatever it be and wherever found, whether in the region of the natural sciences or in that of ethics and theology.

### *The Physical Teaching Implicated with the Spiritual.*

The Bible also shows that its physical teaching is implicated with its spiritual teaching in the closest logical and practical connections, with no possible discrimination between the one as erroneous and the other as true. The full import only of these connections can be discerned by profound study. Ordinarily we lose sight of them. We are so prone to detach Scripture from Scripture that we often neglect or slight large portions which do not at once strike our fancy or interest. We ask, what is the use of Genesis, with its dry genealogies, or Leviticus, with its obsolete ritual, or the Prophets, with their mystical visions? Why read the Old Testament at all, when we have its fulfilment in the New? Or why even take much thought of the Epistles, while we have their core in the Gospels? The words of Christ contain the essential truths, and these are so few that they may be read running.

All the rest we are ready to discard as mere surplusage. So might some masterpiece of dramatic art seem full of irrelevant scenes and dialogues until its plot has been analyzed and its details tested upon the stage. The devout student of the Bible, intent on searching its full contents, will soon find that the seeming medley is in reality a living organism, with its nearest spiritual truths in logical dependence upon its remotest physical facts, and the one in practical relation to the other. He will see its astronomical revelation of a Creator of the heavens and earth, not only distinguishing the true Jehovah from the mere local and national deities of antiquity, but identifying him with the maker of suns and systems in our own time, and thus disclosing the foundations of revealed, in all natural, religion, together with the revealed commandments against heathenism, idolatry, and profaneness. He will see the geological revelation of the six days' work, not merely upholding the narrow Sabbath of the old economy, as commanded from age to age, but projecting the larger Sabbath of the new economy as yet to be realized in the millennial age of peace, and so connecting the whole history of the earth with the history of man. He will see the anthropological revelation of God's lost image in man as at once demanding and sustaining the atonement and the incarnation, together with the whole human half of the decalogue, and the predicted regeneration of both earth and man in the resurrection. Throughout the realm of the sciences he will see the author of Scripture revealing himself as the author of Nature, and building the one upon the other. The whole psychical superstructure of religious doctrines and ethical precepts will appear to him reposing upon its physical foundations in the pre-existing constitution of nature and humanity. Remove but one of those foundation stones, and that superstructure will totter. They stand or fall together. Historically, too, as well as logically, the concession of any scientific error has led to the downfall of the whole biblical system of doctrine.

*The Physical and Spiritual Teaching Alike Non-Scientific.*

It is seldom remarked that both the physical and the spiritual teaching are alike given in a non-scientific form. Often it is said—and said truly enough—that the Bible does not teach astronomy or physics as a science. But neither does it teach theology or ethics as a science. The method and phrase of science are no more, no less, wanting in its physical than in its spiritual revelations. If the former are presented as a mere crude mass of facts and truths without law or order, so also are the latter; and it will be no harder to find the epochs of geology in the first chapter of Genesis than the persons of the Trinity in the first chapter of St. John. If it be granted that the physical truths of Scripture are couched in the popular and phenomenal language of the times when it was written, so also are its spiritual truths veiled in the anthropomorphic and even barbaric imagery common to all rude peoples; and when the Psalmist tells us, "The sun knoweth his going down," he is no worse astronomer than he is theologian when he declares, "He that sitteth in the heavens shall laugh at the kings of the earth." If it be urged that we have left far behind us the contemporary astronomy of the Old Testament, with its spangled canopy of heaven wrought as a marvel of handiwork, how shall we defend its contemporary theology, with its manlike deity so often depicted seemingly as a monster of anger, jealousy, and cruelty? If we are told that we have outgrown its physics, with their cisterns in the earth and windows in the sky opened and shut by angels, what shall be said for its ethics, so long charged with polygamous patriarchs and pro-slavery apostles? If we are warned against a few devout scientists who are endeavoring to harmonize their geology with the Mosaic cosmogony, is there to be no warning for this scandal of great churches and denominations at the present moment adjusting their metaphysics to the Pauline divinity? Is modern theology any more accordant with Scripture than modern geology? In short, there is not an objection to the non-scientific character of the physical teaching which will not recoil with greater force against the spiritual teaching. Whoever, for this reason alone, affirms scientific errors in the biblical astronomy and physics, must be prepared to admit them also in the biblical theology and ethics.

### The Physical and Spiritual Teaching Alike Sincere.

Nor can it be said that the spiritual teaching is any more reconcilable with popular fallacies than the physical teaching. It has been maintained that the divine author of the Scriptures accommodated them to the physical errors of their own times, for the sake of the moral and religious truths to be conveyed. There was no need to correct the false astronomy of the ancient Jews, so long as the phenomenal sunrise and sunset were still true for them and for their age. It was only important to give them true ideas of God and duty, and to leave them to their unaided reason in other matters of mere science and culture. Our Lord Himself is supposed to have thus connived at the story of Jonah, the belief in demoniacal possessions, and even the tradition of the Mosaic authorship of the Pentateuch. He did not come to teach natural history, or medical psychology, or the higher criticism. It was enough for His purpose that He could make the entombment in the whale's belly prefigure His own resurrection, prove His Messiahship by seeming to cast out devils, and enforce His teachings with the great name of Moses. But the risk of such reasoning is that it might prove too much. It might soon bring down the maxim, "False in one thing, false in everything else," upon the head of any teacher who only once should thus deceive his disciples and teach them to deceive others. In the examples given, it would leave the most momentous truths resting through all coming time upon a basis of prejudice, superstition, and falsehood. Moreover, it could be applied logically, as it has been applied actually, to doctrines the most essential; and in the end would reduce Christianity to mere natural religion as adapted to Judaism. It is a matter of history that the so-called theory of accommodation has thus run its course in the schools of criticism. Be it observed, however, that the theory itself is not here in dispute, for the purpose of this argument. You may adopt it if you like; and treat the history of Jonah as a mere nightmare vision with a good moral, the demoniacs as cases of lunacy and delirium, and the literary claim of Moses as an old Jewish legend. But in that case you must be ready to find pious frauds and innocent fables throughout the Bible, and can no longer hold it to be false only in physics and not also in religion and morals. If it were once true for its own time, it would soon cease to be true for our time.

### The Physical and Spiritual Teaching Alike Permanent.

Here it should be noticed that both the physical and the spiritual teaching alike have a permanent and universal import, as well as local and temporary reference. Usually this is admitted as to the biblical theology, despite its antique and rude imagery. We have read the Old Testament forward into the New, and the New Testament backward into the Old, until the God of justice in the one seems consistent with the God of mercy in the other, and all anthropomorphism disappears in a divine ideal of infinite purity and love. But as to the physical sciences, it is sometimes held that the prophets and apostles were so dominated by their environment that they not only shared the scientific errors around them, but may even have expressed those errors in their inspired writings as freely as they have exposed their own frailties and idiosyncrasies. Otherwise, it is said, no revelation could have been received by them or made through them to their own age and country, or indeed to any other age or country. There is a show of truth in such statements. Certainly it would be very absurd to treat the sacred writers as mere amanuenses without thought or individuality; and quite impossible to take them out of their proper setting in the unscientific ages when they lived, and from among the uncultured peoples whom they taught. It is not even necessary to suppose their own personal knowledge greater than that of their contemporaries, outside of the divine communications. But neither is it necessary to suppose them acquainted with the entire purport of those communications. They may have spoken better than they knew. They may not have been fully conscious of their messages, as applicable in other eras and stages of culture. Even in pagan literature the great poets, sages, and philosophers, though writing solely for their own time, have unconsciously written for all after-time. So Homer sang in ancient Greece; and the ages have been listening ever since. So Euclid, two thousand years ago, sketched lines and angles which to-day save the sailor from shipwreck and regulate the commerce of nations. So Plato reasoned in the academy, with little thought beyond his own disciples; and the world's philosophy is still sitting at his feet. No more marvellous would it be had David discerned a divine glory in the heavens which astronomy now illustrates, or Moses perceived a divine order of creation which geology is confirming. Inspiration may at least be supposed to equal genius. Moreover, the claim of inspiration being allowed, the sacred authors at once appear as organs of another and higher intelligence than their own. Avowedly, they often speak of divine mysteries which they knew only in part, and sometimes of a distant past or future which they neither had seen nor could see. Moses, in his vision of the creation, during six days could not have reviewed the whole physical development of the globe; and Isaiah, in his vision of redemption, could not have foreseen, beyond his own foreground, the whole moral career of mankind. Yet behind the words of both Moses and Isaiah was an Omniscience embracing the entire course of nature and of history. No violence would be done to their personality by supposing them the mouthpiece of such Omniscience. As voiced by its greatest teachers, science itself acquires an ever-widening vision of which they had not dreamed. Nor need any mystical sense be claimed for the sacred text in order to give it so large scope and fulness. It is not the mere learned exegete or visionary saint who is now reading between the lines of prophets and apostles. It is the strict scientist who is returning from every conflict with the phenomenal language of the Bible, to interpret that language, as he has learned to interpret the phenomena themselves, in a richer sense and with a wider application. That the heavens declare the glory of God has become only more true since a Newton and a Herschel have illuminated them with suns and planets. That heaven and earth were made in six days is none the less true because a Dana and a Guyot have been retracing those days of Jehovah as long cosmogonic eras. That man was created in the image of God might still be true even though devout biologists should yet prove him to be but the full flower of the planetary life as well as the highest ideal of the Creator. Only the young and crude sciences, wrangling among themselves, are at seeming variance with the Scripture. The older, more complete sciences are already in growing accord with it. Hence it is that the revealed Jehovah still reigns in the astronomical heavens, instead of having been left far behind us as an Israelitish Jupiter in the skies of Mount Zion. For this reason Genesis is still repeating the story of the earth instead of becoming the forgotten myth of some Hebrew Hesiod; and for this reason Jesus Himself is no mere Jewish Socrates of the schools, but the Divine Teacher of mankind. In a word, it is because the Bible, though non-scientific, is not anti-scientific, that it is as true for our time as it was true for its own time, and is likely to remain true for all time to come.

### The Physical and Spiritual Teaching Alike Suitable.

We come next to the more positive argument that the physical teaching, like the spiritual, has been adapted, both in kind and degree, to our wants and capacities. It may be objected to the foregoing view that, after all, as a matter of fact, we get our theology from Scripture, and our natural sciences from nature, and that a mere absence of scientific errors from Scripture does not prove the presence of any scientific verities. This is true, and yet not true. As to theology, it is true that when considered as a metaphysical science of God and divine things its material is mainly to be found in the Bible; but it is not true that as an empirical science of religions it may not find material outside of the Bible in the religious history of mankind. As to the physical sciences, it is true that they are derived mainly from nature as bodies of empirical knowledge; but it is not true that they can find no metaphysical ground and material in the biblical revelations concerning physical facts. On the contrary, a thorough investigation will show that, as we ascend the scale of the sciences, from the simple to the complex, the revealed material increases with our increasing moral needs and decreasing mental equipment. In astronomy, on its metaphysical side, we shall find, at least, some revealed matter, such as a creator of the heavens, whose immensity, eternity, omnipotence, immutability, and glory they declare; in geology, a little more revealed matter, such as the divine order of the material creation, the divine wisdom and goodness which it illustrates, with some moral crises which mark its history; in anthropology, yet more revealed matter, such as the creation of man in the divine image, his vicegerent dominion over nature, his primitive innocence, together with some glimpses of his early history, the origin of races, languages, and arts, and their adjustment in a scheme of universal providence. And so on, through the higher mental and social sciences, we shall meet an ever-growing volume of revealed facts and truths, until we reach the topmost science of theology, where the revealed material becomes transcendent in kind and infinite in extent. Could we here pursue such inquiries, it might be shown that this apportionment of so large an amount of spiritual teaching with relatively so small an amount of physical teaching is not only in strict accordance with the pre-existing constitution of the human intellect, but is itself a proof of the divine wisdom which has presided over the whole revelation.

### The Physical Teaching Also Important.

It only remains now to add that the physical teaching in its own place and for its own purpose is quite as important and valuable as the spiritual teaching. In proving this, there is no need to belittle the great religious themes of Scripture, or to deny a religious aim and purport, even in its physical revelations. Such facts as the origin of the heavens, the formation of the earth, and the constitution of man have a physical side, which has been, indeed, revealed to us in connection with religious truth. Nevertheless, they are, at least, separable in thought for special study under their scientific aspects and in their scientific connections. As a matter of fact, they are thus treated by physicists and by some divines. Without foisting into the Bible any occult meaning, or forcing it out of its due sphere of influence, we may investigate its correlations with astronomy, geology, anthropology, and other sciences, considered as subsidiary and complemental to divine revelation; and the field of such correlations will widen the further we investigate them. Moreover, true as it may be, that religion is the chief topic of revelation, yet it is still true that it touches other great interests of humanity, and serves other high purposes. Although never designed to teach the arts and sciences, it has in fact always promoted them in every stage of their progress. While the furtherance of science, the perfection of philosophy, and the growth of civilization cannot be ranked as its chief ends and issues, yet they may at least be classed as its incidental fruits and trophies. In this guarded sense we shall find that the physical portion of revelation, small though it seem to be, is of the greatest benefit to science, philosophy, and general culture.

### *Evidential Importance of the Physical Teaching.*

There is, first of all, its apologetical or evidential value, to which a passing glance should be given. Civilization is interested in the defence of Christianity; and whatever makes a divine revelation valuable, either in philosophy or in religion, becomes enhanced by the proof of its harmony with human science. When the chief authorities in any science are found favoring such harmony; when its established truths already illustrate it, and its hypotheses can be hopefully adjusted toward it; and when all the sciences are seen taking this general direction according to their different stages of advancement—we gain new evidence of revelation, the highest, perhaps, that can be afforded. It is science itself becoming an unwitting, and sometimes an unwilling, witness at the bar of Omniscience. It is evidence which is strictly scientific in its logical quality and force, since it is derived from the facts of nature, as agreeing with the truths of Scripture. In this age of the arts and sciences it is as timely as the evidence yielded in the age of miracles and prophecies. It meets the modern scientist seeking wisdom, as that evidence met the ancient Jew requiring a sign. It even explains miracles and fulfils prophecies, and thus crowns and completes all former evidences. Without it, indeed, they would themselves fall worthless to the ground. As no miracle could ever prove a falsehood, and no prophecy could perpetuate nonsense, so no amount of miraculous and prophetical evidence accumulated in past ages could uphold a Bible containing scientific errors in the face of modern science. Herein lies the peril of the hour. The timid or rash apologetes who are spiking their guns on the outer bulwarks of scientific evidence, and fleeing into the citadel of orthodoxy to repair its walls, may yet find themselves in conflict with enemies whom they had thought to admit as friends within the ramparts. Schleiermacher long since forewarned us of that " bombardment of derision, amid which they will be ceremoniously interred in their own fortifications." Not by weak concessions to science in this day of abounding science is the Bible to be vindicated. Only by strengthening and insisting upon its scientific proofs can it retain its power, either at the centre of Christian civilization or in the logical crusade of the missionary among heathen religions and philosophies.

### Metaphysical Importance of the Physical Teaching.

But the direct value of revelation, not only as scientifically attested, but as itself a source of scientific verity, lies more within the present inquiry. As such value is largely metaphysical, it may not be readily appreciated by the unthinking reader, who terms anything metaphysical which he does not choose to understand; or by the superficial thinker, who scorns all metaphysics but his own; or even by the special scientist, who abjures metaphysics for the sake of some little fragment of empirical knowledge. But to the profound inquirer, even though he eschew the scholastic metaphysics, it is becoming every day clearer that all physics at length run out into metaphysics, and that every physical science at bottom rests upon some hidden metaphysical basis, underneath the facts or phenomena with which it deals, down in a recondite region of realities and causes which divine revelation alone can disclose. The Bible, indeed, does not teach the empirical part of any such science, its body of phenomena and laws; but it does teach its metaphysical complement, the divine ideas expressed in those phenomena, and the divine causes of those laws. In astronomy it does not teach celestial physics, the figures, motions, and orbits of planets, suns, and stars throughout infinite space and time; but it does teach that divine immensity, eternity, and omnipotence of which the whole celestial system is but a phenomenal manifestation, and without which it would be a stupendous anomaly. In geology it does not teach terrestrial chemistry, the birth and growth of the earth through all its eras and phases, with all its strata, floræ, and faunæ; but it does teach that divine power, wisdom, and goodness which are the source, method, and issue of the whole terrestrial development, and without which it would be at once causeless and aimless. In anthropology it does not teach the human organism, with its laws of heredity and environment, and of the evolution of races, languages, and arts; but it does teach those divine ideals through which man has been passing from the image of an ape to the image of God, and without which he would be a mere failure and paradox. And in the higher mental and social sciences, while it does not teach any psychical processes and laws, it does teach all needed spiritual truth and knowledge. As yet, indeed, these subtle connections between the rational and revealed material of each science have not come clearly into general view; much less have they been logically ascertained and formulated. Nevertheless, the large-minded leaders in all the sciences are at least seeking some more rational ground for them than sheer ignorance or clear absurdity; and not a few of them are finding it practically by studying the works of God together with his Word.

*Philosophical Importance of the Physical Teaching.*

At the highest point of scientific contact with the Bible appears its value in philosophy considered as the supreme science of knowledge or science of the sciences. Here the full appreciation is not only difficult, but barred by prejudice and distaste. We have become so accustomed, wisely enough, to treat philosophy as a secular pursuit, and have so just a dislike to any crude admixture of religion with science, that we may be in danger of the other extreme of leaving at least one-half the philosophic domain under the rule of scepticism and ignorance. Often, because unwilling to mingle sacred speech with scholastic jargon, we may seem to accept theories of knowledge which ignore or exclude revelation, as if there were no such aid to reason. Possibly our agnostic friends, with whom we agree up to a certain point, may sometimes have fancied the fastidious reserve to mean doubt of any philosophy taking religion as well as science within its scope. If this be so, it is time to say, in the frankest English, that while they are building their knowledge upon faith, we are building our faith upon knowledge. It is time to remind them that the little they do know, they know only in part; that the most exact science of which they can boast is filled with crude hypothesis and vague conjecture; that it has been reared through ages of error by a fallible logic; that it depends upon an assumed order of nature which is broken every time they lift a stone from the earth; that it rests ultimately upon universal conceptions which by their own showing are self-contradictory; in a word that, apart from the despised metaphysics and the neglected Bible, it is mixed with credulity and based on absurdity.

It is time also, on our part, to insist that, although we cannot know everything about God, and the soul, and the unseen world, we may at least know something; that the otherwise Unknowable has been made known to us by an intelligible revelation; that this revealed knowledge has been built up for us within the region of facts, through ages of experience, before science was born; that it not only comes to us with scientific evidence, but supports each science, and throughout the sciences yields material without which they would fall, like falling stars, into a chaos and void—in a word, that the inspired Bible is a radiant source of divine knowledge, chiefly within the psychical sciences, but also within the physical, and therefore essential to the completion of philosophy itself as the crowning science of the sciences. Such a philosophy will see no scientific errors flecking that sun of truth which thus lights up its domain, but only paradoxes to dazzle it, should it too rashly gaze, and mysteries to blind it with tears.

It is more than half a century since this discussion began in the schools of Germany, and less than half that time since it passed into the Church of England. In our own country it seems destined to become popular in its course, as well as academic and ecclesiastical. The daily press already reflects a growing interest in questions of biblical criticism, which hitherto have been kept within the province of scholars and divines. Parties are forming, as if some great battle for the truth of Holy Writ were at hand. Its defenders, it is to be feared, are as yet but poorly equipped and marshalled. Their opponents boast of the highest culture of the time; have the exultant sympathy of the whole unbelieving class; and even claim, however unwarrantably, some orthodox allies. In the first onset, doubtless, they will win a brilliant victory. Then may come a great uprising of the Christian masses, as moved by that Holy Spirit who first inspired His Holy Scripture. Whoever shall stand apart from them in such a crisis will not be shunning a religious question alone. In his place he will be deserting some other related interest of humanity. The thinker will be deserting that which for ages has set the problems of philosophy. The scholar will be deserting that which has built up the universities of Christendom. The artist will be deserting that which has yielded the purest ideals of genius. The scientist will be deserting that which has kindled the torch of research. The man of letters will be deserting that which has moulded our English speech and literature. The man of the world will be deserting that which has lent to society refinement, and purity, and grace. The merchant, the lawyer, the doctor will be deserting that which is the ethical basis of their callings. The patriot and the statesman will be deserting that which has given us our freedom and our laws. And the philanthropist will be deserting that which is the very keystone of civilization.

# CHAPTER IV.

## THE EVIDENCE FROM ASTRONOMY.

On entering the field of the Scientific Evidence we are at once impressed by its vast extent and embarrassed with its varied materials. It is as vast as the domain of science itself, embracing both the physical sciences, astronomy, geology, anthropology, and the psychical sciences, psychology, sociology, comparative theology; and it is as varied as the contents of Holy Scripture, extending into the Old Testament as connected mainly with the physical sciences, and into the New Testament as connected chiefly with the psychical sciences. It would be impossible, in a few chapters, to traverse this entire field of investigation, and exhaust all its riches of proof and illustration. We must confine ourselves to the physical sciences, astronomy, geology, anthropology; and from these sciences we shall be able to cull only a few specimens of the evidence which they so abundantly afford.

### *Growth of the Astronomical Evidence.*

Astronomy, as the oldest of the exact sciences, was the first to come into seeming conflict with revealed religion, and has been the first to yield it a large body of striking evidence. In its early stages, as cultivated by the Greeks, it was repelled as false science by the Church Fathers, who continued to expound the astronomical psalms in a strictly literalistic manner and descanted upon the Glory of God in the heavens as there displayed by a star-spangled curtain or canopy stretched over the earth. In its later stages, during the reign of the Ptolemaic theory, it was accepted by the schoolmen who derived the same biblical argument, in a purely phenomenalistic manner, from an illuminated dome of crystalline spheres, which were supposed to revolve around the earth with the sun, moon, and stars attached to them as means of producing the wonderful vicissitudes of day and night, summer and winter. But in the modern stage of the science, with the rise of the Copernican theory of the solar system, the discovery of the rotundity of our planet and its orbital motion around the sun, the whole orthodox conception of heaven, earth, and hell was revolutionized; the literalistic and phenomenalistic interpretation of Scripture was abandoned; the ancient canopy of the sky was rent in twain; the great dome of the crystalline heavens was dashed to pieces; and there issued a breach between the Bible and astronomy, more alarming than any that now seems to yawn between the Bible and other sciences. It was as if the very throne of God had been removed from the firmament, the abode of the angels destroyed, and anything like a revelation to our little world made impossible. Galileo was compelled upon his knees to abjure his discoveries as deadly heresies. Nevertheless, as the new astronomy gradually compelled assent and admiration, efforts were made to readjust it to the Scriptures by a more scientific interpretation, which should magnify divine revelation in consistency with the popular and phenomenalistic language in which it had necessarily been conveyed. It was found that, after all, the rationale of the biblical argument, which the fathers and schoolmen had so crudely conceived and imperfectly used, remained unimpaired, and in fact could now be based upon more unquestionable premises, and unfolded with a more wonderful richness and potency. The divine glory in the heavens, being no longer obscured by a false astronomy and a false exegesis, began to shine forth with all the added brilliance of myriads of suns and planets, and the Scriptures acquired a fuller meaning indicative of the omniscience which had inspired them. The result is, that a science which at first so seriously menaced revealed truth is now yielding it abundant evidence. We shall find by adducing a few specimens, that it affords each of the four species of evidence which were described in the introduction.

## Testimony of Astronomers.

The first is the testimony of the chief authorities of the science. It is not surprising that astronomers, as a class, should be devout and Christian. The grandeur of the starry universe, and the impotence of human reason to comprehend it, conspire to lift their thoughts toward the Creator as its only adequate cause, and justify the poets' verdict that any intellect must be abnormal that can resist such impressions—" An undevout astronomer is mad." Certainly the exceptions can be better explained by some idiosyncrasy, or defect of training, or inveterate prejudice, than by any supposed sceptical tendency in the science itself. If Lalande could jestingly dismiss religious considerations from the field of astronomy, he spake as an atheist and a revolutionist rather than as the accomplished astronomer that he was. It is said that Laplace never mentioned the name of the Supreme Being without a reverent gesture, and when, therefore, the French King remarked that he seemed to have allowed no place for a God in his cosmogonic speculations, it was simply, as a strict scientist, not as an atheist, he replied, that he did not need the hypothesis of a God in so purely empirical and inductive an inquiry. The examples of unbelieving astronomers have been few, and many of them, when historically traced, will be found to have been less astronomers than unbelievers who have made their little knowledge do service to their prejudices.

## Devout Astronomers.

On the other hand, we find that nearly all the great names in the science have been harmoniously associated with the Christian faith. The chief discoverer of modern astronomy, Copernicus, lived as a faithful priest, and died requesting that his epitaph might be the prayer of the penitent thief on the cross, " Lord, remember me when thou comest in thy Kingdom." Galileo did not abjure the Holy Gospels upon which he was forced to abjure the opinion of the earth's mobility. Kepler, as he cried Eureka at the close of his researches into the motions of the planet Mars, declared that he could wait a century for a reader, since the Almighty had waited thousands of years for a discoverer. Newton, after discovering and proclaiming the law of God in the heavens, turned devoutly to study that other law of God revealed in his holy Word. The Herschels, father and son, had their tomb inscribed to that divine faithfulness which is established in the heavens and on earth, and in their family maintained from one generation to another. The brilliant and versatile Arago did not deem it unscientific to support his celestial speculations with religious truths and arguments. The late Stephen Alexander thought of himself as a child spelling out the divine story of the stars, and crowned his life-long studies with a matured confession of his faith. And the great living astronomers, with scarcely an exception, have let it appear that Christian truth is either theoretically or practically combined with their astronomical knowledge.

### Revealed Truths in Astronomy.

The second source of evidence is found in the perfect agreement of astronomical facts with revealed truths. This will appear by simply bringing the two together and observing their correlations; in other words, connecting what has been certainly discovered with what has been surely revealed in reference to the heavenly bodies. On the one hand, it has been discovered, contrary to all appearances, that our earth is a huge globe or planet poised in space with the moon as its satellite; that the sun and stars are also great globes, but immensely larger in size and inconceivably distant; that the stars are innumerable companies of these suns, planets, and satellites, under fixed mechanical laws, careering, with incredible swiftness, through orbits and periods, practically infinite in space and time. On the other hand, it has been revealed, in the common language of appearances, that the heavens declare the glory of God; that by his understanding hath he made them and garnished them by his spirit; that his throne is over the heavens, and in the heavens hath he established his faithfulness; and that he is the High and Lofty One who inhabiteth eternity and whom the heaven of heavens cannot contain. Now, is there any contrariety between these scientific facts and these religious truths? Are they not rather the logical complements or counterparts of one another? In the view of philosophy as well as of faith, what were the vast celestial mechanism without some sufficient cause, such as the revealed Jehovah, to give it rational support and consistency? And what were that revealed Jehovah without some adequate illustration of his infinite attributes, such as astronomy alone can afford? Take either without the other and see what would remain. Take astronomy without the Bible and there would remain a mere causeless and purposeless mass of worlds, sun, planet, and satellite, whirling blindly through the ages toward nothingness. Take the Bible without astronomy, and there would remain the infinite and absolute Jehovah enthroned in the skies of our little planet as the only scene of his abode. But bring the two together, and at once the author of Scripture becomes the author of nature with all his revealed attributes in full manifestation; with his immensity extending through the boundless regions of celestial space; with his eternity unfolding through the endless periods of celestial time; with his omnipotence expending its potential energy in the tremendous forces and velocities of the celestial orbs; with his immutability expressed in the mechanical and physical laws which govern these ceaseless movements; and with his omniscience displayed in a universe of order and beauty and grandeur which all our science has but begun to apprehend. Astronomy thus yields overwhelming evidence in favor of revealed religion.

### Critical Questions.

And this evidence is quite independent of any question raised by literary criticism as to the origin, composition, and inspiration of the Bible itself. The most extreme ground may be taken in regard to such questions. Let it be assumed that Genesis, the Book of Job, the Psalms, and other scriptures which contain astronomical allusions were written by unknown authors, or compiled from pre-existing documents, or derived from some primeval revelation in the form of mere legendary fragments. Yet the fact remains that in this ancient book alone can be found that pure sublime theism which astronomy now requires, verifies, and illustrates. Let it also be granted that our modern astronomy was wholly unknown to the sacred writers, whilst they were freely speaking as organs of revelation, and that the psalmist beheld in the firmament nothing more than a star-lit expanse or an embroidered canopy wrought by the Divine fingers. Yet it will still be true that in the light of science his inspired words have acquired an infinite meaning which no mere human genius could foresee and of which he may never have dreamed when he exclaimed, "The heavens declare the glory of God."

The demonstrated portion of astronomy, known as descriptive astronomy or celestial mechanics, affords evidence of those revealed attributes of Jehovah which imply his relations to the material universe, to illimitable space, time, matter, and force, such as immensity, eternity, omnipotence, immutability, omniscience, together with some incidental proofs of the divine wisdom and goodness in the adaptation of the celestial system to our planet and its inhabitants.

### *Evidential Literature.*

With the rise of the modern astronomy such conceptions were inevitable, if not irresistible in all religious literature. The earlier astronomers themselves, such as Copernicus, Kepler, and Newton, did not scruple to mingle pious reflections with their scientific discoveries. Richard Bentley, the first Boyle lecturer, in his sermons on the Confutation of Atheism, from a survey of the origin and frame of the world, expounded the Principia of Newton against the Epicurean doctrine of eternal matter and motion, at the same time unfolding scientifically that ancient proof of the divine beauty and order of the firmament, the cosmos and mundus, which kindled the adoration of Plato and Cicero no less than of Moses and David. William Derham, the learned Canon of Windsor, whose once popular Astrotheology seems to have been the first distinct treatise of the kind, also demonstrated the being and attributes of God from a survey of the heavens, especially enlarging upon the usefulness of the celestial "globes" as then for the first time becoming apparent in their ascertained figures, motions, orbits, and attractions. The versatile Whiston, in like manner, treated of the Astronomical Principles of Natural and Revealed Religion, on the basis of the Newtonian philosophy. And the same argument was continued by Ray and Paley. Dr. Whewell, in his Bridgewater Treatise on the Connection of Astronomy with Natural Theology, still more scientifically vindicated the benevolent design of the cosmical arrangements against the insinuation of Laplace that it was easy to conceive of a better solar system or of one more advantageously adapted to human welfare. The late Professor Ormsby Mitchell, in his Astronomy of the Bible, not only sought to illustrate the divine omnipotence, eternity, immutability, and wisdom from the celestial mechanism but to discern an occult inspired acquaintance with it in the very language of the Scriptures; finding in the Hebrew expression of Job, "the sockets of the earth," implied knowledge of its diurnal rotation, and in the binding "influences of the Pleiades" an anticipatory allusion to the attraction of the solar system, and other astral systems, about a centre of universal gravity, which Mädler has placed in that constellation. And hosts of popular writers, not professed astronomers, but accepting their discoveries and embodying the results in magazines, lectures, and sermons, are still unfolding the astronomical argument for the being and attributes of deity as revealed in the Scriptures.

### Astronomical Hypotheses.

The third source of evidence is found in the provisional agreement of astronomical hypotheses with revealed doctrines. Leaving the ascertained facts of the science, we now enter the field of its unsolved problems concerning the origin, the development, and the destiny of the celestial universe. As to each of these problems we shall find astronomers holding rival hypotheses with purely scientific motives and from no religious bias whatever. And these hypotheses, being still imperfect and conflicting, might simply be left unnoticed so far as they seem to menace revealed doctrines, but if brought into relation with such doctrines can be hopefully adjusted to them by showing that at their worst they would only require some modification of our existing interpretation of Scripture; that they are already more or less reconcilable with Scripture; and meanwhile, whichever of them shall at length prevail, the one essential truth of Scripture remains untouched and indestructible, if not greatly enhanced and illustrated. In other words, astronomy even in its most problematical and hypothetical portions admits of prospective harmony with revealed religion.

### A Primitive Cosmos.

As to the first of the unsolved problems, the origin of the celestial universe, rival hypotheses have been held almost from the dawn of the science. The one hypothesis is that of a primitive cosmos or mundus, which from the beginning has continued and ever since remained as a finished world of order and beauty. Not a few astronomers, in a strict scientific spirit, such as Galileo, the younger Herschel, Lamont, and Newcomb, have abstained from speculative inquiries into the origin of the heavenly bodies as unknowable, except on metaphysical or religious grounds, and have confined their researches to the existing order of things as now proceeding under fixed mechanical and physical laws. In their view, our solar system, as we now know it, whatever may have been its primitive condition, is a piece of self-adjusting mechanism, ever maintaining its equilibrium against disorder; and the planetary bodies of which it is composed, the sun as a great globe of fire at the centre; torrid Mercury; fair, bright Venus; snow-capped Earth; blood-red Mars; belted Jupiter; Saturn with double rings and moons; Uranus and Neptune, wandering darkly in the outermost void, are but so many different species of cosmic forms with no more trace of transition or development than we can find in the different species of organic forms of plants and animals which subsist side by side in our planet. In like manner, beyond our solar system, throughout infinite space, are innumerable other solar systems, or stellar systems, each star a sun with planets, revolving around some universal centre of gravity, and displaying other cosmic forms as inconceivable to us as the scenery, flora, and fauna of unvisited countries. And it is claimed that the telescope has proved the truth of the hypothesis by resolving the nebulæ or cloud-like masses of the Milky Way into clustered suns, even galaxies of suns, all together comprising a fixed series of worlds, or scale of cosmic types, varying from the crudest asteroid that wanders in space up to the most richly garnished planet that careers around the Central Sun of the Universe.

### A Primitive Chaos.

The other hypothesis is that of a primitive chaos or crude material mass from which the existing universe was developed and is still advancing through various stages of progress. Accepting this Oriental and Hebrew conception, some astronomers, with a speculative turn of mind, like Kepler, Laplace, Herschel and Humboldt, instead of limiting their researches to the heavenly bodies as they now appear, have sought to trace them back under fixed mechanical and physical laws of evolution to their original condition. From their point of view, our Solar System, uncounted ages ago, was a vast nebula or fiery cloud which, as it whirled in swift vortices, cooled and condensed, first into a central igneous body like the Sun; then into rotating rings like those around the planet Saturn; then successively into gaseous and watery globes, like Jupiter and Uranus; and at length into solid shells like that which encloses the fiery core of our Earth as a finished world of mature growth. In like manner the whole sidereal region of space beyond our solar system, with all its constellations, is supposed to be a vast nursery of worlds in different degrees of cosmic development, co-existing like trees in a forest, but so distant that the most brilliant suns can now appear only as lucid dots in a film of light long ages after their rays have reached the eye of man. And it is now claimed that the spectroscope is verifying the truth of this speculation by revealing in the chemical constitution of different stars the successive phases of nebula, sun, and planet, as plainly as you can trace the seed bursting into the leaf and the flower at your feet.

### The Doctrine of Creation.

Now, in more or less direct relation to these two astronomical hypotheses stands the revealed doctrine of creation:— that in the beginning God created the heavens and the earth; that wisdom was with Him when He prepared the heavens; that by His word or reason the world was made and without it nothing was made that was made, and that through faith we understand that the worlds were framed by the word of God, so that things which are seen were not made of things which do appear. And the state of the question is this: If we accept one of these hypotheses our existing interpretation of Scripture remains undisturbed; if we accept the other, it can be favorably modified; but whichever shall at length prevail, the error will have been solely in our fallible interpretation and not in that infallible word of God which abideth forever. Take the hypothesis of a primitive cosmos, or of finished worlds of order and beauty, and then, in accordance with the long received and still popular conception of an instantaneous creation, the whole assemblage of suns and planets will appear starting into being full-born as by a fiat of Jehovah. Take the other hypothesis of a primitive chaos, or of worlds in different stages of evolution, and then, in accordance with the newer and more scientific conception of a continuous creation, an endless variety of suns and planets will be seen ever unfolding the infinite attributes of Jehovah in all their richness and glory. But whichever hypothesis you take, whether you conceive of creation as an act or as a process, it will still be true, as it always has been and always will be true, that "in the beginning God created the heavens and the earth."

### Our Planet Alone Inhabited.

The second unsolved problem relates to the development of the heavenly bodies into habitable worlds; and for its solution two conflicting speculations have long been current. Some astronomers, like Galileo, Herschel, Whewell, and Proctor, have maintained that our planet is the only inhabited world. It has been argued that other worlds do not possess the organic conditions of habitability; that the asteroids and comets are plainly incapable of sustaining life; that the Moon is like an extinct crater without even an atmosphere; that the Sun is but a ball of incandescent mist; that the inner planets, Mercury and Venus, are composed of cinder and slag; that the outer planets, Jupiter and Uranus, are mere globes of water and ice, while our Earth is situated between the extremes of heat and cold, in that temperate zone of the Solar System where alone the life of sentient and intellectual beings has become possible. As to the innumerable suns and planets which are supposed to be clustered together in the constellations, in

Orion, Cassiopea, and Capella, it has been boldly surmised that these are not worlds at all, but mere sparks, meteors, and comets, still coruscating throughout the heavens from the great fire-wheel of that solar nebula of which our planet is the most substantial remnant. And it is also urged that geology, by showing how many ages have rolled away ere the earth could have become ready for man, has rendered the chances as millions to one against any other world than ours being inhabited at the present time.

### Other Planets Also Habitable.

Other astronomers, however, such as Kepler, Newton, Arago, Oersted, Flammarion, have favored the idea of a plurality of inhabited worlds. In support of this idea it has been maintained that there may be forms of planetary life and intelligence for which our planet affords no analogies; that some of the planets at least, like Mars and Venus, have climatic zones, seas, and continents, suggestive of their habitability; that if others, like Mercury and the Moon, have long since passed the habitable stage and become extinct worlds, yet Jupiter and Saturn are but advancing in an earlier stage and will yet become encrusted with strata, furnished with floræ and faunæ, and tenanted by intellectual races; and that even the Sun itself bears thronging inhabitants upon the opaque body hidden behind his dazzling photosphere. It is declared that no limit can be set to the prodigal richness of Nature. With daring fancy the speculation has been pushed into the stellar regions, and the ponderous globes, gross organisms, and meagre furniture of our solar system have been put in contrast with sublimated spheres of light in Cassiopea, Orion, and Capella, where myriads of ethereal creatures are supposed to bask under many colored suns in eternal summer and perpetual youth. And it is even anticipated, in proof of the speculation, that the spectroscope may yet reveal conditions of life on the remotest stars, and that upon some of the nearer planets will soon be descried by the telescope such works of art and genius as have no type or semblance in the wildest romances of our little orb.

## The Doctrine of Angels.

Here again the state of the question is the same as in the previous problem. Two opposite speculations of astronomers are to be adjusted to the revealed doctrine of angels. That doctrine is, that Jehovah is worshipped by the whole host of heaven in the very heaven of heavens; and that the heavens are the abode of the Father and the angels, even of our Father who is in the heavens and of whom the whole family in heaven and earth is named. As yet, we have no final interpretation of these and other like Scriptures and no full comprehension of their meaning. On the first supposition, that our world alone is inhabited, the long received interpretation can be retained. The biblical heavens will continue to be viewed as a mere appurtenance of our earth. The unseen hosts of angels and archangels, dominions, principalities, powers, may be fancied, according to the Dantean conception, ascending rank above rank, toward the empyrean above our atmosphere, where the Trinity is ever enthroned as the object of their ceaseless worship. On the other supposition, however, that other worlds as well as ours are inhabited, this picture would vanish and the old interpretation be changed. Our mental horizon would expand beyond our planet, beyond the solar system, into the very heaven of heavens, until it embraced the whole amphitheatre of countless worlds with the angelical hierarchies dwelling in them as in the many mansions of our Father's house. And to the physical affinities between their dwellings and ours, would be added their spiritual attraction toward our earth as the scene of a special theophany with unfolding mysteries into which they desire to look, and every trophy of which, though but one repenting sinner, they hail with joy. Be all this, however, as it may, to whatever extent we seek to identify the biblical with the astronomical heavens, the revelation standeth sure, that the heavens are the abode of the angelic hosts, and that now unto principalities and powers in heavenly places is made known by the Church that manifold wisdom, the mystery of human redemption which was hidden in the bosom of God from the beginning.

### A Final Chaos.

The third problem refers to the destiny of the celestial universe; and for its solution two opinions have been advanced. Some astronomers and astronomical writers, like Newton, Helmholtz, Stephen Alexander, and Winchell, have inclined to the notion of a final chaos. Amid all the order and beauty of the heavenly worlds they have read signs of decay and warnings of disaster. It has been held that the incursion of comets is ever a menace to the stability of the solar system; that its own perturbations are cumulative and destructive; that the planets are cooling, shrinking, and spinning more feebly in their orbits, and slowly losing their life-bearing powers; that the Moon is already a dead world, with its pallid face upturned to the Sun; that the fires of the Sun itself are steadily dying out; and that sooner or later the time must come when sun, planet, and satellite shall be precipitated together and collapse into the igneous dust from which they sprang. It is taken as an axiom that there can be no perpetual motion in the machinery of the heavens, and that the potential energy of the universe must at length be dissipated. The presage of disaster has been carried beyond our solar system into the sidereal heavens, and the nebulous forms of the broken ring, the fire-wheel, and the spiral are supposed to indicate a stupendous disruption and dispersion of suns and systems throughout those distant parts of the universe. And as if to make the prediction more plausible its advocates have depicted the awful scene which must ensue when inexorable laws have run their course, and the planets shall have tumbled as charred ruins into the sun, and the sun shall have fallen like an exhausted warrior, among the dying stars, and universal night and death shall have settled upon the spent powers of Nature.

### A Permanent Cosmos.

Another class of astronomers, however, like Laplace, Mädler, Mayer, and Poisson, have leaned toward the notion of a permanent cosmos. In spite of any signs of occasional disturbance in the celestial system, they have gathered auguries of all-preserving order and never-failing beauty. The popular dread of comets, they tell us, has already been dissipated by showing their vaporous nature and periodical recurrence; and it has been mathematically proved that the perturbations of the solar system are self-correcting and conservative; that there is no uncompensated shrinkage and cooling of its great masses; that the furnace of the Sun is ever fed by meteors and aerolites; and the planets ever supplied with heat and light to insure their life-bearing powers. It is assumed that there is a perpetual conservation as well as dissipation of the energy of the universe. The hopeful prevision has been extended throughout the stellar regions, where the nebulous forms and star clusters are to be viewed, not as painted in our distorting fancy, but as so many astral systems, revolving with our own solar system, around the bright star in Alcyone, through millennial summers and winters, with ever-changing climates and histories. And as if to crown the splendid vision, it has even been boldly conjectured, that the evolution of nebulæ into planets and dissolution of planets into nebulæ, if they occur, may be periodic rather than catastrophic, a sort of normal birth and death of worlds, throughout infinite space and time.

### The Doctrine of Old and New Heavens.

It will be seen, at a glance, how the two astronomical opinions bear upon the revealed doctrine of the destruction and renewal of the heavens. Each has in it an element of truth which is in accordance with Scripture, while both together tend to unfold its full meaning. On the one hand, the opinion of a final chaos or dissolution of planets, as Helmholtz admits, will answer quite well to the biblical descriptions of the day of judgment, as depicted in popular language, when the sun shall be darkened, the moon shall become as blood, the stars shall fall like meteors, the heavens shall pass away with a great noise, and vanish like smoke, and the elements shall melt with fervent heat. On the other hand, the opinion of an ensuing or fresh evolution of planets is in agreement with the prediction of Isaiah, the vivid picture of St. Peter, and the vision of St. John in the Apocalypse, that after the first heaven and the first earth shall have passed, Jehovah shall create new heavens and a new earth, purged by the fires of judgment, as an abode of righteousness. And then, taking the two opinions together, we shall understand anew the transitoriness of the whole visible heavens as viewed by the Psalmist and the Apostle, in contrast with the eternal Jehovah, who wears them as but the changing garb of his glory: " The heavens are the work of thy hands: they shall perish, but thou remainest: yea all of them shall wax old as doth a garment; and as a vesture shalt thou fold them up, and they shall be changed; but thou art the same and thy years fail not."

### The Stupendous Problems of Astronomy.

The whole speculative problem of astronomy, as now brought before us, has become too vast for the mind of man to compass. The spectacle of evolving and dissolving planets, suns, and galaxies, in our bewildered fancy,

"Glitters like a swarm of fireflies tangled in a silver braid."

No hand of man can unravel it. We can solve the problem only by the aid of revelation. If we yield ourselves to scientific evolutionism alone, it will land us in the pessimistic view of a universe at once causeless and purposeless, beginning in irrational force and ending in impotent reason. But if we blend such evolutionism with the biblical theism we may rise to the view of a universe of order and beauty, originating in the potential energy of one Absolute Will and unfolding the purposes of one Infinite Reason, even that revealed Creator who inhabits yet controls his own creation, immanent yet transcendent, making and unmaking world after world, world without end, yet ever remaining the eternal and self-existent Jehovah, I-am-that-I-am, the Alpha and the Omega, the Beginning and the End, which was and is and is to come, the Everlasting, of whom and through whom are all things, to whom alone be glory.

### Astronomical Marvels.

The fourth source of evidence is found in a comparison of the marvels of modern astronomy with correspondent miracles of revealed religion. Leaving the speculative region of the science and descending from the distant worlds in which as yet we have no conscious interest, we return into the narrow scene of our planet to consider the celestial prodigies which have there occurred in its own history, such as the Arrest of the Sun and Moon at Ajalon, the Receding Shadow on the Dial of Ahaz, and the Star of the Nativity. In a full treatment of these miracles it would be proper to raise and settle some exegetical questions before deciding upon their strictly astronomical character and historical truth. We might inquire if the command of Jehovah to the sun and moon to stand still at the battle of Ajalon was not a mere figure of speech, a bold trope in a poetical narrative, or if it meant more than that the sun should stop shining during the storm which followed, or if the phenomenon was not a long summer twilight caused by a fortunate coincidence of moonrise and sunset, on the mountain of Gibeon and in the valley of Ajalon, or if, instead of being an actual stoppage of the sun, with so tremendous a disturbance of the whole solar system, it may not have been only a brief swaying of the earth and its satellite, having the same optical effect as if the sun and moon had stood still. We might inquire if the phenomenalistic language, "the sun went back ten degrees," at the prayer of Hezekiah, implied actual motion of the sun any more than when we speak of the sun rising and setting; if the phenomenon witnessed was other than a local refraction of the sun's rays on the face of the dial; if that refraction might not have been caused by a passing cloud. We might also inquire if the star which guided the Chaldean astronomers to the cradle of our Lord may not have been a poetical figure for some inward light of the mind pointing toward Messiah as the object of their studies and hopes; or some astrological sign in the constellation of the Fish, which they regarded as the symbol of Judea in the Zodiac, or a new apparent star caused by conjunctions of the planets Jupiter, Saturn, and Mars, which twice occurred, as Kepler has proved, about the time of the Nativity.

### Astronomical Miracles.

Waiving such inquiries for the present, if we take these miracles literally and supernaturally as true astronomical events and prodigies, they will seem no more incredible, *a priori*, than some astronomical discoveries with which science has made us familiar. Grant that there was some disturbance of the relations of the earth and sun at the battle of Ajalon, yet at this moment it is the sun which seems to stand still while the earth goes flying around it swifter than a cannon ball. Grant that the sun's rays became somehow refracted in the dial of Ahaz; yet such rays, as now decomposed in the spectrum, are revealing the secrets of the most distant suns in the universe. Grant that the Eastern Magi discovered a new star in the skies of Judea, yet since then myriads of new stars have been discovered throughout an immensity populous with worlds of light. Remember, too, that these miracles were themselves worthy acts of divine wisdom and not mere achievements of human prowess; that the courage of Joshua was sustained by the evident favor of Heaven; that the faith of King Hezekiah was strengthened by a promise of lengthened days; and that in the divine horoscope of worlds, both angels and men hailed a new-lit orb in the heaven, as but the fit presage of a new-born God upon earth. Add to this, that the proof of astronomy is for most men as much a matter of hearsay and tradition as the proof of revealed religion; come unbiassed to them both, with a mind blank to their impressions, and it will be easier to believe the miracles of religion than the marvels of astronomy.

### Astronomical Difficulties of Faith.

It must be granted, however, that astronomy itself has occasioned some new difficulties of faith, which should now be briefly noticed, in order that its evidence may appear complete. So far as such difficulties inhere in the infinitude of the universe and the finitude of our faculties, neither science nor religion can remove them or be held answerable for them, but may only palliate them and outweigh them with compensating considerations. Since we cannot be as gods knowing everything, it is an act of reason as well as of faith to accept our lowly position in creation and make the best of its advantages and consolations. I shall mention but two of the astronomical difficulties referring you to authors by whom they have been fully treated.

It is thought difficult to conceive of the omniscience of Jehovah as extended throughout the immensity which astronomy has unfolded. The remoteness and multiplicity of the heavenly worlds seem to make general oversight of the universe inconsistent with special notice of our little planet and fitted only to foster unbelief and impunity among its inhabitants. An objector of this temper will soar away in fancy to some neighboring planet from which the great globe of the earth with its seas and continents shall appear no bigger than the sun or moon appears in our firmament. Starting afresh in a flight millions and millions of miles beyond the solar system, he will alight upon some star so distant that the earth will have disappeared and the sun itself become but another star sparkling like Sirius among other suns. Still winging his flight among the stars through unimaginable spaces and times, he will at last reach a point from which the suns of our galaxy of stars, if descried, would seem mere dots and films of light upon the dark expanse beneath him. And then, returning from this dizzying flight, back to our little world, hidden away among clustered suns and planets, like a lost grain of sand upon the shores of time, he will be ready to ask with Eliphas, the sceptical comforter of Job, " Is not God in the height of heaven? and behold the height of the stars, how high they are! And thou sayest, How doth God know? Can he judge through the dark cloud?"

### Illustration of Divine Omniscience.

It sounds like a paradox, but it is the sober truth, that the very height of the stars, astronomically considered, will help us to conceive how God may know and can judge through the dark cloud. The argument or rather the illustration is contained in an ingenious little treatise entitled The Stars and the Earth, and is based upon the phenomena of interplanetary light as produced by waves of the universal ether vibrating from one star to another. It is well known that light, like sound, travels through space at an appreciable rate of velocity, so that when we perceive a luminous body a certain portion of time elapses between the moment of emitting its rays and the moment of its becoming visible to our eye. This passage of light is too swift to appear in the limited distances between objects here on earth, but in the mightier scale of distances between the earth and the planets and stars it becomes readily conceivable. It has been ascertained that some of the heavenly bodies are so remote that they become visible to us minutes after the ray of light has left them; others again so remote that they do not become visible to us until hours have elapsed; and still others so inconceivably remote that long years and ages must have passed ere their rays could have reached the eye of man. We are told that if a star had been shattered to pieces in those far-off regions of space thousands of years ago the catastrophe would as yet be unknown in our corner of the universe, and we might still seem to see the star shining where it had long since been blotted from the firmament. Reversing the point of view from the earth to the stars, if we now imagine our sceptical objector endowed with telescopic vision in his flight of fancy from orb to orb through endless space, he would not descry what is now passing on the earth, but what has already passed hours or years ago, in the days of King Alfred, in the time of our Saviour, in the age of the patriarchs, backward until the new-born earth should burst upon his view at the dawn of creation; and then in his returning flight he would review the scenes of the past forward to the present; thus recalling a universal panorama, ever changing, yet ever the same. In the light of this illustration, as freed from its crude human fancies, we can conceive of a Divine vision or consciousness, at once omnipresent and omniscient, pervading the universe and embracing the secrets of all worlds, through all ages, literally in one everlasting present, in one Eternal Now. With true godly fear, we may say: "And there is no creature that is not manifest in his sight; but all things are naked and laid open before the eyes of Him with whom we have to do." And devoutly may we exclaim: "Whither shall I go from thy Spirit? or whither shall I flee from thy presence? If I ascend up into heaven, thou art there: I make my bed in hell, behold thou art there. If I take the wings of the morning and dwell in the uttermost parts of the sea, even there shall thy hand lead me and thy right hand shall hold me. If I say, Surely the darkness shall cover me; even the night shall be light about me: the darkness and the light are both alike to thee."

## Physical Insignificance of Our Planet.

The other astronomical difficulty to be considered is one which occurs to the believer as well as to the sceptic. It is not the fancy that our earth is too insignificant to attract any divine notice, but that it is too insignificant to have attracted so much divine notice as the Scriptures attribute to it. And it is a difficulty which has weighed upon the greatest minds. The statesman Daniel Webster wished to have inscribed upon his tomb the sentiment that the reason for the faith that was in him had "sometimes been shaken by philosophical argument drawn from the insignificance of man in comparison with the grandeur of the universe." Ordinarily, as wholly absorbed in sublunary affairs, we may not feel this sense of insignificance and desertion in the universe: but if we rise to the contemplation of the astronomical heavens as the same with the biblical heavens, as including not merely uncounted myriads of worlds but as the abode of the Father and the holy angels, it is hard to realize that He should have concentrated the gaze of all intelligent creatures upon this little nook of creation and made it the scene of a special mission and incarnation of his only-begotten Son. In wonder, if not in doubt, we are ready to say with the psalmist, "When I consider the heavens the work of thy fingers, the moon and the stars which thou hast ordained, what is man that thou art mindful of him? or the son of man that thou visitest him?"

## Moral Importance of Man.

The reply which the psalmist gave is the same which must now be given under the full light of modern astronomy. It is to the effect that the moral importance of man in creation and in redemption justifies all the divine condescension toward him, and makes him an object of angelic interest throughout the intelligent universe. The argument has been unfolded by Chalmers, in his Astronomical Discourses, with masterly clearness and fulness. On the assumption that our earth is the only lost world, he likens man to the solitary sheep astray from the heavenly fold, and the one repentant sinner causing new joy among the angels of heaven. Magnify to the utmost the populous immensity which astronomy has disclosed around the narrow stage of our probation. Imagine, as in a vast amphitheatre of worlds, the series of planets, suns, and stars, with corresponding orders of intelligence, angels and archangels, thrones, dominions, principalities, cherubim and seraphim, ascending rank above rank, toward the inaccessible glory of god-head. Then behold the eternal Son descending from that excellent glory to our little orb, becoming united with our lowly human nature, and ascending as our Redeemer amid the triumphing host of heaven, and so magnifying Infinite Love as the crowning attribute of Deity and transcendent marvel of the universe, and we shall no longer ask incredulously, "What is man that thou art mindful of him? or the Son of Man that thou visitest him?" but shall say with reassured faith, "Yet hast thou made him but a little lower than the angels and crowned him with glory and honor."

# CHAPTER V.

## THE EVIDENCE FROM GEOLOGY.

In distinction from astronomy, geology is restricted to our planet, and is, literally defined, the science of the earth, including its mechanical form and structure, its external features of land and sea and sky, the vegetable, animal, and mineral products upon its surface, the strata, floræ, and faunæ imbedded in its crust, the hidden nucleus which it contains, and the physical forces active in producing its climatic changes and structural modifications. In this large sense of the term we shall use it, without confining it to the study of ancient organisms known as paleontology, or to the speculative problems of the primitive earth. And we shall find it yielding the four kinds of religious evidence already traced in astronomy, if less perfectly than that science, because of its own relative imperfection, yet with sufficient clearness and fulness for the purpose of the argument.

### Growth of Geological Evidence.

Geology is a comparatively modern science. Its evidence of revealed truths, like its seeming conflict with them, is of recent date. For many centuries it was in a false bondage to theology. The early Greek speculations concerning the round form of the earth and the agency of fire and water in its formation were rejected as heathen superstitions by the church fathers, who conceived of the earth as an oblong plain with a surrounding sea and crystal roof, and descanted upon the divine wisdom and goodness displayed in such a structure. With the proof of the earth's rotundity, this crude geography fell into ruins; but the schoolmen, like the fathers, went on expounding the hexæmeron, or six days' work of creation, as a mere didactic process for unfolding the divine attributes and enforcing the observance of the Sabbath. Long after the Reformation even geology was still identified with Genesis, and the whole disordered configuration of the globe was attributed to the fall of Adam or the punitive action of Noah's Deluge. At length, within the last century, the discovery of fossil remains and the consequent proof of long cosmogonic eras have emancipated geology from this false exegesis, and issued in an apparent rupture with the Bible which is not yet fully healed by any of the numerous schemes of reconciliation. Nevertheless, through all these crude speculations and futile alliances, the great theistic argument itself has remained logically correct in form, needing only to be reinforced and enriched with better knowledge; and the estranged science is already returning with new and growing evidence in favor of its early faith.

### Testimony of Geologists.

The first source of this evidence is the testimony of geologists themselves. As we have said, at its origin geology was almost a sacred science, more consciously depending upon the Bible than any other natural science. For a long time it was nothing if not scriptural, and it was not strange, therefore, that in the rebound from a false interpretation of Scripture, some of its votaries should be carried into indifference or hostility to Scripture itself. Such cases, when historically traced, can be easily explained. Some of the Italian geologists simply avoided the fate of Galileo by masking their scepticism in a policy of dissimulation. When Buffon was forced to recant his Theory of the Earth, he declared that he offered it as a pure scientific hypothesis, which was not necessarily contrary to the writings of Moses. There is nothing in the works of Hutton but a strict scientific reserve to justify the attacks of the Edinburgh divines, who accused him of atheism. It was but natural that Humboldt and Vogt should have concluded that the Mosaic hexæmeron was an oriental legend or a pious fraud, when the German biblical critics were showing them the way to such conclusions. And the credit which Lyell in his historical sketches gave to other sacred books, whilst silent as to the Scriptures, whatever else it may have been, was not an instance of scientific candor. Duly allowing for all exceptions, it will remain true that geologists, as a class, have not lost their faith in the Bible or even renounced its geological teaching. In proof of this the roll of the science might be called from its beginning. Robert Boyle, the chief founder of the Royal Society, devoted his life to such researches, and bequeathed the apologetic lectureship which still bears his name. The geologist Ray was the first to unite natural history with natural theology. Cuvier, the father of paleontology, fancied himself bidden, like the prophet, to evoke the dry bones of buried nature into life. The greatest of geographers, Ritter, avowedly wrote his magnificent work as his song of praise to God. And the chief masters of the science in our own day, Hugh Miller, Dana, Guyot, Dawson, in the face of previous failure and ridicule, have still intrepidly maintained a general accordance of Geology with Genesis.

### Geological Facts and Revealed Truths.

The second source of evidence appears in the existing agreement of geological facts with revealed truths. The two are so accordant that it will be found difficult to state either without reference to the other. On the one hand are the geological facts: that the earth is a globe covered with sea and land, revolving on its axis and in its orbit, from morning to evening, through summer and winter, and ever teeming with living things, plants and beasts and fishes and birds, yet sometimes having storms, earthquakes, and volcanoes to disturb its general life and order. On the other hand are the revealed truths: that the earth is Jehovah's and the fulness thereof; he made the sea and his hands formed the dry land; that He stretcheth out the north over empty space and hangeth the earth upon nothing; that He causeth the outgoings of the morning and the evening to rejoice, and hath made summer and winter, and openeth his hand to supply the wants of every living thing; that He maketh the earth to quake before Him, turneth up fire under the earth, sitteth on the floods with stormy wind fulfilling his word; yet hath he set his rainbow in the cloud in token of a covenant with the earth, that while the earth remaineth, seed-time and harvest and summer and winter shall not cease.

Are not these two statements logically inseparable, simply opposite half truths of one rounded whole of truth! Look at the geological facts alone, and you will see a world orderly and beautiful indeed, yet without cause or purpose or meaning, without a will or reason or intelligence, or any personality to uphold it, and at times so marred and deranged as to seem but the sport of chance or fast bound in the chains of fate. Look at the revealed truths alone, and you will, indeed, behold an all-sustaining Preserver of the world, ever asserting his presence in nature, yet but vaguely apprehended under its phenomena and with but little intelligible connection with its processes, like a prince who has retired from his realm, or returns into it only to play the tyrant. Then look at both the facts and the truths together, and at once this revealed Preserver of the earth will be discovered as its Creator, with all his attributes in full activity; with His almighty will strenuously put forth in upholding the globe and controlling the play of its mechanical forces; with His exhaustless skill displayed, as with lavish art, in an endless variety of animal and vegetable products; and with His diffused benevolence shown in countless contrivances for the happiness of myriads of sentient creatures. And so the modern scientist, with infinitely more meaning, can take up the refrain of the ancient psalmist: "O Lord! how manifold are thy works, in wisdom hast thou made them all. The earth is full of thy riches."

### Evidential Literature.

While the known astronomy illustrates the physical attributes of Deity as expressed in the inorganic phenomena of the universe, the known geology illustrates also His intellectual attributes as expressed in chemical and organic phenomena, His knowledge, wisdom, and goodness. The literature of the subject is immense. As the geological sciences have advanced, the true theistic argument has become cumulative and bewildering in its magnificent richness. Evidences have been collected not merely of benevolent design, but of supreme intelligence in the mathematical order, the geometrical symmetry, the optical beauty, as well as the wonderful utility, which pervade the whole terrestrial system. Dr. John Kidd, in his

Bridgewater Treatise on The Adaptation of External Nature to the Physical Condition of Man, with reference to the supply of his wants, starting with a view of his comparative helplessness, has ranged through the atmospheric, the mineral, the vegetable, the animal kingdoms, co-ordinating an immense series of facts in proof of the wisdom and goodness of the Creator. Dean Buckland, in his Bridgewater Treatise on Geology and Mineralogy, with reference to Natural Theology, beginning far back in time with the molten earth, has traced its forming layers of rock, metal, and coal as designed for future use, together with the monster floræ and faunæ adapted to its changing climates, ere it was fitted to become the abode of man. The same argument has been unfolded with scientific candor and learning, as well as devout enthusiasm, by President Hitchcock in his Religion of Geology and its Connected Sciences. Professor George Fowne, in his Actonian Prize Essay, has exemplified the wisdom and goodness of God in the chemical history of the earth and its atmosphere, and in the marvellous adaptation of its inorganic substances to the organized beings which tenant its surface. On the same foundation a like illustration has lately been drawn by the Rev. George Warrington, from the phenomena of radiation. Professor J. P. Cooke, in his Graham Lectures on Religion and Chemistry, has gathered fresh testimony from the beneficent uses of oxygen, carbonic acid, nitrogen, and all the constituents of air, earth, and water. Professor Guyot, in his Lowell Lectures on Earth and Man, has sketched the wonderful preadjustment of the whole physical structure and furniture of the finished globe to the races and civilizations which have been cradled in its genial continents, nourished by its cloudy mountains, fanned with its balmy winds, and wafted with growing wealth and power across its mighty seas.

    The invisible beauties of nature, as well as its more obvious utilities, have also been unveiled by the hand of a devout science. The distinguished mathematician, Charles Babbage, in his Ninth Bridgewater Treatise, sought to illustrate arithmetically, by means of a calculating machine, after the manner of Paley, that divine forethought and design which pervade the evolution of the whole terrestrial mechanism, under both law and miracle, and unfolded a secret Book of Remembrance in those ethereal waves of light and sound which perpetuate the impression of every word and deed of man. President Hill, of Harvard, has in like manner united Geometry and Faith, by exposing those vast, intricate problems of form and motion, with which an Infinite Intelligence is ever tasking the devout student of nature. President McCosh, with the aid of Professor Dickie, in his Typical Forms and Special Ends, while not undervaluing the utilitarian arguments of other writers, has chiefly aimed to blend the evidence of order and beauty with that of adaptation and use, as found in the subtle harmonies of number, form, and color which lurk in the crystal, the plant, the animal, gleam in the most hidden atoms and particles, and thus transform the whole earth with a divine intelligence and glory.

The whole argument has been popularized by writers, lecturers, and preachers, who have sought to translate the annual course of nature into a sort of parable of divine grace. It has been framed into the calendar of the natural year by Dr. Hitchcock in his Religious Lectures upon the four Seasons, discoursing upon the Resurrection of Spring, the Triumphal Arch of Summer, the Euthanasia of Autumn, and the Coronation of Winter. It has been woven into the calendar of the civil year by Dr. Duncan in his Sacred Philosophy of the Seasons, joining scientific with Scriptural meditations upon the phenomena of the ever-changing climate and scenery. It has also been adapted to the Christian year by an English layman, Dr. Chapin Child, in a scientific commentary upon the Benedicite, blending the great orchestra of Nature with the liturgy of the Church.

### Geological Hypotheses.

The third source of evidence is in the provisional agreement of geological hypotheses with revealed doctrines. We now enter a region of the science which has been overrun with the wildest and most contradictory speculations concerning the origin, development, and destiny of the earth. The verity of Scripture will stand quite independent of such speculations, even though they be left unnoticed; and the odium of any failure in reconciling them with Scripture should be divided with the geologists who have themselves been conspicuous among the reconcilers and have often misled them by offering some mere conjecture as a scientific truth. Nevertheless, it will be well to show the bearing of these speculations upon the revealed doctrine ever to be conserved and maintained, whichever of them may prevail in the end. It will be found, in some instances, that they already give promise of shedding new light upon biblical truths which they may seem to have menaced.

### The Primitive Earth a Finished World.

The first of the unsolved problems of geology relates to the origin of the Earth; and two rival speculations concerning it have been pursued. Nearly all the early geologists, such as Burnet, Woodward, and Cuvier, and others mainly of the Neptunist school of Werner, accepted the dogma of instantaneous creation as a scientific postulate, and conceived of the primitive earth as a finished world such as we now find it. It was held that as far back as science can take us, our planet was found to have been a solid globe covered with strata, floræ, and faunæ, such as now appear in its mineral, vegetable, and animal kingdoms. The earthquakes and volcanoes which occasionally disturb its order were regarded as relics of second causes employed by the Creator when he divided the land from the sea by upheaving the mountains and draining the waters into a central abyss. The layers of granite, slate, and clay, together with the fossil organisms found with them, were accepted as the sediment and remains of the Noachian Deluge, which as a universal ocean had destroyed all organic life upon the earth. And the view was made plausible by the admitted fact that the superficial strata, including the fossiliferous portions, are largely composed of aqueous formations.

### The Primitive Earth Chaotic.

The later geologists, however, such as Buffon, Humboldt, Lyell, and others chiefly of the Vulcanist school of Hutton, have gradually discarded the dogma of an abrupt creation as unscientific, and conceived of the earth as evolved from a primitive chaos. It is now maintained that science can take us back to a time when our planet was one of the nebulous rings of the solar system; first condensing into an incandescent sphere, and then hardening around its fiery nucleus into a granite shell as the base of the organic species which have since flourished and decayed upon its surface. The fossil remains and serried strata imbedded in its crust could not have been formed and deposited by so transient an event as the Deluge, but are the effects of physical and chemical processes still passing before our eyes. Earthquakes and volcanoes are only surviving expressions of a molten interior mass which the earth has inherited from the primitive nebula. And the opinion is made more probable by the undeniable fact that the great solid masses of the planet are composed of igneous formations.

### The Doctrine of Creation.

It would be interesting, but it might be tedious, to recount the many attempts to harmonize these conflicting views with the revealed doctrine of creation. The first view, that the earth was perfect from the beginning, fell easily into agreement with the traditional conception of creation as an instantaneous act of the Almighty about six thousand years ago, when the heavens and the earth were created in the beginning, as declared in the first verse of Genesis. In order to meet the next statement, in the second verse, that the earth was in a chaotic state, and to explain the marks of disorder which it still presents, it was held that the earth was dragged down from its pristine perfection by the fall of the angels who inhabited it; that then ensued the six days' work of creation in conflict with this satanic agency; and that by the temptation and fall of man came fresh disorder, to be effaced by the work of redemption and ultimate triumph of Christ over Satan. In place of these extravagant interpretations, the second view, that the earth has been evolved from an ancient chaos, is now generally accepted as more in accordance with science and with Scripture. If we conceive of creation both reasonably and scripturally, as a process rather than as an act, and include evolution in its process, then the first verse of Genesis will stand by itself as a declaration of the general doctrine or fact of creation; the second verse will indicate the void and formless nebula in which the earth originated; and the following verses will depict the creative method by which it was evolved into its present finished form. But whichever of the two views we accept, though we accept them both and sift them together, we shall have as a residual truth the plainly revealed statement that the primitive earth was without form and void ere the creative spirit of God moved upon the face of the abyss.

### The Catastrophists.

The second problem is the development of the earth through the geological periods; and before this problem are encamped the Catastrophists and the Uniformitarians. According to the Catastrophists physical processes in the primitive earth were inconceivably swift and violent. Geologists of this school will appeal from the present to the former condition of the planet before it became ready for organic life, when it was a rocky shell enclosing a fiery mass and enveloped in a universal ocean by which were produced its erupted mountains and abysmal seas and of which the volcano and the earthquake are now but faint echoes. After it became ready for organic life, they will tell us, the same aqueous and igneous agencies conspired to render it like a huge hot-house for producing enormous ferns and prodigious monsters of which we can find but a few traces and remains buried in its crust. These fossiliferous strata, moreover, by their position one above another, are supposed to indicate successive destructions and renewals of organic life by means of great planetary convulsions ere the appearance of man. And it must be granted that the distorted surface of the globe and its broken strata, viewed with the occasional freshet and the smouldering volcano, are very suggestive of spent forces which have once acted with paroxysmal violence.

### The Uniformitarians.

According to the Uniformitarians, however, physical agencies in the primitive earth were inconceivably slow and tranquil. Geologists of this school, if we give them unlimited credit in the bank of time, will trace the present globe far back to its gaseous origin, under existing laws at their present rate of action, without a break or catastrophe. The fossil floræ and faunæ preceding the historic period, they tell us, indicate successive dynasties of organic life, the kainozoic, the mesozoic, the paleozoic, or the modern, mediæval, and ancient, evolving one out of another, with the changing climate of the earth, each lasting untold thousands of years. Earthquakes and volcanoes have a conservative effect upon the general balance of sea and land, and are but incidental to the slow process by which new islands and continents are formed as the foundation of new organic systems. Even the most ancient strata, the crystalline rocks preceding all organic life, are but relics of the solidifying crust of the molten globe as it cooled and hardened through long æons of geological and astronomical time. Whatever may be thought of those remote periods, it cannot be denied that during the historic period, at least, the aspect of nature has suggested a steady play of its forces with uniform tranquillity.

### The Six Creative Days.

The most heroic efforts have been made to bring these various speculations into agreement with the revealed doctrine of the six creative days. Without reviewing all of them we shall find, by a glance at them, that the general outcome is already favorable and hopeful. At first the opinion of the Catastrophists, as applied by Penn, Fairholm, Kirby, lent itself naturally to the dogmatic conception of the creative days as a series of stupendous miracles. It had become the orthodox faith, as it is still the popular notion, that about six thousand years ago land and sea and sky, plants, animals, and men, started forth into being, one after another, in six days of twenty-four hours, by successive fiats of Jehovah. And when the evidence of fossil remains was brought to light, it could only be denied or treated as illusory. It was even imagined that since Adam must have been created with an umbilicus, and since the trees must have been created with concentric rings, so the earth itself must have been created in a stratified form, with extinct floræ and faunæ, suggesting a growth through which it had never passed. This was catastrophism run wild, and the miraculous made monstrous. To meet such difficulties, learned divines, like Chalmers, Pye Smith, Andrew Wagner, suggested a long interval of time between the first and the second verses of Genesis, during which all the geological periods might have been unfolded, but which was omitted as not essential in the sacred narrative. After which follows, in the next verses, the account of a new creation, on the chaotic ruins of the old, having man for its centre and performed literally in six days. It was even fancied that this new creation was local and supernatural, in Central Asia, to furnish a paradise for Adam, while the rest of the globe was still proceeding, as of old, under natural laws. But the difficulties of this mode of interpretation, though reduced, were not removed, and it has declined with the decline of Catastrophism among geologists.

### *The Creative Days as Cosmogonic Eras.*

The opinion of the Uniformitarians, as held by Guyot, Dana, Dawson, Hugh Miller, has led to more successful attempts to identify the geological periods with the creative days as divine working days or long cosmogonic eras of the Creator. If to the conception of creation as a process, we add that of an orderly evolution as its method, on the assumption that the author of Scripture is also the author of nature, it will be only a question of detail to harmonize the story of the one with the story of the other. Neither the scriptural nor the common use of the word "day" limits it to a period of twenty-four hours; nor has the enlarged sense of it in Genesis been forced upon modern reconcilers by the claims of science, since it was held on doctrinal grounds by St. Augustine and Bossuet, long before the dawn of geology, as well as by learned Hebraists, like Pusey and Hengstenberg, on grammatical grounds. According to the best of the uniformitarian schemes of conciliation as set forth by the late Arnold Guyot, on the basis of modern astronomical and geological speculation, the biblical cosmogony comprised during the first three days the general evolution of the heavens with their nebulæ, suns, and planets, and during the second three days the special evolution of the earth with its climates, floræ, and faunæ: the former, or astronomical, including the azoic ages, or inorganic era, of matter; and the latter, or geological, the paleozoic, mesozoic, and kainozoic ages, or organic era of life; the whole concluding in the formation of man as the climax of the evolution and the image of the Creator. The seemingly inconsistent appearance of light on the first day and of vegetation on the third day, previous to any mention of the sun, is explained by the cosmic conditions which existed when the gaseous nebula became luminous, and when the still luminous earth could bear forms of plant life, ere the sun had begun to illumine it or the seasons had prepared it for the organic epochs of the three following days. The seventh day of rest, which came after the six days of work, is that historic period of tranquillity and order throughout nature which closed the period of energetic evolution, when God rested from all his work and saw that everything he had made was very good. And since then, from generation to generation, this great Sabbath of God has had its perpetual memorial, image, and accompaniment in the lesser sabbath made for man.

### The Creative Days as Logical Stages.

The clearness, richness, and beauty of this scheme have been widely recognized. It was used by Mr. Gladstone in his controversy with Professor Huxley, concerning the Proem in Genesis. But it does not satisfy all minds. The difficulty of tracing in detail an exact parallelism between Genesis and geology has caused a reaction against such minute interpretation and led to an effort to banish the time-element altogether from the narrative. Profound thinkers, like Michaelis and Reusch, have maintained that the creative days correspond with the geological periods, not as chronological epochs, but as logical stages in the creative process, founded in fact and in reason, but not necessarily to be conceived of as fixed intervals of definite duration. The order is the same in both Scripture and nature: First, a formless waste or the nebulous chaos; second, a division of the earth from the firmament, or the separation of the nebulous planet from the rest of the solar nebula; third, the gathering of the seas and appearing of the dry land to bring forth grass and herb and plant, or the evolution of the terraqueous globe with its sun-like photosphere and commencing verdure; fourth, the sun, moon, and stars to give light upon the earth and to be for signs and for seasons, for days and years, or the establishment of the mature planet in the solar system with its zones and climates, its day and night and summer and winter; fifth, the swarming of the water and air with great fishes and winged fowl or the evolution of the lower animals of the organic scale; sixth, the earth bringing forth beasts each after its kind, and the making of man in the image of God with dominion over the fish of the sea and the fowl of the air and the beasts of the field, or the evolution of the higher animals of the organic scale and the production of man as the most perfect and dominant animal of the globe; seventh, the rest of God from his work, or the repose of nature, since man appeared upon the earth. And this order will hold though it be purely ideal in the mind, though it represent merely the phases of all cosmic growth without special reference to our earth; though it simply depict the existing succession of terrestrial phenomena, sky, sea and land, plants, animals and man; though there be no effort to adjust it to the still imperfect periodology of geological time.

But whichever of the schemes be adopted, whether the history be regarded as real or as ideal, the essential point remains, that the geological order of evolution agrees with the revealed order of creation, and justifies the divine and human Sabbath as the reason given for the Fourth Commandment: "For in six days the Lord made heaven and earth, the sea and all that is therein, and rested the seventh day: wherefore the Lord blessed the Sabbath day and hallowed it."

### Critical Questions.

Let it be here observed, in passing, that this scientific interpretation of the Hexæmeron is in no way affected by any critical questions which have been raised as to the authorship of Genesis or the literary form in which it is cast. Take the most advanced ground as to these questions. Assume that the biblical cosmogony was derived from Hebrew documents, Egyptian hieroglyphs, Assyrian tablets, or other primeval traditions, by some unknown editor inspired to mould them in their present form. Assume, still further, that the narrative is dramatic in structure and anthropomorphic in language; a series of visions or scenes dawning and fading like successive days, with divine fiats ushering and explaining them one after another, as they pass before the fancy of the rapt Judean seer. Nevertheless, the fact remains, that here in this oldest of books is an order of creation which modern geology verifies, and based upon it is a calendar of historic time which has supplanted successively the calendars of Egypt, Assyria, Greece, and Rome; which still rules the highest civilization of our day, which governs every week of your life and mine, and which is imperiously proclaimed from the altars of the Church, whenever we hear the words " Remember the Sabbath day to keep it holy."

### Dissolution of the Earth.

The third geological problem is the destiny of the earth; and two opinions have arisen concerning it. The early geologists, such as Hooke and Ray, predicted the future dissolution of the globe. It had become a sacred tradition that the earth will yet be destroyed by fire, as it had once been destroyed by water, and this tradition was made a basis of scientific prevision. Its portents were found in the combustible material of the earth's surface, and in volcanoes and earthquakes, which seemed to betoken some vast fiery magazine in the under-world, which might at any time burst forth in the flames of a general conflagration. It was ascertained by thermometrical measurement that the heat of the globe increases downward toward the centre, which was supposed to be a molten mass of minerals and lava within a crust relatively no bigger than an egg-shell. Together with these internal sources of combustion were combined atmospherical and astronomical agencies, such as the lightning and the thunderbolt, the meteoric shower, the comet, increasing solar heat, and even stellar radiation throughout the celestial regions in which the sun is journeying with the earth among the stars. It seemed easy enough to find instruments as well as presages of the great disaster.

### Stability of the Earth.

The later geologists, however, such as Herschel, Thompson, and Lyell have been more inclined to believe in the stability of the globe. Repeated failures to fix the date of the predicted conflagration have combined with more thorough geological researches to induce a scientific scepticism as to the interior fires of the earth. It has been maintained that the earthquake and the volcano are not destructive, but conservative agencies, mere safety-valves and vent-holes to preserve the equilibrium of land and sea over any molten mass underneath the ground. The egg-like globe with its fiery yolk could not live even in fancy after it was shown by mechanical and thermal calculations that the earth has cooled from its centre and not from its surface; that its density forbids the notion of a central fluidity; and that there is an equilibrium in its temperature as well as in its mass, to insure its permanence. The atmospheric storm is treated as no more than "a sneeze in man's small universe," and it has even been surmised that if our planet is journeying with the sun among the stars from cold to hot regions of space with aqueous and igneous epochs of development, yet these may be periodic rather than catastrophic, and as superficial in their effects as the annual seasons, only a longer sidereal winter, to be followed by a later, more glorious summer. In the light of science the earth can be made to look essentially solid and enduring.

### *Doctrine of the Old and New Earth.*

The two geological opinions now before us, by their very statement, appear accordant with the revealed doctrine of the destruction and renewal of the earth. What is true in each of them agrees with all that is true in existing interpretation. The opinion of the earth's future dissolution is vividly depicted by St. Peter, though not with a scientific purpose, where he warns the scoffers of the last days, that the heavens which now are, and the earth, by the word of God are stored with fire, against the day of judgment, when the elements shall melt with fervent heat, the earth also and the works that are therein shall be burned up. The opinion of the earth's stability is also countenanced by the Scriptures which declare that Jehovah has a covenant with the earth never again to curse the ground for man's sake, and that the foundations of the earth are so surely laid that it cannot be moved. At the same time, both opinions when sifted together yield the Scriptural conception of a new earth to be formed out of the old, of a palingenesia, or second genesis born of the first, of a paradise regained blossoming out of a paradise lost, and of a general resurrection of material nature in connection with redeemed humanity: " For the creation was subjected to vanity not of its own will, but by reason of him who subjected it in hope that the creation itself also shall be delivered from the bondage of corruption into the liberty of the glory of the children of God."

The whole problem of the speculative geology, we can now see, is but part of the larger problem of the speculative astronomy. In the biblical conception the old and new earth is included in the old and new heavens, as in the scientific conception our planet in its development shares the vicissitudes of the celestial system to which it belongs. And if we adopt the astronomical speculation that our earth is carried by the sun through hot and cold regions of space, during long epochs of ice and fire, then the time must come when our planet shall share in the destruction and renewal of the heavens; when the renewed earth shall become a restored paradise for renewed man, and all the glorious symbolism of the Apocalypse shall be fulfilled: physical pain and sickness and tears shall pass away, and the tree of life shall shed its fruit every month for the healing of the nations.

### Geological Marvels and Miracles.

The fourth source of evidence is in the comparison of the miracles of revealed religion with the marvels of modern geology. The Bible records numerous miracles wrought during the historic period within the province of this science. The exegetical questions preliminary to a full consideration of them are interesting and important, but not essential to the present argument. If the burning of Sodom and Gomorrah with fire and brimstone was a meteoric shower or volcanic overthrow, it has its parallel in the destruction of the dissolute cities of Herculaneum and Pompeii, and is far surpassed in wonderfulness by the fiery cloud and core of the globe during its earliest geological period. If the Deluge of Noah was a local freshet destroying the then known earth with the Adamic race, rather than a universal ocean, yet geology asks us to believe that such an ocean once invested the whole planet, followed by glacial epochs more marvellous than anything narrated in Scripture. If the miracles of the Exodus, such as the crossing of the Red

Sea, the quail and manna and fountain in the desert, and the conquest of Canaan, were simply exceptional but natural phenomena, and if the mighty works of our Lord within the realm of nature, such as the Draught of Fishes, the Feeding of the Ten Thousand, the Stilling of the Tempest, were only natural processes accelerated or arrested by divine wisdom and skill, yet the whole earth around us has been transformed with greater marvels of human science and art, such as tunnels, bridges, and canals, iron steamers ploughing through stormy oceans, prodigious harvests and luxuries, continents reclaimed and barbarous regions civilized, all which would have seemed more incredible to an ancient Hebrew peasant than the miracles of his day can now seem to a sceptical critic. And the belief in such miracles, instead of being an act of stupid wonder, becomes intelligent and reasonable, when it is remembered that all of them are radiant with divine meaning; that the destruction of Sodom and Gomorrah was a deserved judgment; that the Deluge was but the opening act in the great scheme of human redemption; that the following signs and wonders under both the Old and the New Testament served to distinguish the true religion from false religions, and cause their prodigies to disappear as mere lying wonders or feats of magic; and that they still live as revelations of divine truth and love in the faith and culture of our own times. To an unprejudiced mind, coming to the question with a fresh knowledge of both Scripture and nature, the marvels of geological science would seem less conceivable, less probable, as well as less sublime, than any correspondent miracles of revealed religion.

### Value of the Geological Evidence.

If the geological evidence seems less exact and perfect than we found the astronomical evidence, it is because, as we anticipated, geology is a less exact and complete science than astronomy. While astronomy deals with simple mechanical problems, geology is entangled in complex, physical, chemical, and organical problems which seem as yet almost to defy analysis. But this necessary imperfection or immaturity of its speculative section being duly considered, its evidence is already great and promising. Indeed, it may be asserted, in spite of current impressions to the contrary, that the harmony of modern geology with the Bible is already greater and more promising than the harmony of modern theology with the Bible. In the first place, the friendly differences among geologists, between such extremes as Catastrophism and Uniformitarianism, are much more reconcilable with one another and with Scripture than the polemic disputes of divines between such extremes as Catholicism and Protestantism, Calvinism and Unitarianism; and, in the second place, the established truths of geology, already harmonious with Scripture, rest upon strictly scientific evidence which cannot be unsettled; while the established truths of theology, such as theism and revelation, rest largely upon speculative evidence which is now being undermined by agnosticism and criticism. In other words, geology, scientifically considered, is a much more advanced and exact science than theology scientifically considered, and therefore much more accordant with revealed religion.

### Geological Difficulties of Faith.

Geology discloses the infinitude of God in time, as astronomy discloses it in space, and occasions a like difficulty of faith in conceiving of the eternity of cosmic time as compared with the brevity of historic time on our earth. If we admit a chronological element into the creative days of Genesis, as unfolded by the Uniformitarian geologist, we shall soon be lost in the maze of long æons of astronomic and geologic time, when the earth was passing through successive stages of matter and life, which no human eye could behold, and which make

> "Our noisy years seem moments in the being
> Of the eternal Silence."

The difficulty is not merely exegetical. The word "day" is used in the narrative, as elsewhere in Scripture and in common speech, in various senses, as the day of cosmic light, the day of solar light, the historic day or age of indefinite duration, or as a mere scenic day in the Mosaic vision of creation. Nowhere, necessarily as the day of twenty-four hours. The difficulty lies deeper than any verbal usage. It inheres in our earthy standards of measuring time, and we can get relief only by emancipating ourselves from those standards. This we may do by a little effort of the imagination. It is a well-known illusion that the time seems short or long according to our circumstances. In an expectant mood we say the minutes are like hours; in a mood of enjoyment, the hours are like minutes. We dream of long past years in a night of slumber; but on a bed of pain, we think the morning will never come. In other words our mental measure of time, within limits, is ever contracting or expanding, and in fancy may leap beyond those limits. Let us make the effort. With the contracting measure, descend through the ranks of inferior creatures, and we shall come to an ephemeral insect, with whom one day is as our threescore years and ten. Descend still lower with the microscope, and we shall reach an animalcule, born, living, and dead in a minute, with whom one day would be as a thousand years. With the expanding measure, ascend through the ranks of superior creatures, and we shall arrive among angelic beings older than the patriarchs, with whom a thousand years are as our threescore and ten. Ascend still higher, and we may approach those eldest children of creation in the planets and stars, with whom a thousand years would be as one day. Then, by the aid of such fancies conceive of a Being as independent of the limitations of time as of space, whose life is measured neither by the millennium nor by the minute, who can alike contract his powers among atoms and seconds or expand them through worlds and ages, and it will seem literally true that with Jehovah one day is as a thousand years, and a thousand years as one day. And in all lowliness may we say, " We spend our years as a tale that is told. For a thousand years are in thy sight but as yesterday when it is past."

There is a kindred difficulty of faith occasioned by the biblical predictions of geological events, such as the destruction of the earth by fire, the descent of the Son of Man in the clouds of heaven, and the day of judgment. In the light of Uniformitarian speculation such descriptions will be regarded but as the dramatic scenery of prophecy, rather than as literal events which are probable and imminent. We look around us upon the present tranquil aspect of nature, as she has been proceeding under fixed laws during the whole historic period, and behold no sign of any great disaster. With this impression we look backward to the six days of creation and find them no longer a single week crowded with wonders, but extending through long geological periods and processes. With these double impressions of the uniformity of Nature, we gaze forward to the great events of the world's future as sketched in a prophetic picture without perspective, and the day of judgment will seem but another historic period, and the coming of the Son of Man a moral crisis rather than a visible pageant. And when to all this is added the scientific scepticism of our times in regard to such catastrophies, it will seem as if St. Peter had but anticipated the precise exigency of our faith: " Knowing this, that there shall come in the last days scoffers, saying, Where is the promise of his coming? for since the fathers fell asleep, all things continue as they were from the beginning of the creation."

The reply then given to such scepticism is the reply to be given now. We might almost say that the Apostle reasons like a geologist. We may at least say that he reasons in a manner not inconsistent with the facts and best theories of geology. He first takes Catastrophist ground against the scoffers by appealing to a past aqueous condition of the globe and to its present igneous condition: "All things have not continued as they were from the beginning of the creation. For this they willingly are ignorant of, that by the Word of God the heavens were of old and the earth standing out of the water and in the water, whereby the world that then was, being overflowed with water, perished. But the heavens and earth, which are now, by the same Word are kept in store, reserved unto fire against the day of judgment and perdition of ungodly men." The apostle next takes Uniformitarian ground for the encouragement of believers, by reminding them that the present historic period of redemption, in the scale of the Divine being, is but like one of the days of creation and now serves as a day of salvation, a season of amnesty or era of grace: " But, beloved, be not ignorant of this one thing that one day is with the Lord as a thousand years and a thousand years as one day. For the Lord is not slack concerning his promise, as some men count slackness, but long suffering to us ward, not willing that any should perish, but that all should come to repentance." And, then, the apostle warns both saints and sinners that the end of the historic day of salvation is ever imminent, and will be attended by a great geological catastrophe: "The day of the Lord shall come as a thief in the night; in which the heavens shall pass away with a great noise, and the elements shall melt with fervent heat, the earth also and the works that are therein shall be burned up." Twenty centuries have not lessened the probability of that event. Nothing is at once so certain and so uncertain. But whether it come in this year or in the next year, in this century or in the next century, in the millennium or in the next millennium, is practically immaterial: its spiritual lessons are the same to us as to our predecessors or may yet be to our successors. It is ever true for us and for all men, that the things which are seen are temporal; that we are living in a world which is transient and probationary: in a world which has enough of beauty to charm the wicked in their infatuation, but not enough to reward the righteous for their fidelity; in a world which has enough of suffering to chasten the saint yet not enough to punish the sinner; in a world which is all scarred through the ages with signs of disaster and portents of judgment; and in a world which even now bears within its bosom the fiery seeds of its decay and ruin. "Seeing then that all these things shall be dissolved, what manner of persons ought ye to be in all holy conversation and godliness."

# CHAPTER VI.

## THE EVIDENCE FROM ANTHROPOLOGY.

The complex study of anthropology has its roots in natural history and its branches in all the human sciences. In distinction from geology, the science of the earth, Anthropology, as literally defined, is the science of man. It is further definable as the last and highest of the biological sciences, being restricted to the human organism in distinction from all other animal organisms, which in their turn are distinguishable from still lower organisms. As thus viewed at the head of the organic scale of our planet, it includes the study of the human body, of its structure and of its functions, known as anatomy and physiology; and it comprises the whole human species, with all its physical phenomena and varied development in different climates and periods of culture. From this last most comprehensive point of view, it may be divided into three sections or subordinate sciences: Ethnology, the science of races; philology, the science of languages; and archæology, the science of ancient arts. It is from each of these three anthropological sciences that we shall be able to gather evidence in favor of revealed religion.

### *Growth of the Anthropological Evidence.*

For many centuries the whole science was little more than a mere biblical study such as still figures in systems of divinity. Its chief source of knowledge was the Bible, and its horizon was bounded by Christendom. The Greek notion of antipodes, or human beings on the other side of the globe with their feet opposite to ours, was repelled by the Church fathers as a pagan myth inconsistent with the descent of all mankind from Adam.

It was also the orthodox faith, all through the age of the schoolmen and far into the age of the reformers, that the whole human race had been renewed from the loins of Noah after the Deluge and dispersed from the Tower of Babel over the face of the earth in different tribes and nations, with increasing confusion of languages and ever-lapsing forms of faith and culture. At the same time, all physical pain and death throughout animate nature were referred to man's apostasy, and the occasional diseases and abnormities of the human frame were treated as direct expressions of the divine vengeance. Under such a ban the science could offer but little proof of the divine wisdom and goodness. It was not until the religious prejudice against dissections had declined, that demonstrative anatomy and physiology could reveal the wonderful structure and life of the human body. And it was not until geographical discovery had proved the existence of other human races, languages, and arts than those known to history, that ethnology, philology, and archæology could gain a fair field of research and begin to disclose these sources of religious evidence which we have found so abundant in astronomy and geology. If its yield of evidence shall prove less impressive than in those sciences, it will be owing to its own greater complexity and relative imperfection.

### The Testimony of Anthropologists.

It is sometimes alleged that the testimony of anthropologists is largely unfavorable. The studies of biologists, especially of physicians, are supposed to blunt the spiritual perceptions and give a bias toward materialism and atheism. But the very reverse might be argued, if only on the principle of contrast. There is nothing in gross physical organs and functions to suggest the finer psychical powers and feelings, but rather much, in any normal constitution, to cause their vigorous recoil and self-maintenance. Nor have anthropologists, as a class, been materialists and atheists. The few exceptions may be explained as due to no legitimate effect of their researches, but to some sinister influence. Drs. Nott and Gliddon betrayed a political prejudice, as well as religious animosity, in their ethnological writings concerning the African slave as compared with other races. Haeckel, Büchner, and Vogt have assailed the biblical anthropology in the tone of Voltaire, but with unscientific virulence and coarseness. It was not as a strict biologist, keeping in his own lines of inquiry, that Huxley ran against the scriptural doctrine of man's place in Nature, but as an agnostic metaphysician and lay preacher wandering *ultra crepidam*. Leidy, Cope, and Marsh may have left no direct religious testimony. But many of the greatest names in anthropology, carrying with them the most weight, are avowedly on the side of revealed religion. This is true not only of numerous missionary ethnologists, linguists, and antiquarians who have become authorities in the science, but of its direct founders and their successors. The great naturalist Linnæus declared that he stood mute with amazement at the inconceivable Divine wisdom displayed throughout living nature. Prout and Bell devoted their physiological attainments to the high argument for a God. Prichard and Agassiz did not disdain to include the Scriptures among their sources of ethnological knowledge. Richard Owen, styled the Newton of natural history, is said to have collected The Testimony of Comparative Anatomy and Zoölogy to the manifold wisdom of God. Carpenter, in his classical work, has asserted the spirituality and immortality of the psychical principle in the very realm of human physiology. And a host of other biologists might be named, some still living, who, while keeping in their own province with scientific rigor, still leave an ever-open door beyond it into the outlying domains of revealed truth.

### Anthropological Facts and Truths.

The perfect agreement of anthropological facts with revealed truths can be easily shown without being fully unfolded. It will be enough to bring together the chief of those facts and truths in order to see that they belong to one another inseparably in any sound philosophy. Before us, on the one hand, appears a consummate system of human physiology recapitulating in man the whole organic scale of advancing types beneath him and exhibiting him as the most perfect organism in the world; on the other side, man is revealed to us as created in the image of God, inspired with a living soul, and receiving dominion over the beasts of the field, the fishes of the sea, and the fowls of the air. Sunder these two congruous statements, and at one extreme civilized man will seem but a developed animal in the satanic image of an ape, while at the other extreme the Divine image in man may be asserted, but as yet only dimly discerned. Then reunite the two statements, and at once the perfect human creature will stand forth as the very masterpiece of the Creator, radiant with His glorious wisdom in every part and faculty—in the eye, the ear, the hand, the tongue, the heart, the brain, and, high above all, the godlike soul. He will himself realize his delegated sovereignty over the whole inferior creation, and, conscious of his divine likeness, be ready to exclaim: "I will praise Him; for I am fearfully and wonderfully made, and that my soul knoweth right well."

### Evidential Literature.

While geology illustrates, as we have seen, the divine power, wisdom, and goodness throughout the earth, anthropology comes to carry that illustration to its fit climax in man, at the summit of living nature,

> "The beauty of the world! the paragon
> Of animals!"

The literature of the argument has grown with the growth of the anthropological sciences. Among its classics should be placed in the first rank, as not yet quite obsolete, the work of Archdeacon Paley, who, while not neglecting other provinces of natural theology, devoted himself especially to the admirable mechanism of the body, as illustrated by that of a watch, to examples of prospective contrivance for the care of the young, to the phenomena of instinct, to the marvellous adaptations and compensations among the different organs of the animal economy, and to the more general relations between all animate and inanimate nature. The Rev. William Kirby, in his Bridgewater Treatise on the Creation of Animals, beginning at the lowest foundations of the argument, dwelt with careful minuteness upon the functions and instincts of infusories, polyps, radiates, cephalopods, etc., as alike resplendent with marks of divine wisdom. Dr. Peter Mark Roget, in the treatise on Animal and Vegetable Physiology, ascended higher in the organic realms, enlarged upon the benevolent intention of the Creator to secure the welfare of individuals as seen in the conservative and reproductive functions, both mechanical and vital, of the different species of mollusca, articulata, and vertebrata. Dr. William Prout, in the treatise on Chemistry, Meteorology, and Digestion with reference to Natural Theology, drew his argument from the preadjusted proportions of air, water, and land for the sustenance of life, the adaptations of climate to the inhabitants of the different zones, the correspondence between the external mechanical organs and the internal digestive functions of carnivorous or herbivorous tribes, and the vital relations between plants and animals and the general economy of nature. Sir Charles Bell, crowning this series of treatises with his masterly monograph on The Hand, has traced its beneficent design as the distinguishing member in the human frame, the organ of touch and sensibility, the instrument of mechanical and artistic skill, and the prime mover in all progress and civilization.

The problematical agreement of anthropological speculations with revealed doctrines is still in the early stage of disturbing long-received interpretation of Scripture. But it has its hopeful precedent in the more advanced sciences with which it is connected, and it is beginning to give promise of a like ultimate harmony. We shall find this to be the state of the question in reference to each of the three unsolved problems of the origin, the development, and the destiny of mankind.

### The Constancy of Species.

As to the origin of mankind, two rival hypotheses are in the field. The early anthropologists, such as Linnæus, Cuvier, and Agassiz, held to the constancy of the human species in distinction from all animal species. It had become a scientific tenet, as well as a religious tradition, that about six thousand years ago plants, animals, and man sprang into being by successive fiats, and have ever since continued invariable, each after its kind, through all climates, ages, and conditions. The naturalists of that day laid a foundation for this tenet by showing anatomical resemblances between mummied and extant specimens of the cat and the dog in Egypt, with an interval of thousands of years, and by showing such resemblances between the same domestic animals and their wild ancestors, the tiger and the wolf, notwithstanding any differences of a superficial nature. It was also claimed that the infertility of hybrid varieties of plants and animals, obtained by artificial selection, was adverse to anything like natural selection or gradual transmutation of species; that it would be as absurd to argue the descent of cats from fishes at the present day as in past geological epochs; and that the differences between fossil and living species indicate successive creations and destructions of organic life by means of cataclysms or other great terrestrial convulsions. On the basis of such reasoning, leading ethnologists, like Blumenbach, Prichard, and Agassiz, have maintained that both savage and civilized man, like the wild and domesticated brute, have retained the same anatomical structure under all diversities of complexion and in all climates—Asiatic, European, American, African—while physical and psychical differences reveal an impassable gulf between animal and human species, forbidding any possible evolution of the one into the other. Philologists, also, like Wilhelm von Humboldt and Max Müller, have denied the animal origin of language, and referred it to the human reason alone, the talking parrot and educated elephant being wholly insusceptible of hereditary improvement or civilization. Archæologists, too, of the same school, such as Champollion and Ferguson, have traced genetic affinities between the ancient monuments of Asia, Europe, and America; have described primitive man as lapsing through golden, silver, and brazen ages into a savage state; and have insisted that the oldest skulls and other human remains, instead of proving his bestial origin, give hints even of religious ideas and customs. To all this evidence against human development has been added the proof of a positive degeneracy. Such writers as Hugh Miller, Gobineau, and Argyll have maintained that civilization always appears as communicated from one people to another, never as inherently developed; that the loss of ancient arts, especially of religion, as by the Hottentot and the Esquimaux, is due to adverse climate and moral corruptibility; that some races are in a state of permanent inferiority, and that all races, like all individuals, are doomed under fixed physiological laws to decline and die. In a word, it is held certain that, within the historical period, there has been no evolution of animals into men, but rather a degeneracy of human races in a descending scale from man as made in the image of God toward man as debased into the likeness of an ape.

### The Evolution of Species.

Anthropologists of the other school, however, as strenuously maintain the development of animal into human species. The traditional belief in a primitive creation of fixed orders of plants, animals, and men has been undermined by scientific research and scepticism. The way was opened by naturalists, such as Lamarck, Hooker, and Wallace, arguing for a continuous variation of species throughout the organic scale, by means of the steady adjustment of organism to environment— the beech supplanting the pine, and the rose the wild thorn; the stranded tortoise growing into the turtle, the high-browsing cattle into the giraffe, the fleet wild goat into the gazelle; nature ever selecting and preserving the best breeds or the fittest to survive in the circumstances. It was explained that mummied and living cats have not changed because their environment, the climate of Egypt, has not changed for thousands of years, and that no cataclysm or convulsion has effaced the fossil evidence of species evolving into species through long epochs, with the changing climate of the globe. Advancing upon such reasoning, biologists, such as Darwin, Huxley, and Haeckel, have found man's place in nature at the climax of this organic evolution, and have sought proof of his animal origin in the phases of his fetal development, in the expression of his physiognomy, in the mental and moral traits which he shares with the cat, the dog, the parrot; in his anatomical resemblances to the higher simian species; and especially in a relic at the base of the vertebral column indicating his descent from a tailed, ape-like man, arboreal in his habits, becoming erect and dexterous, but still wanting the distinctive faculty of human speech. As if to supply this want, philologists, like Sleicher, Yäger, and Royer, have traced language back through fossil dialects and phonetic types to its sources in animal cries and imitative acts such as the pairing-call of birds and the gesture language of monkeys, and have suggested that it is only a matter of sufficient time to develop under linguistic laws the chatter of scolding apes in a primeval forest to the comedies of Molière on the modern stage. Archæologists also, such as De Perthes, Stevens, Westropp, have looked for primeval man as a half-animal savage in caves and lake dwellings; have sketched his slow descent in connection with changing climates, through ages of stone, of bronze, and of iron, according to the cast-off implements used in his progress, and have surmised that the first man who struck one pebble against another to give it more regular form gave the first blow of the chisel which produced the marbles of the Parthenon. The whole argument, biological, linguistic, antiquarian, has been made cumulative by philosophical writers, like Lubbock and Lyell, who have discovered traces of incipient culture in the most barbarous tribes, as well as of original barbarism in the most cultured nations, and have asserted a gradual transmutation of species, languages, and arts from the earliest mammalia of the pliocene period to the civilized man of our epoch. In short, it is now claimed that evolution reigns not only throughout the whole paleontological scale of animal species, but also through the historic scale of human races, from the low forehead of the anthropoid ape up to the vertical brow of the Apollo.

### The Doctrine of the First Adam.

Such are the two anthropological opinions which stand related to the revealed doctrine of the First Adam. As yet, they are still so imperfect and conflicting that they cannot be fully reconciled with that doctrine; nor is such reconciliation necessary or very important. But they contain grains of truth which should be sifted from them in order that we may understand the exact state of the question. The first opinion long reigned in biblical interpretation, as we have seen; and even after the absurdity of a sudden creation of organic species began to be shown, the evidence was resisted or evaded. Devout biologists, like Agassiz and Owen, continued to conceive of the serried orders of plants and animals, as but so many divine archetypes or ideals successively produced and realized at intervals, in anticipation of man, as the last and highest ideal of the Creator. And more fanciful writers, like Schlegel and Delitsch, have described great geological convulsions as birth-throes of the earth in bringing forth monster floræ and faunæ before the sudden manipulation of man as a clay effigy to be inspired with a living soul and impressed with the divine image. It is probable that Milton's graphic picture of such a creation still largely pervades the popular mind. But the opposite opinion of the evolutionists has lately been gaining ground. Intelligent interpreters of Scripture, such as Winchell, Henslow, and Mivart, have already blended evolutionism with creationism, throughout the inorganic realms of the first three days, when heaven and earth and sea were formed; then, throughout the organic realms of the last three days, when fishes and beasts and birds were formed; and so have carried evolution to the point where man was created as the last of the divine works. If now we conceive of that creation of man as a process rather than as an act, and make the sixth day of creation as indefinite in time as the preceding days, the animal organism of man will emerge, not like a dead statue amidst living nature, but as the consummate flower of her whole physical evolution. And then his special endowment with psychical qualities and divine resemblances will follow as new miraculous acts or subsequent processes during the historic period. This interpretation had been foreshadowed by patristic and scholastic writers, long before science could have compelled or suggested it; and it is grammatically in accordance with the Scriptures. It is distinctly said that man was formed out of the dust of the ground, and his connection with animate nature is implied in the dominion assigned to him over the fish of the sea and the fowl of the air, and every creeping thing upon the earth. Be this as it may, whichever of the two opinions we adopt, whether we regard the human organism as the last of a series of creative ideals or of developed types, the language of the biologist could scarcely be more accurate than the devout phrase of the psalmist: "In thy book all my members were written which in continuance were fashioned when as yet there was none of them."

## Unity of the Race.

The second problem relates to the development of mankind into a plurality of races. The elder school of anthropologists held strictly to the physical unity of the human species. The dogmatic tradition of a descent of all mankind from Adam and Eve had become accepted as a scientific postulate, and in support of it was arrayed the crude physical science of that day. The way was opened by naturalists such as Adelung and Linnæus, basing the unity of each organic species upon its fixity. It was assumed that plants, beasts, and birds as primordial creations were propagated from Paradise or from the Ark of Noah over the whole face of the earth, each keeping its structural likeness, through all changes of climate and culture and in spite of any geographical barriers or terrestrial convulsions. By similar reasoning, the ethnologists, such as Cuvier, Prichard, and Bachman, maintained the organic unity of the human species. It was argued that since cultivated plants (the vine, rice, and wheat) and domesticated animals (the swine, dog, and horse) are everywhere found associated with man, they must have originated with him somewhere in Central Asia, since he would be organically inferior to them if he could not cope with adverse climate, as well as other animal species, which had spread from pole to pole around the globe. Such writers also maintain that the common origin of the Caucasian, Mongolian, and Ethiopian races, or white, yellow, and black races, of Europe, Asia, and Africa was indicated by their anatomical sameness and fertile intermarriages, notwithstanding any physiognomical differences, such as the color of the skin, the texture of the hair, or the angle of the face, all which were merely the effect of climate, habit, and culture. The philologists, in like manner, such as the two Humboldts, Latham, and Bunsen, held to the common origin of languages as well as races. It was maintained that affinities of speech are sure proof of the affinities of the most widely separated races, as well as of their radiation from the same geographical centre, and attempts were made to trace back the existing dialects of Europe, Africa, and America through various linguistic stages to the one primitive tongue and pair in Central Asia. The archæologists, also, in different continents, have referred ancient monuments and traditions to a common source in the East as the cradle of civilization. It was claimed, not only that the culture of European nations, but also that of China, Hindustan, and Thibet, had been early derived from Central Asia; and that the Indian mounds and Mexican temples of America betray the same Asiatic origin with the cromlechs of Britain and the pyramids of Egypt. To all this biological, linguistic, and antiquarian testimony might be added that of strict evolutionists, like Lyell, Haeckel, and Pouchet, who are ready to admit, if only sufficient time be allowed for the stone, iron, and bronze ages, that mankind may have descended from one pair.

The later school of anthropologists, however, has advocated a plurality of human races. Geographical discovery combined with biological research to suggest the existence of other tribes of men than those mentioned in Scripture and included within the pale of orthodoxy. The naturalists, such as De Candolle and Pennant, began the argument by maintaining that all plants and animals could not have migrated from Eastern Asia over wide oceans into adverse climates; by showing that they have structural differences forbidding a common descent; and by dividing the earth into botanical and zoölogical provinces, each producing its own flora and fauna or specific forms of vegetable and animal life. On the ground of such analogies, ethnologists, such as Agassiz and Forbes, have maintained a plural origin of human races, as well as of plants and animals. They have shown that a geographical distribution of all tribes and nations from one parent, from Adam or Noah, was physically impossible; that it would imply incredible fertility within the period allowed for it; that it is forbidden by anatomical diversities in the hand, the profile, and the skull as well as in the color of the hair and the skin; and, therefore, that the great Asiatic, European, American, and African races, together with the floræ and faunæ severally connected with them, must have been separately created or produced in the continents where they are found. Philologists, likewise, such as Pott and Sleicher, have advocated a plural origin of languages as well as of races. They have argued that there are no such affinities of human speech as point back to one primitive tongue and pair; that any words common to different peoples may be referred to maritime adventure and commerce, as in our modern languages; that the aboriginal dialects of America, unlike the mixed tongues of Europe and Asia, are as distinct and local as its animal products, and consequently that each continental species must have had its own native tongue at the beginning. Archæologists, also, such as Pulsky, Romans, Le Plongeon, have contended for a multiple origin of arts, as well as of languages and races. They have insisted that any resemblances between the American and the Asiatic monuments and traditions, instead of indicating historic descent, are purely accidental or ideal; that the Mexican temples, so far from being imported forms, are native products antedating the oldest ruins of Europe and Asia. They have even surmised that astronomical and geological conditions then existed which indicate an ancient tropical flora and fauna at the pole and point to Central America as the true cradle of civilization, which, they maintain, flowed eastward, with the changing axis of the earth toward the sun, until it reached Asia and Europe, whence it is returning with the westward march of empire in our day. To all this ethnological, philological, and archæological evidence, it should be added that leading progressionists, like Agassiz and Gobineau, have frankly admitted a plurality of races, while still adhering to the ideal, moral, and religious unity of the species.

### Doctrine of the Fall of Adam.

It is, perhaps, premature to attempt any very accurate adjustment of these complex speculations to the revealed doctrine of the fall of mankind. If they seem now to menace that doctrine, as popularly understood, it should be remembered that they are still largely hypothetical and conflicting; that it would be safe to await their further development; that they are not likely to disturb existing interpretation of Scripture more seriously than it has been disturbed by other more advanced sciences with which it is now in harmony; and that the present state of the question is already as hopeful as the case admits or requires.

The first opinion, the physical unity of the race, has long

been practically identified with orthodoxy. It has been both
the dogmatic and popular belief that a single individual, Adam,
was the sole progenitor of the whole human species; that by
eating forbidden fruit in the garden of Eden he involved all
mankind in sin and misery; that the whole corrupt race was
swept from the earth by the Deluge, except Noah, his family,
and the animals in the ark; that his three sons, Shem, Ham,
Japhet, became respectively the ancestors of the Asiatic, European, and African races; and that by the confusion of tongues
at the Tower of Babel, all existing tribes and nations have
become dispersed over the globe. In support of these tenets
learned commentators have calculated the stowage of the Ark
with reference to the fauna of that period; have traced back
all languages to the one inspired Hebrew as spoken in Paradise ere it became broken into jarring dialects at Babel; and
have found fulfilment of the predictions of Noah in the Shemitic nations of Asia as the great religious peoples, in the
Japhetic nations of Europe as the colonizing peoples, and in
the Hamitic nations of Africa as the enslaved peoples, servants
of servants. And notwithstanding the discovery of other races,
languages, and arts in the Western Hemisphere, intrepid
efforts have been made to make them fit into the sacred record,
by connecting the monuments and traditions of Mexico and the
Pacific Islands with Noah's Ark and the Tower of Babel, by
claiming Polynesian and American languages as debased dialects of the one primitive Hebrew, and by identifying the
North American Indians as the expelled Canaanites or lost
tribes of Israel. Like St. Augustine, such divines seemed ready
to deny the very antipodes rather than imperil their dogmatic
conception of a physical unity of the race.

### Physical Unity of Mankind.

But the accumulating difficulties of such interpretation have
at length caused a reaction toward the opinion of a plurality of
human races. Scientific students of Scripture, such as Pye
Smith and McCausland, on the basis of the devout speculations
of Agassiz and Guyot, have admitted the existence of co-Adamite races mentioned in the Bible as dwelling in the land of Nod
and the cities of Enoch, and even of pre-Adamite races, not

mentioned in the Bible, but now surviving as the African and Patagonian savages, still in the paleolithic, or early stone epoch of human development. The contention is that the Adamite race, or Caucasian Jewish people, was divinely selected as the choicest breed of mankind and brought under a special supernatural economy, with a view to the ultimate regeneration of all other races and nations. It is claimed that this interpretation is not inconsistent with the statement of St. Paul that God hath made of one (blood) all men, since it is still literally true of all human races that they have the same physiological structure, and even psychical capacity, though created or developed at different geographical centres. Nor is it necessarily hostile to the doctrine of the First Adam, since Caucasian Man would still represent all mankind in the old economy and become a figure of Christ as the Second Adam in the new economy, while the mystery of original sin remains the same inscrutable fact as on the other hypothesis. Moreover, the creation of man in the divine image, like the other creative works, may be conceived of as a continuous process or gradual development of man toward the likeness of God, during the present historic period.

### The Divine Image in Man.

Such interpretation is by no means to be brushed aside as a modern make-shift or exegetical device. It can be based upon a distinction long since made by theologians between the divine image as lost or restored, as original or developed. And it may derive grammatical support from learned Hebraists, such as Hävernick, Pusey, and the late W. H. Green. If we take the first chapter of Genesis as a general revelation of the creation of the heaven and earth and man, the second chapter will follow as a more special revelation of the primitive state of man after the heaven and the earth had been created. In form it is didactic and topical, rather than historical and chronological, and the time-element may be disregarded. It sets forth at first the primitive earth becoming habitable and cultivated like a garden, the primitive man as derived from the ground and inspired with a living soul, the normal relation of man to organic nature, the development of language, and the institution or ideal of marriage in a state of innocence and purity. Then follows, in the third chapter, a description of the corruption of human nature through the appetites and passions under Satanic influence, and its consequent condition of labor, sorrow, and death. The scene is laid in Eastern Asia, some time early in the historic period; but as an ideal picture of primeval man it might almost be conceived without regard to time or place; and the adjustment of the pre-Adamite, co-Adamite, and Adamite races becomes a mere question of detail which may well await the more complete researches of anthropologists.

Such is the present mixed state of this question. We need not adopt either of the two hypotheses before us; but whichever we may favor, whether we regard the unity of the race as physical or as psychical; whether we conceive of the scriptural Adam as a progenitor or as a representative of mankind; whether we think of universal depravity as a primitive event or as a present condition—in either case it remains undeniably true, as St. Paul tells us: " In Adam all die."

### Critical Problems.

Let it now be added that this remaining truth stands sure, whatever critical or literary questions may be raised. Accept, if you like, the newest theories in regard to such questions. Treat the first and second chapters of Genesis as separate documents by separate authors, an Elohist and a Jehovist, with a Redactor to weave them together as we now find them. Treat the whole story of the Fall of Man as a divine allegory—the tree of knowledge as a sacred symbol, the talk of Eve with the Serpent and of Jehovah with Adam as an inspired parable—nevertheless, here in these archaic writings, under this simple imagery, is a portrait of primitive man, which stands alone in history; which has outlived the myths and legends of the mightiest nations, Assyrian, Egyptian, Grecian, Roman; which still colors the civilization of our age; which our anthropology is but beginning to verify; and which the strictest evolutionist must adopt whenever he reads the words: " The First Adam is of the earth earthy."

### Physical Decline of Mankind.

The third problem of anthropology relates to the destiny of mankind. The elder school has looked for a physical decay and extinction of the species. The classic myth of a decline of the race through golden, silver, and brazen ages into a degeneracy requiring its destruction by divine judgment, has been followed by scientific presages of a coming ruin through purely physical causes. As some astronomers have predicted a diminishing heat in the sun which sustains the earth; as some geologists have detected a decreasing fertility of the earth which sustains its plants and animals; and some naturalists have discerned a loss of prolific vigor in cultivated plants and domesticated animals—so some anthropologists, from every quarter of their domain, have gathered signs of a like deterioration of man. Ethnologists have told us of extinct nations and starving tribes in hostile climates; of hybrid stocks dying out through infertility; of the imbecile sons of brainy ancestors; and of a sensuous luxury which is enervating the finest breeds of men. Philologists have spoken of barbarous dialects perishing without a memorial; of debased fragments of the pristine speech of Eden; of dead languages with only a ghost-like survival among the living tongues; and of classic literatures waning away under the reign of patois, slang, and vulgar fiction. Archæologists have said that they everywhere find the remains of a high primitive civilization and even of lost arts which surpass the proudest monuments of modern skill. It is claimed that the fine arts are now only living upon past ideals, and that the industrial arts are fast using up the fertile soils and coal-beds and precious mines upon which all our civilization depends. In short, if we listen to such Cassandras of science we must expect a time when man shall have exhausted the earth upon which he dwells, and make it but the tomb of all his greatness.

### Physical Improvement of Mankind.

A later school, however, is looking forward to a physical improvement and perfection of the species. The utopian dream of social perfectibility is based on the newest anthropological science. Advanced naturalists of the evolutionary school have been predicting a future when artificial selection shall have replaced natural selection everywhere but in the sea; when cultivated plants and animals shall alone survive, and the earth become a garden for man. Ethnologists of the same school have argued that the higher human races are ever improving; that the lower are lifted up by the higher, as fast as they blend with Hebrew, Greek, Roman, Norman, Saxon blood; that genius, like religious faith, is hereditary and transmissible; and that with growing knowledge and virtue, the world will yet be stocked with a breed of heroes, sages and saints. Philologists, with the same forward glance, have looked for signs of steady improvement in the cultivated literary dialects as ever reinforced with the new blood of vulgar speech; in the growth of a universal language through commerce and linguistic study, and even in our vernacular English as the destined perfect speech of civilized man. Archæologists, though looking backward, have sketched stone, iron, and bronze ages of the Man of the Past as but a platform on which to project the silver and golden ages of the Man of the Future. Some speculative writers have imagined the whole geological development of ever-refining floræ and faunæ and human races issuing at length in a perfected Man to be as ethereal as the empyrean around us; and have even fancied him, with new psychical powers, migrating through the ethereal medium to the planets and to the sun itself, in still higher stages of cosmic development. In a word, if we could follow such visionaries of science into those remote periods and regions, we might descry the Future Man careering with the earth as in a triumphal chariot among the stars.

### The First and Second Adam.

Wild as these two speculations may seem to be, yet they have points of affinity with the revealed doctrine of the First and Second Adam. On the one hand, the notion of physical decline and corruptibility is countenanced by those Scriptures which speak of the First Adam or of degenerate humanity; of the fall of man and nature from Paradise; of the ground as cursed for his sake with thorns and barrenness; of the whole earth becoming so corrupt as to require the cleansing baptism of the Deluge; of the confusion of tongues and dispersing of peoples as a divine frustration of their impiety; of their continued lapse and corruption through following ages, and of a final judgment of mankind when the earth shall be burned up with all the works that are therein. On the other hand, the notion of physical improvement and perfectibility is also countenanced by those Scriptures which speak of the Second Adam or regenerate humanity; of Christ representing man in the New Testament as Adam represented him in the Old Testament; of the new man in Christ as fulfilling the image of his Creator; of his regeneration as completed in the resurrection; of nature as sharing in the resurrection, supplanting the thorn with the rose, causing the wilderness to bud and bloom, and at length appearing as a new earth wherein dwelleth righteousness. And when we bring together these two notions of humanity as corrupted and as perfected, we shall hear the voice of science echoing the words of Scripture as repeated in the solemn Office of Burial: "As in Adam all die, so in Christ shall all be made alive. The first man is of the earth, earthy; the second man is the Lord from heaven. And as we have formed the image of the earthy, we shall also bear the image of the heavenly. There are also celestial bodies and bodies terrestrial; but the glory of the celestial is one, and the glory of the terrestrial is another. There is one glory of the sun and another glory of the moon and another glory of the stars; for one star differeth from another star in glory."

### Anthropology and Angelology.

The whole problem of anthropology, as now set before us, is plainly involved in the larger problem of astronomy and geology. Since man is physically connected with the earth, and the earth is physically connected with the sun and the stars, he cannot but be included in their development and somehow share in their glory. And this vital connection, though unseen, is deep laid in Scripture as well as in Nature. It has been recognized by fanciful writers who are fain to associate anthropology with angelology or the revealed doctrine of angels. Accepting a scientific theory before referred to they have imagined pre-Adamite races of fallen angels dwelling in Central America unknown ages ago; have traced their diabolical reign in the heathen religions of the long Adamite period; and have anticipated a post-Adamite race of glorified men and angels mingling together on the scene of the new heaven and earth. Whatever we may think of such speculations, it is undeniable that the Scriptures do afford hints and glimpses of a commerce between celestial and terrestrial races. We look backward to the new-made earth and man, and we hear the morning stars singing together and the Sons of God shouting for joy. We look upward from the cradle of the new-born God on earth, and we hear a multitude of the heavenly host singing glory to God in the highest; and we look onward to the renewed man and earth of the Apocalypse, and we hear a new song of Moses and the Lamb ascending from every kindred and people and tongue under the whole heaven.

### Miracles of Anthropology.

We have still to consider the religious evidence afforded by modern marvels of anthropology as compared with the ancient miracles wrought within its province. Mere exegetical questions concerning them need not now be discussed, and it will suffice to cite but a few of them. Let the ark of Noah have all the living freight that ever was imagined, and it would not exceed the floating hotels upon our oceans. Let the Tower of Babel rise through all the stories that have been depicted, and it would be over-topped by some heaven-defying structures in our cities. If Jonah lived three days in the whale's belly, yet it would be no more incredible, *a priori*, than the life of every unborn infant, and geologists can tell us of ancient sea-monsters beside which the largest Mediterranean fish would be a minnow. If Balaam's ass spoke, yet other animals are now known to speak, and some linguists would argue that all speech is a developed animal function. The confusion of tongues at Babel and their miraculous fusion at Pentecost are no more astonishing than some linguistic phenomena of our own time. The miracles of healing under the Old and New Testaments are matched by the wonders of surgery, vaccination, and chloroform. Granted that you do not understand the divine method of performing these miracles, no more does a savage or a child understand your methods of curative skill. But what you can understand is the divine motive in these miracles, especially as explained in some cases by our Lord and his apostles. In the story of Jonah you can find universal lessons of humanity, duty, and faith. In the ass of Balaam, in the ark of Noah, and the Tower of Babel you can discern landmarks in the divine process of selecting and perfecting the high religious races from which you are sprung. In the Pentecostal gift of tongues you can find a symbol and a pledge of the future unity of churches and nations. In the healing of the sick and lame and blind and deaf and imbecile and insane you can see the source and sanction of the great philanthropies which distinguish our civilization. In all the humane miracles of our Lord you can behold displays of divine truth and love which have long since caused the magic and thaumaturgy of other ancient nations to fade away as forgotten dreams in the childhood of the race.

### Difficulties of Evolutionism.

It is in anthropology as a region of human interests and passions that the most determined stand is taken against the advancing theory of evolution. In astronomy and geology as regions of mechanical force and organical life it has been comparatively easy to accept the theory, but it is thought derogatory to the dignity of man to admit his animal origin and contrary to Scripture to conceive of the divine image as impressed upon him by other than a single act, sudden and miraculous. The question should be approached with caution and yet with candor. Without raising difficulties before they meet us, or making concessions before they are needed, we shall find it wise to forecast the possible course of opinion and be prepared for every contingency. In spite of instinctive and dogmatic prejudice it may yet be shown that the evolution of the human from the anthropoid species during the prehistoric period is not necessarily inconsistent with the biblical picture of paradisaic man as formed out of the ground in connection with the animals; nor would his continued evolution during the historic period toward the divine image, individually and socially, be inconsistent with the doctrinal conception of universal man as originally corrupted through satanic cunning and as still permanently depraved but for the uplifting power of divine grace. It should be remembered that the whole human evolution outside of the Old and New Testament history is at its best brilliant but abortive, while inside of that history, under supernatural guidance, it has been steadily approximating the highest ideals of religion and virtue. The most advanced evolutionism is thus reconcilable with the most advanced Christianity, and we may therefore serve notice on our evolutionary friends that when they have reached the utmost goal of their researches they will find us there to welcome them with the Bible in our hands. Meanwhile we bid them godspeed in their scientific labors, whatever be the issue.

### The Problem of Physical Evil.

Anthropology also brings with it a peculiar difficulty of faith in reconciling the divine benevolence with the occurrence of physical pain and death throughout the animate creation. The old unscientific orthodoxy accepted such evils as expressions of vengeance for sin and remote effects of the fall of man. In this spirit Milton depicts a physical crisis at the moment when Eve reached forth her hand to the forbidden fruit and

". . . Nature, sighing through her seats,
  Gave signs of woe that all was lost."

Thereafter the seasons were deranged; beasts and birds became ferocious and carnivorous; and disease and death reigned throughout the living world. Science, however, has dispelled somewhat of this gloomy illusion, not only by proving that animal pain and death existed long before the appearance of man, but that they are themselves inherent in physiological laws and the inevitable issue of natural processes. On this scientific basis Paley has vindicated the divine benevolence against the apparent malevolence of poisonous plants and venomous animals by showing that they incidentally serve some good purposes and are so compensated and alleviated in the general economy of living nature that it is still ever true that " The tender mercies of the Lord are over all His works."

But in the inner consciousness of man there is a profound connection between sin and spiritual death which distinguishes him from the brutes; and if he is more acutely sensitive than they, he also has rational and moral resources which they do not possess for coping with physical evils. To pursue the argument in this direction we should need to enter those higher mental and moral sciences which as yet have not come within our view, and we must therefore limit the argument to man as a purely sentient being endowed with an æsthetic faculty which is exquisitely adjusted to the impressions of external nature through the senses and the imagination.

### Æsthetic Impressions of Nature upon Man.

It is but a low, narrow view of the material creation which would make human utility its sole object or confine its benevolent design to the mere supply of animal wants. Of what use to man are the flowers that bloom on Alpine heights, or the microscopic crystals which melt away in the snow, or the telescopic wonders which are hidden in the far-off stars of heaven? The beautiful has been strewn with lavish hand throughout the universe where there can be no hint or thought of the useful. "The Lord rejoiceth in his works," though neither man nor angel behold them. Like some perfect artist who has wrought the most invisible details of his work with exquisite finish and feeling, He stayed His creative hand only when His ideal was fully satisfied: "And God saw everything that He had made, and behold it was very good." And He would have His human creatures to share in His joy of creation. Not only has He given them creative imagination, but He has adapted the universe around them to their versatile fancy with endless variety and ceaseless vicissitude. The three physical sciences which we have reviewed conspire to show how "He hath made everything beautiful in its time."

### The Scene of Human Life.

Behold in the light of astronomy how beautiful is the scene of human life! This goodly fabric of heaven and earth, with its alternate night and day and returning summer and winter, occasioned by the mutations of the solar system, has been fitted up as a theatre of man's action, for his rational amusement no less than for his physical maintenance. It has indeed grown old and familiar, and in this dull workaday world of ours may long since have lost that subtle charm which the poet so feelingly laments—

> "There was a time when meadow, grove, and stream,
> The earth and every common sight,
> To me did seem
> Apparell'd in celestial light,
> The glory and the freshness of a dream.
> It is not now as it hath been of yore;
> Turn wheresoe'er I may,
> By night or day,
> The things which I have seen I now can see no more."

And yet might we recall such early impressions or could the face of nature around us be changed, how different would be its effect upon our æsthetic sense! Were we placed upon a sandy desert under a cloudless summer, or on a snowy waste beneath a sunless winter, how insupportable would be the monotony of life! We forget that it is by the orderly revolution of the earth upon its axis and in its orbit that the spectacle of the world becomes for our entertainment a magnificent stage with its scenery shifting day after day, from sunrise to sunset, through the blue sky of noon and the starry night, and year after year from the verdure of Spring to the snows of Winter, through the sheen of Summer and the splendor of Autumn.

### The Course of Human Life.

Behold also in the light of geology how beautiful is the course of human life! These successive periods of Childhood, Youth, Manhood, and Age, as predetermined by the organic conditions of our planet, are like so many acts of the great drama in which man as the actor is ever changing with the changing scene. The decline of their impressiveness through familiarity and custom is depicted by the same great poet as in mythical vision,

> "Heaven lies about us in our infancy,
> Shades of the prison-house begin to close
> Upon the growing boy,
> But he beholds the light and whence it flows,
> He sees it in his joy;
> The Youth—who daily farther from the East
> Must travel—still is Nature's Priest,
> And by the vision splendid
> Is on his way attended.
> At length the Man perceives it die away
> And fade into the light of common day."

But as the dawn will return after the day has faded, and the Spring will follow the snows of Winter, so the parent is renewed in the Child, and the Man lives again in the boy. Were it otherwise, could eager youth at once seize the sceptre of manhood, or active manhood at once break down in childishness, how would the development of human nature be marred and blighted! How dreary would life be without the brilliant hopes of youth and the tranquil memories of age! The natural seasons of growth and decay in man, like those in nature, come and go, each in its own order and with its own charm.

### The Story of Human Life.

Behold at length in the light of anthropology how beautiful is the whole story of human life. The varied experiences, of pain and pleasure, of care and mirth, joy and sorrow, summed up in the one great contrast of life and death, and so largely modified by our physical organism and environment, these form the dramatic interest of the checkered tale which unfolds through summer and winter, from childhood to age. That we do not appreciate its full attractiveness and realize how all things are working together for our good is because we cannot always see the grandeur of the plot but lose ourselves in its bewildering details. Yet as we could not have the day without night nor the summer without winter, and as we need youth to fit us for age, so we may not have true joy without sorrow, and need even death rightly to appreciate immortal life. Did we ever live in sympathetic unison with man and nature, the whole manifold spectacle of the world around us, whether in sunshine or shadow, would be suffused with spiritual interest and feeling like that expressed for us by our great Christian poet:

> "Thanks to the human heart, by which we live,
> Thanks to its tenderness, its joys and fears,
> To me the meanest flower that blows can give
> Thoughts that do often lie too deep for tears."

Learn, then, O querulous man, that it is thy right and thy duty to be happy. Give glory to the Creator while enjoying the beauty of His creation.

# INDEX OF AUTHORS

## WHOSE OPINIONS HAVE BEEN CITED.

Abelard, 60.
Adelung, 209.
Agassiz, 202, 204, 207, 210, 211.
Alexander, J. A., 141.
Alexander, Stephen, 170.
Anselm, 50, 51, 52.
Aquinas, Thomas, 52, 55.
Argyll, Duke of, 11, 205.
Arnold, Matthew, 16, 22, 24, 26.
Audæus, 60.
Augustine, 50.

Babbage, Charles, 183.
Bachman, 209.
Bacon, Francis, 12, 25, 41, 44.
Bagehot, 20.
Barret, 61.
Beattie, 34.
Bell, Charles, 202, 204.
Bentley, 16, 121, 163.
Berkeley, 5, 9, 20.
Bernard, 20.
Blount, Charles, 14.
Blumenbach, 205.
Boethius, 50.
Bolingbroke, 17.
Bossuet, 53, 124.
Boyle, 55.
Bradlaugh, 48.
Briggs, C. A., 101.
Brougham, Lord, 11.
Brown, 52, 57.
Browne, 15, 59.
Bruno, 48.
Büchner, 47, 202.
Buckland, Dean, 183.
Buel, 53.
Buffon, 180, 185.
Bunsen, 38, 209.
Burnet, 185.
Butler, 5, 9-44, 105, 126.

Calderwood, 57, 63.
Carpenter, 202.

Carus, Paul, 61.
Chalmers, 11, 27, 38, 52, 54, 58, 177, 188.
Champollion, 205.
Chandler, 15.
Chapman, 15.
Charnock, 55.
Child, Chapin, 184.
Chubb, 16.
Cicero, 121.
Clarke, Samuel, 12, 51, 52, 53.
Coleridge, 52.
Colliber, 20.
Collins, 14.
Comte, 3, 4, 5, 48, 60.
Conybeare, 15.
Cook, J. P., 183.
Cope, 202.
Copernicus, 160.
Crocker, 62.
Cousin, 53.
Cudworth, Ralph, 15, 52.
Cumberland, Bishop, 20.
Cuvier, 181, 185, 209.

Dana, 181.
Darwin, 43, 206.
Dawson, 181.
De Candolle, 210.
De Perthes, 207.
Derham, William, 163.
Descartes, 38, 51.
DeWette, 121.
Dickie, 184.
Diman, 57, 62.
Diodorus, 55.
Disraeli, 122.
Dorner, 58, 63.
Draper, 5, 101.
Duncan, 184.
Duns, 51.

Edwards, 52.
Eichhorn, 121.

Emory, 11, 27.
Epicurians, The, 59.
Ernesti, 121.

Fairholm, 188.
Fenelon, 53.
Ferguson, 205.
Fichte, 53.
Fiddes, Richard, 53.
Fiske, John, 56, 60, 62.
Fitzgerald, 10, 11, 20, 25.
Flint, 54, 58, 62.
Forbes, 40.
Foster, 20, 55.
Fowne, George, 183.

Gale, Theophilus, 15.
Galileo, 165, 167.
Gaunilo, 51.
Gibson, Stanley, 56.
Gillespie, 53.
Gladstone, W. E., 9, 20, 30, 190.
Gliddon, 201.
Gobineau, 205, 211.
Green, W. H., 213.
Grew, 55.
Guyot, Arnold, 181, 183, 189, 212.

Haeckel, 47, 206, 210.
Hallam, 20.
Hamilton, Dean, 53, 56, 60.
Harrison, 48.
Hävernick, 213.
Hegel, 51.
Helmholtz, 170.
Hengstenberg, 189.
Hennel, 28.
Henslow, 208.
Herbert, 14, 15, 52.
Herder, 121.
Herschel, 165, 166, 167, 190.
Hill, 184.
Hitchcock, 183, 184.
Hodge, Alexander, 61.
Hodge, Archibald, 58.
Hodge, Charles, 52, 57, 62.
Holbach, D', 47.
Holyoke, 48.
Hooker, 206.
Hugh of St. Victor, 55.
Humboldt, 166, 180, 185, 204.
Hume, David, 55, 56, 57.
Hutton, 180.
Huxley, 4, 43, 131, 190, 206.

Jacobi, 61.
John of Damascus, 55.
Josephus, 73.

Kant, 4, 51, 56, 57, 60.
Kepler, 160, 166.
Kidd, John, 182.
Kirby, 185, 202.
Krause, 51.

Lalande, 160.
La Mettrie, 47.
Lamarck, 206.
Lamont, 165.
Laplace, 38, 99, 163, 166, 170.
Latham, 209.
Leibnitz, 25, 38, 55.
Leidy, 202.
Leland, 15.
Le Plongeon, 211.
Leslie, 15.
Linnæus, 209.
Littlejohn, Bishop, 54.
Locke, 13, 15, 51, 55.
Lotze, 54.
Lowman, Moses, 53.
Lubbock, 207.
Lyell, 180, 192, 207, 210.

McCausland, 212.
McCosh, 57, 184.
Mackintosh, Sir James, 11, 18.
Mädler, 170.
Mahan, 57.
Malcolm, 27.
Malebranche, 53, 124.
Mansel, 48.
Marsh, 202.
Martineau, 21, 28, 58, 63.
Maurice, 27.
Mayer, 170.
Maxwell, 58.
Melito, 60.
Mendelsohn, 53.
Michaelis, 190.
Mill, 5, 56, 57, 58.
Miller, Hugh, 181, 205.
Mivart, 208.
More, Henry, 15.
Morgan, 15.
Müller, Max, 205.

Newton, 55, 99, 170.
Nott, 201.

Occam, 51.
Owen, Richard, 202, 207.

Paley, 163, 202.
Pattison, Mark, 18, 20, 25.

Penn, 185.
Pennant, 210.
Plato, 50.
Poisson, 170.
Pott, 210.
Pouchet, 210.
Prichard, 202, 205, 209.
Proctor, 167.
Prout, William, 202, 204.
Pulsky, 211.
Purinton, 63.
Pusey, 189, 213.

Quintilian, 35.

Raimund, 60.
Ray, 163, 180.
Reid, 54, 57.
Reusch, 190.
Ritter, 181.
Roget, Peter Mark, 203.
Romans, 211.
Row, 57, 62.
Royer, 206.

St. Augustine, 101, 189.
Schelling, 4, 51.
Schopenhauer, 61.
Schurman, 50, 62, 63.
Scott, Sir Walter, 33.
Scotus, 51.
Secker, Archbishop, 18.
Shaftesbury, 13.
Shedd, 53, 57.
Sherlock, 16.
Sleicher, 206, 210.
Smith, Goldwin, 23.
Smith, Pye, 188, 211.
Spencer, Herbert, 4, 26, 48, 56, 57, 60, 61.
Spinoza, 51.
Steere, 16.
Stephen, Leslie, 18, 22, 27, 29.
Sterling, 57.
Sterret, J. McBride, 63.
Stevens, 207.

Stewart, Dugald, 54, 57.
Stillingfleet, 52.
Stoics, The, 59.
Strauss, 66, 69, 71, 72, 78.
Strong, 52.
Swedenborg, 4.

Tertullian, 60.
Tholuck, 25.
Thomson, 58.
Thompson, 192.
Toland, 14, 15.
Tyndall, 14, 43, 58.

Ulrici, 53.

Vogt, 47, 180.
Voltaire, 65.

Wagner, Andrew, 188.
Wallace, 206.
Warburton, 15.
Warrington, George, 183.
Wayland, 11.
Webster, Daniel, 177.
Weisse, 53.
Wesley, John, 17.
Westropp, 207.
Whewell, 3, 5, 163, 167.
White, Andrew, 5, 101.
Whiston, 163.
Wilkins, 20.
Winchel, 53, 170, 208.
Wolf, Christian, 51.
Wolff, 5, 55.
Wollaston, 53, 55.
Woodward, 185.
Woolston, 14, 16.
Wundt, 4, 57, 58.

Yäger, 206.

Zenophanes, 59.

www.ingramcontent.com/pod-product-compliance
Lightning Source LLC
Chambersburg PA
CBHW030817230426
43667CB00008B/1251